FLAGSHIP *HOOD*

Alan Coles has been a journalist since the age of 16 and his interest in naval affairs began during National Service when he was a court martial and board of inquiry shorthand writer with the Mediterranean Fleet. Journalism has taken him to the *Manchester Evening News* and Fleet Street with the *Evening Standard* and the *Daily Mirror*. He and his wife ran a South Devon newspaper group for six years and he is now a lecturer in journalism at University College, Cardiff.

Ted Briggs, MBE, joined the Royal Navy in 1938, aged 15, and served for 35 years, being promoted to lieutenant. He was with the *Hood* for the last 22 months of her existence and was one of only three survivors when the ship sank. He is a well-known member of the *Hood* Association. He lives in Hampshire.

TO THE MEN OF THE *HOOD*,
WHO LIVED AND DIED IN HER.

Here lies a most beautiful lady,
Light of step and heart was she,
I think she was the most beautiful lady
That ever was in the West Country.
But beauty vanishes; beauty passes;
However rare it be;
And when I crumble, who will remember
This lady of the West Country?

Epitaph by Walter de la Mare

Flagship *Hood*

The Fate of Britain's Mightiest Warship

Alan Coles and Ted Briggs

ROBERT HALE · LONDON

© Alan Coles and Ted Briggs 1985
First published in Great Britain 1985
Reprinted 1985
First paperback edition 1988
Reprinted 1990
Reprinted 1996

Robert Hale Limited
Clerkenwell House
Clerkenwell Green
London EC1R 0HT

British Library Cataloguing in Publication Data

Coles, Alan
  Flagship Hood.
  1. Hood (Ship)—History
  I. Title   II. Briggs, Ted
  623.8'252'0941   VA458.H6

  ISBN 0-7090-3542-X

3   5   7   9   10   8   6   4

Photoset in North Wales by
Derek Doyle & Associates, Mold, Clwyd
Printed in Great Britain by
St Edmundsbury Press Limited, Bury St Edmunds, Suffolk
Bound by WBC Book Manufacturers Limited, Bridgend

Contents

List of Illustrations

Credits

R. Ellis, 1; Central Press, 2, 3, 25, 26 32; *The Times*, 4, 23;
John Bush, 5, 6, 7; H. Holderness, 8, 12, 16, 24; E. Smith,
14; T. Dunster, 15; The Imperial War Museum, 17, 21, 22;
Musée de la Marine, Paris, 30.

Plans

Acknowledgements

Without the diaries, logs, reminiscences, anecdotes and yarns of the men who served in HMS *Hood* – and there was a total of more than 15,000 who trod her decks in the twenty-two years of her life – this book would have run aground.

Official records can be too terse, lacking in colour and unrevealing, although, of course, we repeatedly referred to them to check the dialogue and correspondence we had with former ships' companies, and it is the language of the upper and lower decks which exhumes the days of glory of Britain's maritime enigma.

All manner of ex-Royal Navy men have contributed and their names are listed in the reference section at the back of this book. But we would like to pay special thanks to the following:

Members of the *Hood* Association, and in particular to their secretary Harry Purdue; John Bush, Harry Holderness, C. Harper-Smith for the supply of pictures from their private collections; Anique Wilson and John Smith, of Plymouth Maritime Library, who made available to us splendid research facilities; Ken Doble, assistant editor of the *Western Morning News* for reading the manuscript and help in obtaining one of the last pictures of the *Hood*; P.S. Strudwick, of the Ministry of Defence; Rose Gerrard, of the Department of Photographs, Imperial War Museum, Lambeth; the staffs of the Public Record Office, Kew, Greenwich Maritime Museum, British Museum Reading Room, and Colindale Newspaper Library; The Bodley Head, for permission to quote from Baron Burkard von Mullenheim Rechberg's book *Battleship Bismarck*; Mrs Mary Ford for helping with research into the *Hood's*

memoriam; Mrs Marian Hall, for assistance with correspondence and to our wives, Clare Briggs and Gay Coles for
their forbearance of a very masculine subject, and for
prodding our memories at the same time.

And finally, to each other, for inspiring the other in
moments of dejection when long roads of research came to
an end in a blank wall, with an almost indiscernible egress in
it.

Ted Briggs
Alan Coles
November, 1984

Prologue

The first time that Ted Briggs saw HMS *Hood* was from the beach at Redcar, Yorkshire. It was the summer of 1935. He was twelve and impressionable. The *Hood's* grey paint, almost bleached white in the shimmering sun, accentuated the rakish, clipper-like bows which flared extravagantly and aristocratically down to the foremost twin fifteen-inch turrets, whose burnished tampions glittered as she swung at anchor. The bulk of her superstructure and conning tower arrested the eye and denoted the power behind the clear-cut beauty, and at the same time seemed to decrease the bulk of her two huge funnels. She appeared to slim down going aft, although this was an optical illusion, where two more twin turrets were softened by the creaminess of the awning over the quarterdeck, which was low in the water compared with the rest of her. Picket and motor boats puttered around her; occasionally a bugle call blared out, or a boatswain's whistle shrilled across the sea.

The last time that Ted Briggs saw HMS *Hood* was from a fiery, oil-coated sea in the Denmark Strait. It was the spring of 1941. He was eighteen and frightened. He gasped for air as his head broke the surface. He trod the freezing water for several seconds before hearing the hissing of a hundred serpents. He turned his head, and fifty yards away there reared the vertical bows of the *Hood*, like a grisly grey headstone. That was all. The rest of her was torn open, somewhere beneath him. On the shattered bows both gun barrels of one turret were slumped disjointedly. There was no sign of the other turret. Then the flame-seared bows, the paint bubbling, as if under the heat of a giant blow-lamp, were sucked down savagely and speedily. Around him shells shrilled across the sea. Below him were dying 1,418 men out of a complement of 1,421.

Seldom can a man's life have been fashioned by one ship, but today Ted Briggs, one of the only three survivors, believes that his destiny was determined by his first glimpse of the world's most powerful warship – that first, to him, magical moment when he saw her anchored off the mouth of the Tees. He remembers: 'I stood on the beach for some considerable time, drinking in the beauty, grace and immaculate strength of her. "Beauty" and "grace" seem rather ludicrous words to describe a vessel of such size, particularly one whose primary function was for destruction. But I can honestly say I never could, nor indeed can even today, think of more suitable words to describe her.'

Boatmen were charging holidaymakers five shillings a time for a trip around the *Hood*, and Ted ran home to try to cajole the money from his mother. He cried bitterly when she refused, but then he could understand it. His father, a house painter, had died after falling from scaffolding three months before he was born. His mother, who had a thirteen-year-old daughter to bring up as well, had no spare cash for Ted's outings. But the *Hood* already haunted him, so he ran back to the beach to offer the boatmen his services as an oarsman as they rowed the trippers round. They laughed him away.

Because he could get no closer to the battle cruiser than the sands of Redcar, he decided the only way was to join the Royal Navy, and the next day he applied at the recruiting office, but he was told he was too young and to return when he was fifteen. Three years later he did just that, realizing that it would be too much of a coincidence to expect to be sent to the *Hood*. But in 1939, after training at HMS *Ganges*, there came a surprise draft to the ship of his dreams.

This was the *Boys' Own* type of start to his naval career at sea in the *Hood*, about which more words had been written than any other warship in peacetime. The beginning might have been novel-inspiring; the ending seemed more fictitious.

PART I

The Frightener

by Alan Coles

1

God is Helping the Navy

To understand the fate of HMS *Hood* is to understand the indecision of her planning and building, the clash of opinions in the Royal Navy, the failure of the Admiralty to implement suggestions to improve her and their inability to heed the lessons of Jutland. She was conceived too early, developed too late and died in battle outmoded by her enemies. Her pedigree was bastardized twenty-five years before she met the *Bismarck* and *Prinz Eugen* by an Admiralty hierarchy who wavered over construction of a new class of battle cruiser and allowed the *Hood* to become a reality – the world's biggest warship and Britain's biggest naval bluff, untested until the moment of demise.

Planning began secretly in November 1914 with realization that Britain's power – and with it supply lifelines – was being underwritten by the hitherto unforeseen potential of the U-boat. The first hint came from Lord Fisher, that contentious, yet visionary, architect of the modern Navy, who had been recalled as First Sea Lord. On 5 March 1915 he wrote to Vice-Admiral Sir David Beatty, commander of the battle cruiser squadrons: 'We have laid down 187 new ships since November, four of them battle cruisers of 33 knots and 15-inch guns and all of them will be fighting within a year. God is helping the Navy.'[1]

Super-optimist Fisher was at the peak of spiritual confidence. It was to be another four years before the *Hood*, the first and last of her class, was to take to the sea. Yet his confidence in battle cruisers inspired the planners.

But just what were battle cruisers? Originally they were intended to carry guns of a similar calibre to battleships, but there the comparison ended. Basically they were designed to be used as fast, lightly armoured 'scouts' to blast out of the water cruiser screens protecting capital ships.

And so in 1915 began a general survey of admirals for the requirements for a world-beater. Admiral Sir John Jellicoe, commander-in-chief of the Grand Fleet, sent a detailed memorandum on the need for heavily armoured ships, on 8 February 1916 – ten months before he became First Sea Lord. He favoured high speed in a hard-hitting vessel – in other words, the battle cruiser.

Within a week of receiving Jellicoe's analysis, the Admiralty instructed Sir Eustace H. Tennyson d'Eyncourt, the forty-seven-year-old Director of Naval Construction, to evolve six designs. The common denominator was that they should be capable of docking at Rosyth, Portsmouth and Liverpool, and there should be twelve 5.5-inch guns and two torpedo tubes. For the first three designs the main armament was laid down as six 'fifteen-inch B guns', which would mean an increase in draught and the loss of a quarter of a knot in speed. The term 'fifteen-inch B guns' was a hidden reference to secret eighteen-inch armament.

By March 1916 the Admiralty endorsed what was known as Design 3, by E.L. Attwood, but the shaft horsepower of 160,000 was too high. The blueprint was changed – for the first of many alterations – to 144,000 shaft power with the introduction of small tube boilers for the first time in a large ship, but the anticipated speed was maintained at 32 knots by reductions in displacement and draught. The amendments satisfied the board, and on 7 April 1916 they approved the design, which was virtually an average of the dimensions and specifications of the six. Her length was to be 860 feet, as against the shortest of 757 feet and the longest of 825 feet of the others, with a displacement of 36,500 tons, compared with the lightest of 32,500 tons of the rest.

On 13 April it was agreed to build four Admiral-class battle cruisers – the *Hood*, *Anson*, *Howe* and *Rodney*. The order for the *Hood* was acquired by John Brown at Clydebank, and on 1 September 1916 the keel of the world's largest warship was laid.

Disagreement followed. The first centred on secondary armament, although it had become generally accepted that four turrets would sprout eight fifteen-inch guns and not the mysterious 'eighteen-inchers'. The secondary armament was intended to be twelve guns, allowing the combination of six firing ahead, five ranging astern and seven on each broadside. Because two guns were to be mounted on the shelter deck on the centre line, one of them would have been forced to shoot over the ship's boats on the broadside, subjecting the craft to splinter and blast damage. This led to re-aligning, and the chance was taken to step up the guns to sixteen, which brought another wrangle.

The 6-inch, 5.5- and 4.7-inch all had their devotees, but because of the 5.5's easier loading this calibre went on the final specification. Four were to be positioned at the level of the shelter deck, and the other twelve at forecastle deck level.

These were minor alterations compared with those forced on the Admiralty by Jutland on 31 May 1916, when three inadequately armoured battle cruisers, the *Indefatigable*, *Queen Mary* and *Invincible*, were blown up as plunging shells ripped through their decks. In two separate decisions the board endorsed d'Eyncourt's ideas for improved protection. On 13 September these proposals included thickening the eight-inch belt by four inches, doubling the three-inch section and putting an extra three inches on the barbettes, which had been planned as nine-inch. On 2 October more modifications were made to upgrade the protection on eight deck sections and the main turrets.

It increased displacement by four thousand tons, although no one had yet thought about paring her weight to maintain a speed of more than thirty knots. By November Beatty had become commander-in-chief of the Grand Fleet and not only followed Jellicoe in this capacity but also took a consuming interest in the prototype *Hood*. With Jutland's repercussions still resounding, he maintained she was still under-armoured, particularly on the magazine crowns, the forward section of the lower deck and the longitudinal magazine bulkhead. All his ideas for improvements were rejected.

Jutland made designers aware of the need to 'trunk off' magazines to the open air, so explosive gases would be blasted outwardly, instead of causing havoc in the hull. Pigheadedly the Admiralty insisted this was defeatism and should not be considered in the design of British warships because 'enemy shells are meant to remain outside British

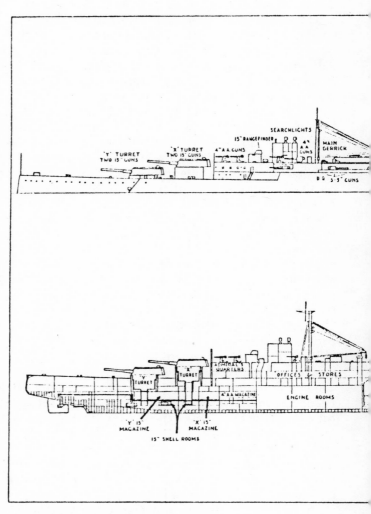

Sectional sketch of the *Hood*

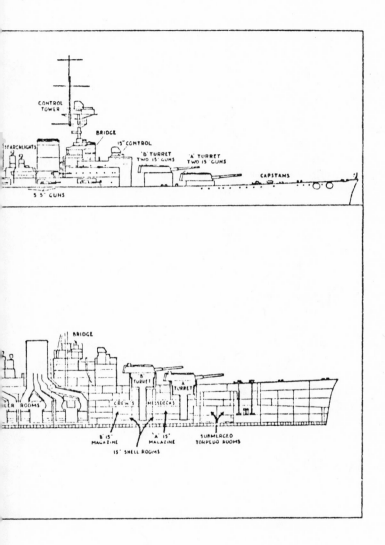

magazines'. And so explosion trunks were not built into the *Hood*.

After conferring with yard officials, the Captain Superintendent of the Clyde District forecast the *Hood* would be ready for trials by November 1918. The Admiralty appeared to be having second thoughts about completing the other three sisters, for on 9 March 1917 they intimated that work on them was not to be given priority. The Director of Naval Ordnance, Rear-Admiral Morgan Singer, was having a closer look at the growing *Hood*, too. He was concerned that the fifteen-inch and 5.5-inch magazines were above their own shell-rooms. He was able to obtain a reversal of the positions in the forward section, yet amazingly was satisfied with the lay-out aft. Here the fifteen-inch and 5.5-inch magazines remained above the shell-rooms because the DNO thought it essential at the lowest end of the ship as the higher positions were an inbuilt defence against mines and torpedoes. It was one of the most important decisions not to have been made! The *Hood* became the only 'modern-day' ship with magazines over the shell-rooms, and it was to cost the Navy their most prestigious vessel and the lives of more than fourteen hundred.

Beatty entered the armoured argument again and in June 1917 averred first that the protection was too weak and second that main turret roofs should be armoured for a depth of six inches. This was too late to invoke as the roofs had been manufactured. Only one of Beatty's six proposals was accepted – and this was the minor one that all sliding doors on bridge decks should be altered to hinge hung.

By now the word had gone round the fleet and the Admiralty that the *Hood* was a waste of money because she did not seem to be superior to the *Queen Elizabeth* class battleships. D'Eyncourt's answer was that she would have thicker protection on her sides and barbettes. In comparison with the *Queen Elizabeth* she had improved deck armour, the equivalent of twelve-inch, against the thirty-degree descent of shells, while there was guaranteed tube protection. The major factor was that the *Hood* could call on an extra six knots.

It was typical of the confused thinking that not until 10 January 1918 were test firings made against plates which were replicas of the five-inch roof armour of her turrets and inch-thick magazine crowns. And it was only Beatty's insistence that ensured three tests were made with 13.5-inch armour-piercing shells and with the new, secret Vickers' fifteen-inch projectiles. The results proved the inadequacy of the armour, and after the second test the experts revised their thinking and doubled the magazine crowns' protection to two inches. All this was happening a month before the *Hood's* launching. And all the time extra weight was being added until at last it was conceded that the funnel uptakes' armour above the forecastle would have to go. It was still not enough, however, and the tonnage allowance for fuel was pared.

More modifications, which meant moving the foremast twelve feet and lowering the bridge six feet, were circulated by the Admiralty and agreed a fortnight before launching. D'Eyncourt asked the Controller if Beatty should be consulted about the alterations. The reply reflected the resentment of having the commander-in-chief interfere with construction. The Controller said: 'I had thought of sending your drawing up to the captain of the fleet [Beatty], but on the whole I think it better not to do so, as he would probably not agree to the proposal about the conning tower, but pick out some other feature from your drawing which he would like altered.'[2]

And so on 22 August 1918 the longest ship built for the Navy rattled down the slipway at Clydebank after being launched by Lady Hood, the widow of Vice-Admiral Hood, who was killed when the *Invincible* exploded at Jutland. The 860-foot hull of steel and iron, weighing 21,920 tons, dwarfed everything surrounding it as throngs of shipyard mateys cheered, whistled and waved their caps.

But the *Hood's* blue blood had been diluted as one modification followed another. Because they feared this bowdlerizing might occur in the three sisters, taking up acres of yard space, the Admiralty cancelled them on 27 February 1919.

The experts still had a new battle cruiser, rapidly becoming antiquated, to play with. More shell tests were going on against the two-inch armour, which was to be incorporated in the magazine crowns. They were to be the most revealing of all and were to be the spectres which haunted senior officers in war. In conditions similar to a range of $10\frac{3}{4}$ miles, a fifteen-inch shell was fired at the replica. The shell streaked through the seven-inch armour, the one-inch backing and also the plates representing the two-inch sloping main deck and three-inch bulkhead. Worse still, the burst was thirty-one feet behind the seven-inch protection. This was final confirmation that the *Hood's* armour was woefully weak.

Yet another modification followed with three-inch armour on the sides of the main deck, with the plating of the barbettes going up to five inches thick. More shell tests were carried out, and this time the shell was deflected. To counteract the extra weight, it was agreed that four 5.5-inch guns should be removed. But these alterations still did not offer improved protection *over* the magazines.

D'Eyncourt's opinion was sought, and he was wholeheartedly for more armour on the main deck and over the magazines, which would further increase the *Hood's* weight by 440 tons. Meanwhile another series of gunnery tests were made to determine the penetrating power of sixteen-inch shells after which it was estimated that another thousand tons of steel would have to be added. It was impossible to balance this by shedding more 'fittings', and from this stage the designers and specialists forgot the problems of perfect protection, if any were possible. The *Hood* might have had the sleek, fast lines of a revolutionary battle cruiser, but she had become an inadequately armoured battleship, although never classed as one.

9 January 1920 was named for her to take the water under her own power. The week before, forty-three-year-old Captain Wilfred Tomkinson, a hero of Zeebrugge, where he had commanded HMS *Warwick*, arrived from the battle cruiser *Lion*, which was being paid off, and began familiarizing himself with the giant vessel. Advance parties of seamen and stokers also joined. Among them was Able Seaman L.E. Brown, who was to become a lieutenant. He recalls: 'Even though she was still in dockyard hands and not properly clean, the *Hood* was a delight, I had just come from a coal-burning cruiser, grimy with dust, dingily lit, with restricted headroom and overcrowded. Now I found

myself in a roomy, clean ship in which you could get lost. She was so big that notices giving directions to the upper deck were posted. There was a barber's shop, cinema, canteen, book-shop, chapel and soda bar, but what amazed us most was we could get fried fish and chips from a large galley range. Every Friday it was Cornish pasties for supper.'

The *Hood* left the fitting-out basin at 12.45 p.m. It was frosty, and heavy sleet and a driving cold wind knifed into working parties on her exposed forecastle. There was no ceremony, although the dual managing directors of Brown's, Sir Thomas Bell and Sir William Ellis, with members of the Clyde Navigation Trust, were on the bridge with Tomkinson. Neither were there any feelings of emotions among the workmen who watched her leave the dock she had occupied for four years. Not a cap was lifted, not a cheer was raised. Most mateys were glad to be rid of her; others considered she was a waste of £6,025,000, which would have been better spent on merchant shipping. As four tugs, under instructions from pilots Andrew Robertson and John Spence, shunted her into position, a desultory gleam of sunshine relieved the drabness.

Suddenly her stern tow-rope to the tug *Dalmuir* snapped, but she behaved after a new rope was fixed, and she was slowly eased along the Clyde until the tugs slipped her at Greenock at 3.30 p.m., when the 144,000 s.h.p. engines took over. At Greenock Customs House Quay and Prince's Pier came the first hint that the world's largest warship would attract the world's largest crowds. Both piers were crammed with flag-waving people.

On the way to Rosyth, came the first indication, too, that the ship was a wet one. With waves of fifteen feet and a Force 8 wind, water constantly rushed over the forecastle, deluged over her first breakwater and cascaded spray on the foremost turrets. And all this was happening when she was not fully laden and more than three feet short of her mean draught. Tomkinson soon realized she was not going to be the easy ride designers had predicted. He was also worried about fierce vibration in the spotting-top above him. These two deficiencies remained all her life.

Between now and 29 March, her commissioning date, more of the 967 ship's company joined. The first batch came from the *Lion*; then they arrived thick and fast from all the bases, although her home port was to be Devonport. Lieutenant Brown remembers: 'She needed a lot of working up and practice in gunnery and torpedo firing, and we were kept hard at it for the first two months. At first we were a happy crew, and everyone was keen to make her efficient. Commander McKinnon gave all the encouragement we needed.'

Lachlan McKinnon, the son of a parson, was indeed someone to inspire. As a young lieutenant he had been an instructor to the Turkish Navy and had been dubbed 'McKinnon Bey'. At Jutland he was the gunnery officer of the *Indomitable*, and his sterling service projected him towards the executive appointment in the *Hood* and in later years was to take him to become Rear-Admiral Commanding the Second Battle Squadron.

After McKinnon and Tomkinson had put both ship and crew through their paces, the *Hood* went into Rosyth's No. 2 Dock again on 15 April for the last of pre-cruise inspections. Dockyard experts probed every section of her structure. They found nothing to undermine their confidence. On 15 May the mighty *Hood* was ready to show her might to the world.

2

'The Happiest Ship'

The first ship's company were probably the *Hood*'s happiest. Most were thankful to have survived the war and to be in the cleanest and most luxurious vessel of any fleet. The nucleus from the *Lion* had already established comradeship and brought loyalty and pride. As she was to be a show ship, divisional officers soon began selecting promising athletes who could be relied on to ensure she was top-dog in the fleet and exemplary in behaviour ashore.

On her first passage south, athletes were singled out for soccer, rugby, running, boxing, hockey and regatta training. They had plenty of space, for three times around the ship equalled a mile. But the cutter crew needed little training to lift the Home Fleet's Rodman Cup on her first stop at Portland. The *Lion*'s oarsmen, who had won it in 1919, were transferred complete to the *Hood*, together with their cutter, *Dipping Lug*, and by stroking at the rate of thirty trounced the *Tiger*'s crew by three lengths. It was the ship's first victory in a long line of successes that was to make her the Navy's sporting palace.

She still had to visit Devonport, her home base, but surprisingly sailed past the mouth of Plymouth Sound and anchored off Cawsand opposite on 17 May 1920. The reason was soon apparent. It was here next day that she was joined by Rear-Admiral Sir Roger Keyes, the audacious former chief of submarines, who had commanded the Zeebrugge raid and who was about to hoist his flag in the *Hood* as leader of the Battle Cruiser Squadron. At forty-eight, Keyes had already been marked down by Beatty as a future First Sea Lord, and now it was no coincidence that he had Tomkinson as flag captain. The two had forged a friendship in the *Fame* eleven years earlier, when Tomkinson was first lieutenant and Keyes his captain. From then on Tomkinson's progress followed Keyes' rising star. It had always been an harmonious partnership, and this commission was to be no different.

On 19 May the *Hood* at last showed herself to Devonport when she moved in alongside Nos. 6 and 7 wharves, which were too small to handle her efficiently. Unknown to the crew, Keyes had orders to prepare her for a mission to Reval (now Tallin) in Estonia, where she was to act as a 'frightener' to the Bolshevik fleet. It was the first of many sorties in which she was to be used in this role. The *Tiger* and a destroyer flotilla were to accompany her. The men were told the squadron were going on an official visit to Scandinavia, but in fact it was to be the forerunner of a more serious Baltic adventure.

This first overseas voyage was meant to be not only a show of power to Soviet forces but also a goodwill trip to Sweden, Denmark and Norway, but it was badly planned, mainly because of the *Hood*'s size again. With the *Tiger* and nine of the newest destroyers, she arrived at Kioge Bay, near Christiania (now Oslo) on 1 June. Only then was it realized that because of her draught she could not steam close inshore. Nevertheless, although she anchored several miles away from the port, she was visited by King Haakon and Queen Maud, the sister of George V, and encountered her first meeting with thousands of visitors who were to set the pattern for 'open ship' for the rest of her peacetime service.

Next stop was Kalmar, two hundred miles from Stockholm, and as she entered Swedish waters, a squadron of aircraft swooped around her in salute. Among the busiest of the ship's company were the sailors who manned the three-pound Hotchkiss saluting cannon. They were firing twenty-one-gun salutes for kings and admirals and seven-gun salutes for consuls more than twice a day for a week.

The *Hood* made smoke of a different kind on 13 June when Keyes exercised the squadron in hide-and-seek tactics. More festivities were ahead at Apenrade two days later, when the area was handed back to Denmark by Germany. The day after came the first death aboard the *Hood*, when Petty Officer Stoker Sidney Hingston succumbed to pneumonia. His body was transported to Britain before the battle cruiser arrived at Copenhagen on 18 June. The now familiar routine was gone through – comings and goings of consuls, mayors and senior civics, the thunder of saluting guns and finally a two-hour inspection by the King and Queen of Denmark. The rounds of visits continued unabated.

It was at Copenhagen that Keyes was told that the squadron's mission was to be curtailed. The Government decided that, as the Baltic states had agreed to live at peace with the new Soviet régime, Britain should not take any more offensive actions against Russian ships. This lifted the blockade of Petrograd Bay, and with it the undeclared naval war on the Soviets ended. Instead the squadron were ordered to Christiana again for another visit by Haakon before sailing home.

By now the crew considered themselves the élite of the Navy, and off Rosyth on 5 August they were called on to provide search parties and armed guards to board the surrendering German ships *Helgoland*, *Westphalen* and *Rügen*. Six days later, at Lamlash, off the Isle of Arran, the *Hood* won the Battle Cruiser Regatta.

Then came the long haul to Penzance and back to Plymouth, where the watches alternated for summer leave. The autumn became another working-up period with more gunnery and torpedo trials off Portland. On 11 November the *Hood*'s marines were afforded the first of many honours, which were to become onerous later, when they supplied the guard of honour for the funeral of the 'unknown warrior' in Westminster Abbey. These heady days were not to last much longer, for at the end of 1920 it was announced that the Navy would revert to the peacetime system of manning by crews from one depot, which meant the splitting of the *Hood*'s company.

The final cruise for the combined hearties of Chatham, Portsmouth and Devonport came in January 1921 – inaptly named the annual Spring Cruise – to Vigo, Arosa Bay and Gibraltar. It was overshadowed by tragedy from the start, after a gale confined the Atlantic Fleet – the Battle Cruiser Squadron with them – to Torbay until 20 January. Then on the first day out the submarine *K5*, which was exercising with the *Hood*, failed to surface 120 miles south-west of the Scillies. All that was found was oil, two pieces of timber and a ditty-box lid. But the sixty-five officers and men were not forgotten. On the return voyage Keyes, an old submariner, ordered a church service to be held over the spot where the submarine had disappeared. The squadron assembled in a rough circle, engines were stopped and wreaths dropped on the sea.

The ceremony might almost have been a requiem for the men who were to remain in the *Hood* after the depot reorganization and departure of Keyes. Lieutenant Brown, who left with the rest of the Portsmouth and Chatham ratings in April, says: 'We were sorry to say goodbye to such a fine ship. I still feel it was one of the happiest ships I've served in.'

His sentiments were not echoed by the Devonport men, nor by the officers who were to serve in her for the next two years.

3

Atmosphere Most Bolshevik

The new men had heard of the reputation of Rear-Admiral Sir Walter Cowan, the fifty-year-old little quasi-hero of the Baltic, who had bottled up the Soviet fleet two years earlier and planned its partial destruction at Kronstadt. He was something of a bully, highly strung, irritable and plagued by a quick temper as fiery as a timber-dry forest, and he had high ideals for enforcing strict discipline and efficiency. Yet he was shy, reserved and difficult to communicate with.

Cowan's sharp temper brought summary justice, and he had been in three mutinies before his flag flew in the *Hood* on 31 March 1921. The first was in 1913, when he commanded the battleship *Zeelandia*. He had been in her only a month when a new executive officer ordered twelve stokers to do work normally given to seamen. The stokers refused to clean upper deck brightwork because they were not given time to wash after coaling ship. Discipline was restored by marines, who put them in cells, and Cowan was cleared of responsibility, but his actions led to a legal blunder. Sir Lewis Bayly, the admiral commanding, ordered a court martial of the twelve, and eight were imprisoned for two years, with hard labour, but it had been forgotten that Cowan, a firm believer in summary punishment, had stopped their leave and given extra drill. The Admiralty revoked the court findings because the stokers had been punished already by Cowan, an error of judgement for which the little commanding officer received their lordships' displeasure.

In June 1919, when in charge of the Baltic Force in the cruiser *Delhi*, Cowan was faced with a more serious outbreak and indicated to the crew of the gunboat *Cicala*, who refused to sail up the River Dvina, that he was ready to fire on them. The gunboat proceeded according to his orders.

Six months later the disaffection spread to the *Delhi*. The crew, already complaining about lack of food, were expecting to return to Britain, but instead the ship was ordered back to the Baltic. When she was due to sail, only a quarter of the ratings went to their stations. The remainder locked themselves in the recreation deck. For hours the *Delhi* did not move; then Cowan threatened to blow up the ship. The men turned-to and she put to sea. The officer mainly at fault was Captain Geoffrey Mackworth, who could be as peremptory as Cowan and had not bothered to explain to the crew why they were not going home. Yet it was the promotion-conscious Mackworth whom Cowan chose to be his flag captain and commanding officer of the *Hood*.

The men and officers were to be the targets of Cowan's tempestuous endeavour. What he planned was sarcastically underlined in this instruction to the chaplain, the Reverend Arthur Gilbertson: 'I hope you will not have the litany in my flagship; but if you insist, will you please omit the petition where we ask to be delivered from battle, murder and sudden death. Hang it! I've never been trained for anything else.'[1]

The crew did not like what they heard and saw of the admiral, the captain and the ship. For many it was like leaving one barracks for another, with the promise of long hours of cleaning paintwork and brass. The *Hood*'s general messing system – known as 'Jago's' after Warrant Officer Alphonso Jago, who devised it – was also unpopular because it meant that individual messes were not able to arrange their own menus and that everyone 'ate the same'. Lieutenant S. Donovan, then a telegraphist, says of the system: 'We accepted it reluctantly. No longer could we collect mess savings at the end of the month as a result of economies we made in each mess by not catering for those on leave or ashore.'

Because Cowan had witnessed the spread of Communism in Russia, he was one of the first admirals to see 'reds in the hammocks', and he was to encounter an example of it in Scotland during May 1921 when the *Hood* was in Rosyth. Her stay coincided with the rail and coal strikes, so the Government ordered Cowan to prepare to put ashore patrols to protect essential services because a General Strike or riots were feared.

Three battalions, composed of seamen, marines and midshipmen, were placed under control of Commander Lionel Wells, DSO, the squadron gunnery officer. They were to be deployed in Cowdenbeath, where there had been a riot at Kinlassie Colliery a month earlier, but the problem was that a sympathy strike was expected by Scottish Motor Transport bus drivers, and the shore patrols had no way of getting to the mining areas. Cowan solved this by arranging instruction in bus-driving for the midshipmen. The late Commander James Gould, then an eighteen-year-old 'snottie' who was among the learner-drivers, recounted: 'None of us had driven a car more than a few times – and some not at all. And the buses then had a vertical acceleration lever and only a hand-brake. We found them awkward to drive.'

Only one midshipman was required to act as an emergency bus-driver, however. When the shore parties were told to move out under cover of darkness from Rosyth, one bus was without a civilian driver, so Midshipman Edgar Armstrong took over on the tortuous route to Lochgelly, where they were to be billeted in a school. Armstrong's driving was carefully controlled until he reached the school; then the bus ran into a large stone post.

The sailors did not need their rifles to win over the population. Admiral Sir Guy Sayer, then a *Hood* midshipman, who was sent to guard the Forth Bridge, relates: 'The miners were rioting at Cowdenbeath, but the tension was eased by our seamen, who challenged them to soccer. That was how the sailors always dealt with trouble around the world. Their interest was sport and hardly anything else.'

'My landing party patrolled the bridge because it was in danger from saboteurs. The atmosphere was most Bolshevik. We were billeted at Dunfermline Station and slept in first-class carriages. We mounted guard on trains in the guards' vans and at the entrances to corridors as trains crossed the bridge.'

Miners attempted to sabotage the buses by emptying the radiators, but the matelots carried water bottles and merely used them to refill the radiators. To improve relations at Lochgelly, a dance was put on for the townspeople, and the

Hood marines band were sent to play. The miners banned their wives and daughters from attending, however. 'But there were still plenty of girls who turned up,' says ex-marine 'Windy' Breeze. 'The band also improved the situation by giving concerts. When we left, there was many a Scots lass in tears.'

Cowan had more serious matters to deal with, mainly because of the tight discipline he was enforcing through Mackworth. The dissatisfaction of strikers spread to the *Hood*, and on his rounds Commander Richard Lane-Poole encountered a passive demonstration, represented by the decorating of a seamen's mess with red bunting. Cowan and Mackworth were furious and interpreted this as a sign of revolution and an inducement to mutiny. Able Seamen John McKirdy and Thomas Guthrie were court-martialled for 'mutinous practice' but were acquitted. This did not satisfy the admiral nor the captain; they then charged Stoker John Hall with inciting men to commit an act of mutiny and even had Master-at-Arms Walter Batten court-martialled for 'concealing a mutinous practice'. Hall was made responsible for this incident and sentenced to three years penal servitude. The case against Batten was not proved.

'This was indicative of the unhappy state of affairs onboard,' says Sayer. 'Most regrettably the *Hood* became renowned as a very unhappy ship, mainly because of the clash of temperament between Cowan and Mackworth. Yet we midshipmen were a happy bunch in the gunroom.'

Life there is reflected by the reminiscences of Commander Gerald Cobb, who joined her as a shivering midshipman, clothed only in his No. 1 snottie's uniform, known as the 'bumfreezer', one rough day off Lossiemouth. 'The senior midshipmen were a tough lot,' he claims. 'They lived up to the squadron's semi-pornographic song, which they gave vent to at appropriate moments.' The most acceptable version ran: 'Away, away with sword and drum – Here we come, sons of rum, looking for someone to shoot up the bum in the Battle Cruiser Squadron.'

Mackworth demanded high standards from his callow charges. In their first week aboard they were expected to know details of tonnage and armament, and the length and speed of the *Hood*. They were lectured if they became lost and wandered around the ship, which to many was like a small town.

After assessing the aftermath of the strikes, Cowan tightened discipline still more in his squadron. He issued a memorandum to the captains of the *Hood*, *Tiger* and *Repulse* with the aim of 'producing a better and more complete understanding and uniformity of thought, procedure and action among us and increase thereby the efficiency and discipline among ships' companies'.[2]

When Mackworth invoked the clamp-down orders of Cowan, it was the wardroom which felt the full authority of their captain. He berated in the log officer-of-the-day Lieutenant Lloyd Gilling, a member of the Australian Navy, for not seeing that a salute by the *Thunderer* was returned by the *Hood*; he reprimanded Marine Major George Woodcock for going ashore when his company were warned to stand by as an armed guard, and he 'corrected' Lieutenant E.V. Major for slackness and inattention when officer-of-the-watch.

After seeing Mackworth's tantrums, many of the crew suspected he drank. Midshipman G. Blundell, who was to become a captain himself, was later to say of Mackworth: 'At drill or during evolutions he raved and ranted, shouted and interfered. He had a habit of waving his telescope and yelling: "I want to know why." Once the chief yeoman, who had just arrived on the bridge, was hit on the head accidentally by the telescope and knocked out, when the captain was having one of his paroxysms.'

The 1921 summer cruise was cancelled, but the *Hood* and battle cruisers exercised off Gibraltar. After being worked hard, the ship's company expected to relax, but Mackworth did not ease up. In August he logged Acting Lieutenant Francis Proudfoot for showing too much compassion in not arresting a drunken stoker. The entire wardroom were later criticized for 'laxity of duty', and petty officers were lectured about their conduct. Neither did the lower deck escape. Close-order drill was ordered in full uniform in the high summer humidity of Gibraltar.

Cowan added to the ceremonial burden of the marines and seamen by not restraining his passion for parades. On the 'Rock' he became a close friend of the governor, Sir Horace

Smith-Dorrien, and together they would ride into Spain to hunt, another of Cowan's fervent pursuits; this comradeship led to his staging parades during which he and the governor would be on horseback. Cowan organized the smallest details himself. He chose the music and worked out the way the men should march, and the speed of their steps.

After one arduous duty it is recalled by Breeze that 'someone pushed the ship's mascot, which was a goat, through the skylight on to the admiral's bed'. The culprit was never discovered, although Mackworth went to extraordinary lengths later to apprehend a marine who made him the butt of a pointed practical joke. The captain was in the habit of suddenly asking for six marines to report for special duties. One day through the post he received a package containing twelve lead soldiers. Attached was the message: 'Marines for use of Captain Mackworth.' According to Breeze: 'We all had to give a sample of our writing to compare with that on the parcel. All our leave was stopped.' Again, the joker was never found.

The goat originally belonged to Cowan, who won him during a rifle contest but then presented him to the ship. This shaggy, shambling animal gobbled cigarette ends from spit-kids and chewed ledgers in the ship's office, oily cotton waste and emery paper. Often he lurked in passageways and butted sailors, but he met his match after an encounter with the bulk of the engineer commander, who picked him up and dumped him in the waist on the main deck. The favourite goat story of Captain H. Watch, then a paymaster midshipman, is: 'He was on the scrounge in the gunroom when a member gave him a lot of bread dipped in gin. The goat gobbled it up and became so temperamental and tipsy it took five people to remove him.'

Resentment at being the 'pusser' work-horse not only of the fleet but of their showy admiral was still apparent in the *Hood* at the start of 1922, when she was about to go on the usual spring cruise to the Mediterranean. As a preliminary, when the battle cruisers gathered at Falmouth on 17 January, Cowan circulated another of his 'tighten up' memorandums to Mackworth and Captain Frederic Dreyer of the *Repulse*, on the cuts and reductions about to descend on the fleet, which he insisted 'must be accepted without protest and complaint'. Cowan underlined his fears of the Navy's deterioration by adding: 'The men realise that many of the officers do not know enough of the Service to get their best from them and so do not always give their best. Ships' companies will be far happier and in better spirits if their best is extracted from them.'[3]

The *Hood's* men would have argued with Cowan on this score. They felt that too much was being extracted from them, and there was another round of full ceremonial scheduled at Gibraltar, Malaga, Alicante and Toulon.

On the way home from it all, the *Hood* was anchored in Arosa Bay, near Vigo, in March when an SOS was received from HMS *Surprise*, the commander-in-chief China's yacht, which was caught in a tempest as she returned to Britain to pay off. Cowan ordered the *Hood* to make steam 'with all despatch' and asked the *Surprise's* commanding officer by wireless whether she could make Arosa. The reply was that the ship might capsize if she were turned beam-on to the sea. The *Hood's* engine-room raised power in the remarkably swift time of two hours – four was statutory – and left at full speed. Commander Gould recalled: 'It was one of the most spectacular examples of rough weather I've ever seen. The bows were going under water up to the forecastle breakwater, where the doors were carried away. Water was coming green over A turret and spray plumed up to the bridge. We reached the *Surprise* about noon, and she really looked more comfortable than us.'

The *Hood* steamed abreast and to the windward of the ex-Russian luxury yacht to give her lee, and oil was poured on the sea to help calm the waves. She remained with the *Surprise* for five hours into the darkness until the storm moderated and she could put into Vigo. Not content with having all hands standing by, Mackworth called out the sea-boat's crew at midnight for exercise!

Examples of Mackworth's malevolence continued. Pay-Lieutenant H.V. Evans was 'corrected' for incurring charges for wine in both wardroom and gunroom; Lieutenant A.R. Cadell was also 'corrected' for allowing a drifter to go alongside, while Lieutenant-Commander Ronald Studd, DSO was castigated for an 'indiscretion'.

There was more dissension in the messes when the

summer cruise was cancelled, with the probability of the *Hood* being confined to the barren northern waters of Cromarty. Then joy – instead, with the *Repulse*, she cruised to Gibraltar. It was here that the commander-in-chief, Admiral Sir John de Robeck, a friend of Cowan's from their days in the sailing brig *Seaflower*, ordered the admiral to take the two-ship squadron to Rio de Janeiro, which during September would celebrate the centenary of Brazilian independence. The highlights were to be an 'Olympic-type Games' between ships of all nations. Cowan described his mission as being 'to strive for first place amongst them in every way in every honour open to us'.[4]

It was fair weather across the Atlantic, and the admiral ordered a general turn-to in training for all athletes in the *Hood* and *Repulse*. The men's mood swung from the gloom of home waters, and they entered the mission willingly and happily. But there was tragedy when Boy Alfred Field, who was seventeen, disappeared overboard off St Vincent in the Cape Verde Isles on 22 August. It was an accident which was to be repeated several years later, similarly without explanation.

Admiral Sir Robert Elkins, a midshipman at the time, kept a detailed log of the visit to Rio, where the *Hood* arrived on 3 September 1922. He described how the battle cruisers steamed in on a dull day and fired twenty-one- and fifteen-gun salutes. Next came Japan's *Idzumo*, then the American battlewagons *Maryland* and *Nevada*, which had to 'search around' for anchorage, and the Argentine battleship *Morino*. On Thursday 7 September, the official day of independence, the *Hood* shattered the peace of the port at 6 a.m. with a twenty-one-gun salute and was dressed overall. Later there was a march-past in the city. '*Hood*'s battalion was the smartest,' Elkins boasted.[5]

The weekend – again heralded by twenty-one-gun salutes from the *Hood* as the president went afloat in the cruiser *Barbarosa* – was the pinnacle of festivities and fame for the British. On the Saturday Elkins crowed: 'In every regatta race our competitors walked through, the Japs and Americans being nowhere. That is the sort of thing which raises British prestige, which has suffered here just lately at the hands of the Yanks.'

Sunday was not a day of rest. It was set aside for the skiff races. 'Hood won the midshipmen's cutter, but the Yanks won the seamen's cutter by six strokes,' Elkins had to admit. He was more exultant after the athletics on the Monday. 'Hood won eight out of the 15 events, knocking the Yanks into a cocked hat. The tug-of-war was a walk-over for the Hood.'[6]

Yet the 'games', intended to build goodwill, ended in a fiasco which caused a rift between the British and Americans. The final event was boxing, and on it depended whether the United States or Britain won overall. With one bout to go, the British squadron, to which the Hood provided five boxers, led by four wins to three. Victory hung on whether the Hood's champion, Stoker Petty Officer Spillar, who also held the Navy and British amateur titles, could beat his American opponent. Commander Gerald Cobb, who was in the stadium, which contained four thousand yelling, partisan sailors, remembers: 'Spillar advanced to touch gloves with his rival – as all boxers in previous bouts had done – when the American immediately struck Spillar with a straight left, followed by a right hook. Curtains for Spillar. Uproar!'

The fight was declared 'null and void', but to calm the riot, Cowan climbed into the ring. 'Only a very appropriate speech by him, followed by his calling for three hearty cheers for the American Navy, saved what would have been a tricky situation,' says Cobb.

As a farewell the Hood arranged an illuminated water pageant in Botofoga Bay, then, on 14 September, she sailed away, carrying three silver cups won by her athletes. Commander Gould thought the parting showed a lack of courtesy, however. 'When we left we were escorted by some elderly Brazilian destroyers, but as we passed the Pan D'Assucan at the entrance we went on to more than twenty knots and left them behind. I thought this very bad manners.'

The crew's behaviour had been exemplary, yet Mackworth was not prepared to reward the officers and men. Punishments for trivial offences continued, and he even logged the chief surgeon. After a two-hundred-mile trip to São Paulo, with more ceremonials, the delights of the West

Indies lay ahead for the *Hood* and *Repulse*, but on the ten-day passage there was no respite. 'We carried out almost continuous evolutions or exercises in competition with *Repulse*, who usually beat us,' said Gould. 'We spread and furled awnings, sometimes twice a day at sea. We all thought this a poor tribute for our excellent showing in Rio.'

For twenty days they cruised through the West Indies, calling at Trinidad, Barbados and St Lucia. It amazed Elkins that, despite a severe storm in Barbados, hands were still required to paint ship, while Watch noted in his log that one clumsy rating in the foretop faced the wrath of the captain for spattering the visiting bishop's wife with paint.

The restless Cowan did not care for the peace of the Caribbean, and when news reached him that the Navy were sending ships to restrain the Turkish dictator Mustapha Kemal from expelling Greeks in Asia Minor, he cabled Beatty, the First Sea Lord, that the *Hood* was ready to start for the Mediterranean. Instead the battle cruisers were ordered to Gibraltar and then home.

After returning to Devonport on 4 December, the *Hood* linked up with the Atlantic Fleet in time for the annual competitions on the 1923 spring cruise. Cowan boasted that the ship 'won the three Bs – band, breadmaking and boxing.'[7] What he did not divulge was that she did not take part in the regatta. Able Seaman Robert Hector, who joined for passage to Britain, reveals: 'The crew were unhappy, and because of unrest between her three divisions and a lack of co-operation, there was no entry for the regatta.'

Cowan was delighted again, however, by the *Hood*'s boxers. The championship rested on whether six 'middies' could win their section. The admiral went to their dressing-room and told them they had to go out and win. 'Six more flaming young tiger cubs you never saw,' he said. 'One after another they whirled in, scorning all defence and won the fleet competition by the skin of their teeth. I was so very proud of them and an hour later looked them over – a mass of cuts, closed eyes and bruises, but full of joy and pride, as was I in them.'[8] Among the midshipmen was Admiral Tyrwhitt's son John, and Cowan wrote to the boy's father, telling of his victory.

As Cowan left Gibraltar in the *Hood* for the last time, she passed through the fleet formed in two lines, with all crews cheering. It was ,a hypocritical farewell, for when the ship arrived at Devonport, the men were thankful to know that by May they would have a new admiral and captain.

4

Matelots' World Booze

The Admiralty called it 'the Cruise of the Special Service Squadron'. The Conservative Press referred to it as 'the Empire Cruise'. The popular tabloids labelled it 'the World Cruise'. But the matelots had their own pet-name – 'the World Booze'. It was a combination of all four.

Unwittingly the men of the *Hood* and *Repulse* were responsible for a voyage which had never been attempted by the modern Navy. Their public relations exercise in Brazil had been highly praised in Admiralty circles, and Sir John de Robeck, commander-in-chief Atlantic Fleet, was convinced a tour of greater magnitude would tighten Commonwealth ties.

Vice-Admiral Sir Frederick 'Tam' Field, who was chosen to lead the mission, which would take him nearly forty thousand miles, hoisted his flag in the *Hood* on 19 May 1923, as a replacement for Cowan, who had finished his two-year term and was not given an immediate appointment. He brought with him Captain John Im Thurn, who created a new atmosphere and imbued a binding comradeship among the crew.

Although there were question marks over Field's health and his ability to lead, he was a well-mannered diplomat and ambassador, highly capable of facing the demanding schedule ahead around the world. He had just handed over as Third Sea Lord and Controller at the Admiralty and was aware of the financial stringencies which were dissecting the Navy. He had chosen a strong captain, although milder in his approach to discipline than Mackworth. Under Im Thurn the *Hood* changed overnight. His leniency was underlined by the story which circulated about Bandmaster Henry Lodge, who was hard up and decided to raffle his motorcycle. It was an offence against King's Regulations for anyone to promote 'private business' or to gamble, so when Im Thurn found out, he should have court-martialled Lodge. Instead he merely cautioned him. The bandmaster was popular in the ship, and his escape from the captain's justice improved the popularity rating of Im Thurn.

The planning of the voyage took a year, and as a 'work-up' the *Hood* and *Repulse* visited Oslo and Stockholm in July 1923 before returning to Torbay on 22 July for the largest gathering of the fleet for years. Six other warships were to accompany the *Hood*. They were the *Repulse*, which formed the other half of the Battle Cruiser Squadron, and the cruisers *Delhi*, *Danae*, *Dragon*, *Dauntless* and *Dunedin*, which was to be handed over to the New Zealand Navy.

Gunnery and torpedo practice was forgotten during preparations for the tour which would take her across the Atlantic, Indian and Pacific Oceans. Instead spit, polish and paint were the orders of the autumn days of 1923. The fifteen-inch guns were enamelled and so highly polished that they reflected the cleaners' faces. It became a ship's joke that one officer-of-the-day was seen flicking specks of dust from the brilliant guns every time he passed. The huge quarterdeck was sandstoned until it was spotless. For the first time the crew were issued with tropical kit, while cups and saucers replaced old basins and white oil-cloth table covers brightened messes. Stewards unpacked 2,700 extra glasses (1,300 for champagne), 1,500 forks, 1,000 teaspoons and 2,000 plates. Two days before departure several trouble-makers, who could not be trusted on this goodwill trip, were drafted to barracks. If the ship were clean, so were the crew.

At 7 a.m. on 27 November, which was grey, cold and misty, the *Hood* weighed anchor and entered Plymouth Sound, followed by the *Repulse*, the *Delhi* and the *Dauntless*. The *Danae* and *Dragon* were delayed by fog at Sheerness and did not join until 8 a.m. next day. But the weather smoothed the way after this. Time was taken up by preparing for the thousands who would inspect the ships in ports as diverse as Suva and San Francisco, Zanzibar and Vancouver. The vital statistics of the *Hood* had to be collated and interpreted in understandable language, so simple phrases were devised for the 'guides'. The 'phrase-book' contained information such as: the width of two trains could fit abreast in either funnel; if she sank upright at the bottom of the Channel between Dover and Calais, eighty feet would still be seen of her; she generated enough power to light a small town; the weight of her two hundred miles of electric cables was a hundred tons; the fifteen-inch guns were nearly twenty yards long, cost £16,000 each, hurled shells higher than Mont Blanc and every time they fired cost £1,200 at the rate of six fifteen-inchers a minute; it took six hundred pounds of bread, seventy-five pounds of butter, four sides of bacon and a hundred gallons of tea to breakfast the crew.

The squadron descended on Freetown, Sierra Leone, at 8 a.m. on 8 December to sample the first influx of visitors. V.C. O'Connor, a special writer and scholar who was seconded to the *Hood* to chronicle her travels, described the entry into harbour thus: 'Her cleanliness reached the point of superlative perfection and gallons of grey paint had been laid in successive layers on the revolving drums of her armoured turrets. The emery-polished muzzles of her guns shone like silver. Her crest – a bird (a chough) and anchor – had been overlaid in gold and picked out in colour; her officers in white uniforms, Royal Marines in khaki, were drawn up on parade, the officers with drawn swords.'[1]

It was a microcosm of the rest of the cruise. Saluting cannon racketed across the harbour; the governor's aide visited Field in the *Hood*; Field visited the governor ashore; the governor visited the *Hood*. And then for five days the ships – and the *Hood* in particular – were invaded by the mixed population. 'But by carefully balancing entertainments and receptions he (Field) managed to leave both sections pleased and flattered,' O'Connor reported.

The *Hood*'s first dance was not an inter-racial success, however. Only '25 white lady partners turned up,' complained a local paper.[2] But the shortage of dancers was less of a worry than the stultifying heat, which turned messes into kitchen ranges. Everyone was relieved to leave this 'white man's grave' for the cruise to Cape Town. On the way nearly a thousand officers and men who had not crossed the equator before were initiated. As the *Hood* stopped, Field marched up to the dais of Neptune, played by Chief Signal Boatswain Alfred Punshon, saluted and went down on his knees to receive the fictitious ribbon and 'Order of the Bath'. In order of seniority, officers followed to accept their 'honours'. Then those wearing uniform, who had not been 'over the line' – and they included Captain Im Thurn – dashed to their cabins to change into bathing-suits. Meanwhile an enormous bath, ten feet high, was erected on the quarterdeck. One by one the novices were beaten over the head by inflated football bladders, shoved on a stool, lathered and shaved with a wooden razor, tipped off and sent skimming along a soapy slide into the bath, where grimy 'bears' ducked them repeatedly. Even Im Thurn did not escape. By 1 p.m. 950 had been received into Neptune's fold. Champagne and sliced oranges closed the ceremony.

The six days at Cape Town, which included Christmas, began badly on 22 December. A dense fog shrouded the squadron as they approached Table Bay, and buoys were streamed so the seven ships could keep station. Nevertheless, they were welcomed in by five fighter planes. The ceremonial rituals, which were to be paraded in every place of importance, were gone through again, and the men savoured their first real taste of Commonwealth hospitality as they were invited to concerts, dances, race meetings, teas, excursions and picnics and competed at cricket, tennis, soccer and boxing.

Field soon got into the swing of making inspiring speeches. During a welcoming banquet in the city hall, he congratulated South Africa on its 'baby navy' but warned the country that it needed at least one light cruiser. 'South Africa should build up a seagoing force to guard her trade routes,'[3] he suggested. His speech was tumultuously applauded, but not by the Afrikaans Press, which ignored the visit.

It was feared that during Christmas sailors might run riot ashore after drinking throat-searing Cape brandy. But after festivities the city police chief acclaimed: 'We have never known Christmas or New Year so free from any signs of rowdyism in native quarters.'[4] He put it down to the fine disciplinary example set by matelots and the dignified march of nine hundred seamen and marines. Yet two men from the

Hood were so attracted to Cape Town that they deserted and were never caught. Ex-Able Seaman E. Hughes, later to be a recruiting officer, recalls: 'One night I was on my way to the *Hood* with a mate when we disagreed on the quickest route back. So I went in one direction and he in another. I never saw him, nor heard of him again.'

A warship as powerful as the *Hood* had never been seen off the coast of South Africa, and authorities at every port clamoured for at least a glimpse of her. The battle cruisers remained the centres of attraction as they continued on to Zanzibar, and after they left Durban a slogan-minded grocer advertised a branded coffee: 'Don't be Hoodwinked — Repulse substitutes.'

At Zanzibar the ships had their first royal welcome when the Sultan, Sayyad Khalifa ben Harud, sailed out in his yacht at the head of a long line of native craft. The procession of war canoes circled the *Hood*, which reciprocated by dressing overall and firing a twenty-one-gun salute.

The three-thousand-mile haul across the Indian Ocean to Trincomalee, Ceylon, took nine days. Continuous heat was taking its toll. The sick-bay was full with exhaustion cases, and there was lassitude among most men. At 'Trinco' the squadron were given their first 'holiday' for two months. There were no ceremonies and no guns to disturb the tranquillity of the green-wooded, landlocked harbour. Protocol yielded to quiet talks, private parties replaced banquets, visitors were kept down to two thousand; the loudest explosions were from the rifles of officers on safari.

At Port Swettenham, twenty-seven miles from Kuala Lumpur on the Malaysian peninsula, only one channel through the mud-banks was navigable. As they steamed slowly at dusk on 4 February the heat was unrelenting, as it had been for the five-day passage parallel to the equator. The cooling plant for the fresh water system did not function, and the water remained hot. The unpleasantness worsened when a leaky condenser tube allowed sea-water into the drinking-water. The men tasted salt in their custard, prunes, tea and 'limers'. Lieutenant C.R. Benstead grumbled: 'Only in the beef-steak pie was it tolerable.'[5]

The brine, heat and mosquitoes were too much for Able

Seaman Lee. He died of malaria and was buried in the town's cemetery. It was the first death of the tour in the *Hood*.

Singapore was one of the most important ports of call for Field because the British Government were still undecided about building a great naval base there. The authorities ashore foresaw the visit as a preliminary to the establishment of the base, and a huge, red illuminated 'Welcome' sign on the pier reflected their eagerness to entertain the Navy, not just for eight days but for all time. Crowds were five deep on the pier. The port was at its sparkling best. Beggars, who normally slept by the war memorial, were shoved away and the memorial cleaned. The council, worried about the appalling incidence of venereal disease – said to be 'rampant among all classes' – licensed all brothels before the squadron patronized them. In the *Hood* a lecture was given about 'catching a dose'.

Special racial arrangements were made for 29,000 to look over the *Hood*, whose 860-foot length was pegged out on a recreation ground to show citizens her massiveness. Red tickets were issued to Chinese, green to Europeans, who had special days reserved, yellow for Eurasians, white for Indians, Ceylonese and Japanese, and pink for Mohammedans. Nothing was to mar the maritime honour accorded to Singapore – and nothing did.

Field had to allay many fears that a naval base there would be a 'pistol pointing at the heart of Japan'. He delivered so many speeches that at the end of the stay he was ill with a sore throat, like several other officers. The sick-bay was still full with heat casualties, and it was estimated there was a twenty-five per cent efficiency loss. 'The level of vitality lowered; men fumbled over work and accidents became more frequent,' reported O'Connor.

Soon after a brief stop at Christmas Island the *Hood* encountered her first stretch of 'bad seas'. The battle cruiser was living up to her reputation of being a wet ship. The night midshipmen were afforded the honour of being dined by the wardroom, a great wave broke into the starboard battery and water cascaded over officers' feet as they sipped cocktails.

The eight-week Australian tour looming was to be the most demanding, and the welcomes the most breath-taking.

Each town and city seemed intent on outdoing each other for entertainment. The rivalry was exemplified at Fremantle, Western Australia, the first call. The squadron arrived on 27 February, and next day the *Hood*'s ceremonial marchers were required to slog through two parades. The first was in Fremantle at 10.30 a.m.; then they entrained for a twelve-mile journey to Perth, where they marched again through the city in leaden heat.

Before the squadron sailed, Sir James Mitchell, the state Prime Minister, invited: 'We want many of your sailors to come out here and live. To Australia the Navy means everything.'[6] The *Hood* took with her a new mascot, Joey, the wallaby, who was given to the crew. 'He became a great favourite,' Lieutenant Benstead recounted. 'He pirouetted on his tail, boxed, loped into the wardroom to eat newspapers and cigarette ends, which he loved ... Later on the cruise Joey would go ashore and dutifully return again.'[7]

Across the Great Bight the *Hood* did something she had never done before – she began to roll for the first time within the memory of her oldest inhabitant. She met a long swell on the beam and rolled seventeen degrees to each side of the vertical. Normally her length rode two or three waves at a time. Although not excessive – light cruisers swayed to the extent of twenty-seven degrees – it caused chaos in cabins and messes. Electric fans crashed on decks, books clattered from shelves, framed photographs smashed. The rolling went on for three days.

The sea became friendlier near Adelaide, but transportation problems were not eased for Im Thurn because there was insufficient depth in harbour and the *Hood* had to anchor 5½ miles out. She lay there two days before moving to within two miles of the pier at Glenlg to ensure thousands of sightseers could make trips to her more easily. The squadron received 69,510 visitors, and the city returned the courtesy by making every facility free for 'jack ashore'.

From Adelaide on, the *Hood* was engulfed by emotional waves of hysterical welcome, coinciding with Australia's new sense of importance as a self-sufficient country still valuing links with Britain. Whole populaces went to see the *Hood*, and the sightseers provided the crew with sights they would never forget. Even so, the eight-day stay at

Melbourne tried the patience of everyone.

The *Hood* and *Repulse* with the light cruisers arrived off Port Phillip Heads at 6 a.m. on St Patrick's Day to run into the peak of ovations. A flight of RAAF fighters appeared off the Cellibrand Light, and hundreds of small craft swept out to greet them. Sirens shrieked and a great roar went up from half a million people on the shore. By noon a crowd of a hundred thousand had overrun Princess Pier, where the battle cruisers berthed. They pushed through a police cordon and surged over the *Hood* thirty minutes before she was officially 'open'. Thirty thousand trampled over her. In the next week 200,000 trod her decks. Youths straddled the guns and scaled the mast – one youngster shinned up to the admiral's flag at the foretop. An intricate ropework rigging streamed the hordes through the correct channels. Shipboard privacy was always limited; now the officers could not find any. As they sipped tea in the wardroom, the skylights and scuttles framed peering faces. 'Sometimes it took officers 20 minutes to cross the cabin flat, a distance of ten yards,' Benstead claimed.

Through the crowds one day was carried Signal Boatswain Punshon, who had played Neptune so strenuously as the *Hood* crossed the equator. He died of a heart attack in hospital the day before the ship departed.

Many friendships were formed and clung to as the ship left. A broad web of streamers was spun between her and the pier. As the men held on to the ends, well-wishers ashore let out more coloured ribbons until they trailed in the sea and broke.

As the voyage continued, newspaper comment was to bother Field more than any other criticism, but he was amused by one fable, which he had to deny in Hobart, Tasmania, the next stop. Benstead wrote of its origin: 'An amusing story was told of a bluejacket who unconsciously assisted the slander. On the day of *Hood*'s arrival a woman approached him and said: "My poor man – how many more years have you to serve?" He replied: "Twelve years, mum" ' This was believed to have given birth to the rumour that the men were recruited from prison. The supposition was dispelled by Paymaster Commander Frank Horsey, Field's secretary, who was instructed to give a special interview to the *Hobart Mercury*.

Contrary to what fellow sailors back in Britain might have thought about the 'world booze', by the time the *Hood* reached Sydney it was becoming onerous, especially for the 'snotties'. Many of them, like Captain Blundell, then a midshipman, were permanently tired. He explains: 'I was running a picket boat, which meant solid work from 6 a.m. to 2 a.m. or midnight. And on my day off it meant entertaining visitors or being entertained ashore. The shore entertainment was a terrible duty. The official dances were a nightmare at which one had to stay until about 1 a.m. Sometimes I could hardly stand up, having had little sleep for several days. The job of laundering and keeping our clothes spotlessly clean was also a nightmare.'

Others also had dress and supply worries. Mark Penfield, the admiral's valet, looked after thirty suits for Field. Bill Collier, a young able seaman who was to become a lieutenant-commander, was a tailor and stitched more than three hundred new uniforms for seven shillings a time. Victualling officers had to make advance arrangements to ensure the *Hood* acquired enough stores to provide daily 1,400 pounds of bread, 1,000 pounds of meat, 1,500 pounds of potatoes and 130 pounds of butter.

Awaiting the *Hood* at Sydney were fifty-seven bags of letters from home, the largest mail for one ship ever handled in Australia. 'Half a million watched the squadron's entry. Just like a coronation,' wrote one journalist. The arrival accompanied the Labour Government's abandonment – later to be changed – of plans for extending Singapore as a base. This led Field to give Australia the assurance that Britain would be prepared to provide capital ships, like the *Hood*, to safeguard Empire sea lanes, if the Dominions supplied the cruisers. The Australian Government's reaction was to agree to construct two ten-thousand-ton cruisers. Field's response was to arrange for the new HMAS *Adelaide* to sail with his squadron for the next five months, with five Australian midshipmen each in the *Hood* and *Repulse*.

On the passage to New Zealand the 'snotties' were flooded out again – this time their gunroom was inundated by high seas. At Wellington, where the *Dunedin* was handed over to the New Zealand Navy, all civic functions were cancelled

because the men and officers were so fatigued. It did not stop
Admiral Lord Jellicoe, the Governor-General, motoring from
Auckland and making the trip back in the battle cruiser with
his flag flying alongside that of Field. Jellicoe was responsible
for breaking a *Hood* tradition when Field gave an official
dinner to him onboard and invited Lady Jellicoe and her
daughter Lucy: it was the only time during the cruise when
women were permitted to dine in the admiral's quarters, and
Field, an expert conjuror, performed tricks for them.

Auckland typified the Kiwis' kinship with Britain. One
afternoon 35,000 rushed the dock-gates and took the police
with them. They ran on to the wharf and charged the *Hood*'s
gangway. Mounted police were called and the ship's fire
brigade stood by with levelled hoses ready to turn on to the
masses. Benstead's view was: 'The crowd, without
displaying the slightest resentment at this curious expression
of our appreciation, laughed loud and long at a speech made
by our No. 1, which was meant to be a serious rebuke, and
went back.'

For six idyllic days the crew next relaxed at Suva, Fiji,
where ancient ceremonies of fire-walking, banyan parties
and drinking the explosive kava were revived.

The next 3,133 miles to Honolulu were broken by a call at
Apia, Western Samoa, where the *Hood* was ringed by canoes
full of girls. For the next two hours the ship was overrun by
'pure white beautiful Samoan girls', enthused O'Connor, the
official scribe. 'A seaman, or marine, or boy would take them
in hand, showing them around.' But at midday this sailors'
paradise ended when all the Samoans were ushered over the
side and the squadron got under way again.

The approach to Hawaii was the most unpleasant the
warships experienced. In the *Hood* the heat in the after flats
was up to a hundred degrees and remained there until she
arrived in Honolulu. The Americans put on the finest
display of airpower the sailors had seen, with thirty-two
seaplanes circling overhead as the squadron dipped into
Pearl Harbour and moored alongside. But the *Hood*
misbehaved, when she pulled out one of the strong bollards
on the new jetty as she secured.

Hawaii, eventually America's fiftieth state, was under
'prohibition', and in deference Field ordered the *Hood* to

cancel the crew's rum ration and the serving of all alcohol in the wardroom. But the 'dry' ball in the ship was attended by eleven hundred. Hundreds of motorists drove on to the wharf to watch the *Hood*'s concert party perform on the forecastle. Applause was screeched on car klaxons. Amid the euphoria of the visit there was one disgrace for the sportsmen of the *Hood* – they were beaten at cricket by a team of baseball players.

A different reception awaited the *Hood* in Victoria, British Columbia. English roses and lilies replaced the leis, while overcoats and woollen scarves were the dress of the day. Although the welcome was far from cold, Field was criticized in Canada's House of Commons in Ottawa. He had said at a Navy League luncheon in Victoria: 'If I were a farmer out here I should be anxious for trade routes to be protected ... and two cruisers on this coast would be invaluable.'[8] Not a lot was made of this statement on the Pacific coast but it was picked up by newspapers in eastern Canada and built up to the degree that he was telling Canada she should equip two cruisers for duty in the Atlantic and another two in the Pacific.

The *Hood* steamed in to a typical Vancouver 'hello' on 25 June. She was greeted by the now familiar squadron of planes, but they dropped twenty-one smoke bombs and ignited a shower of rockets. Tourists flooded in from as far as the southern states of America for shenanigans which included a gyro marathon, aquaplaning, cycle races, a contest for the 'perfect physical culture girl' and athletics. Again the *Hood*'s sporting types lost a national game when the soccer side bowed to the Royal Canadian Mounted Police.

Vancouver was a foretaste of the North American ballyhoo the Navy could expect, but on a bigger scale, in San Francisco, for as the squadron turned south again, Californians awaited them with the type of welcome normally reserved for kings. Yet the *pièce de résistance* beneath the Golden Gate went wrong. Again came the planes, again they dived on the *Hood*, but a golden key of the city which was supposed to be dropped on the quarterdeck plopped into the sea. The enthusiasm of the thousands who jammed the cliffs was understandable. It was the first British squadron to anchor in an American harbour for forty years. And in a public address to the city, which was traditionally anti-British, the mayor decreed: 'We surrender our city unto you. We capitulate.' It did just that. At its biggest dance five thousand pretty girls were hand-picked by a chaperon committee to partner sailors; newspapers appealed to Boy Scouts to dig up worms to improve the diet of the *Hood*'s kiwi, although the bird was suffering from worms and did not need any extra, and pleaded with visitors not to shake hands with Field because 'he has a sore right hand from greeting thousands'. The *Chronicle* filled four pages with squadron news and even included a column in a mixture of cockney and naval jargon. By the time the squadron sailed out on 11 July they had completed the most successful public relations operation ever by the Navy in the home of publicity.

The ship's company yearned for home now, although in front was the longest lap, the 3,442 miles to Balbao at the entrance to the Panama Canal. When the *Hood* arrived, it was doubtful whether she would get through the locks without damage. The width of the chambers was 110 feet, which gave a clearance of 30 inches on either side. To help her slip through, the sides were smeared with pounds of soft soap. O'Connor related: 'After waiting her turn the *Hood* entered the first lock and only just fitted in; she was then pumped up in a short space of time while the gates closed ... and so on to the next lock. She was towed very slowly by four little engines, called the mules, which it seemed could climb walls.' Tolls at 50 cents a ton amounted to $22,399.50c.

At noon on 24 July the two battle cruisers anchored off Colon breakwater at the canal's eastern end. They were still sweltering and remained in this state of sweatiness until the cool breezes of Jamaica rustled through them four days later. Nevertheless, the men were suffering from torpidity after a march in full dress through Kingston.

The temperature was in the hundreds again when the *Hood* cruised towards the eastern coast of Canada, yet by the time she reached Halifax on 5 August it was cold, and the drastic dropping of the temperature brought influenza. The sick-bay was full again, and many officers were confined to their cabins. Although the visit was synchronized to commemorate the 175th anniversary of the city's founding, it was the gloomiest part of the cruise for Field, who now heard that his speeches had triggered controversy in Britain. A Canadian newspaper article headlined 'Admiral Field tells Canada what to do' was seized on by Socialists. The *Daily Herald* ranted: 'We cannot recall a previous experience where the commanding officer of a squadron has been permitted to flaunt personal opinions in public on matters of state policy. Are we to understand they are the view of the Board of Admiralty and that he has been acting under instructions?'[9]

Yet Field, the disciple of naval power, was surprisingly defended in the French nationalist city of Quebec, where the *Hood* arrived on 19 August. A newspaper trumpeted headily: 'In her mass and speed and perfection of armament the Hood symbolizes the valorous determination of war-weary Britain to maintain intact for the good of mankind the far flung Empire she has built up through the centuries ... so that the Briton who watches her majestic course finds himself humming snatches of Land of Hope and Glory and breathing the prayer God that made thee mighty, make thee mightier yet.'

The men of the mighty *Hood*, however, were not feeling mighty when they left the city for the journey down the St Lawrence to St John's, Newfoundland. Nine and a half months of fêting, feasting and fatigue had jaded them, so they were diverted for fifteen days to Topsail Bay, a lonely location where Im Thurn let them slip back into normal routine without temptations ashore.

Finally, at 4 p.m. on Sunday 21 September, the band struck up 'Rolling Home' as the battle cruisers weighed anchor and headed out to the Atlantic. Field wirelessed the Admiralty for permission to try to break the Atlantic crossing record but was told it would be a waste of fuel. In mid-passage the ship suddenly shook so violently that the captain was called to the bridge. The cause was never explained, although one theory was that she had hit a whale.

A week later the Special Service Squadron were together again as the cruisers which visited South America rendezvoused seven miles off the Lizard. Sailors lined the rails to cheer each other as they parted company off the Eddystone Light.

The *Hood* had crept away at dawn on 27 November 1923 and crept back into Devonport Dockyard at dawn on 9 September 1924. She had covered 38,153 miles, crossed the equator six times, received 752,049 visitors and entertained 37,770 at parties and dances, while the full squadron had received 1,936,717 public visits. It was a journey never to be repeated by a modern naval force.

But the ceremonies were not over. Members of the Admiralty arrived to congratulate Field on the success of the mission and give him the news that the King had made him a knight commander of the Most Distinguished Order of St Michael and St George, with Im Thurn becoming a companion of the order. A more personal ceremony was performed in the ship's chapel, where Paymaster-Commander Horsey's son was christened in the ship's bell. The same afternoon wives, sweethearts and families poured over the gangway for a special reception. Among them was Mrs R. O'Sullivan, the daughter of a petty officer, who remembers: 'My dad gave a whistle and Joey, the wallaby, came bounding along. He nuzzled around my dad's pocket until he took out his tobacco pouch and gave him a pinch of tobacco. Joey was addicted to it.'

The wallaby became a *Hood* celebrity, and many legends were spun around him. Mr E. Hughes yarns: 'He was handed over to the ship's butcher who fed, cleaned and taught him good naval manners. He wandered around but was never again allowed between decks. If you said "Put 'em up," he would get into a fighting stance. One sailor tried to fight him, and in no time Joey's claws ripped his trousers like a pair of scissors.

'One day at sea the butcher gave him a piece of meat with a spoonful of mustard on it. Joey gulped it down and then jumped into the sea. The cutter was lowered and he was saved.

'Two years later he became a nuisance when he started escaping on to the jetty, so he was given to a zoo.'

The rest of the *Hood*'s menagerie, also destined for zoos, included a ring-tailed opossum, a flying squirrel, two beavers, two pink cockatoos and several parrots. Miss

Aperty Australis, the kiwi, did not survive the voyage. In search of food she was said to have pecked the armour plate and died from injuries.

5

The Genius of Gunnery

While the Special Service Squadron were away on their extravagant cruise, Britain had changed and was about to change again. In December 1923 the first Socialist Government were returned to power, but under Prime Minister Ramsay MacDonald it failed to acquire the confidence of the country and just nine months later fought a General Election.

For the 'professionals' in the *Hood*, the new Conservative Government under Stanley Baldwin in October 1924, seemed something to rejoice about. With a Chancellor of the Exchequer like Winston Churchill, who immediately struck sixpence off the pound in income tax, they could expect to retain their status with the blunting of the notorious 'Geddes axe'.

At the beginning of 1925, after a three-month overhaul at Rosyth, the *Hood*, still flying Field's flag, rejoined the fleet for the routine spring cruise to Gibraltar.

On the way to the Rock the ship was detached for another ambassadorial duty, the last which Field was to carry out. Portugal was celebrating the four-hundredth anniversary of the death of the explorer Vasco da Gama, and the *Hood*'s battalion led the march-past of foreign navies in Lisbon. To Midshipman Gould, accompanied by his colleagues Normand Luard and Alexander Bingley, fell the honour of being a standard-bearer at the head of the parade. 'I was only given a couple of hours' notice,' said Gould. 'And the sling which the ensign rested in didn't fit me. Mounted police roughly cleared crowds in front to make way for us. Unfortunately our band was not there, and it was difficult to march to the foxtrot which the French band played. My father was surprised to find my picture in *The Times* next day.'

On the way back to Plymouth, the *Hood* thrashed into a full power trial, and despite calm weather, the officers came in for a soaking. The ship suddenly went over a shallow and dropped nearly fifteen feet. This created an enormous bow wave, which flooded the quarterdeck. Gould remembered: 'Speed was reduced, amid a lot of noise from the lifting safety valves. The after hatch had been left open and a lot of water came in, flooding officers' cabins and even getting down the spirit-room.'

The midshipmen's quarters were also constantly being swamped, but not by the sea. One of the chest flats was adjacent to a bathroom, which had a faulty ejector pump. This brought flooding in the bathroom and consequently the flat. Clothing was always floating in the area. 'We ran a communal wardrobe there and put on anyone's dry clothes which were available and fitted us,' says Commander Neville Cambell, a cadet at the time.

By May 1925 Field was due to say farewell and become Deputy Chief of Naval Staff, which was to lead him to his ambition of being First Sea Lord. The new leader of the squadron was fifty-one-year-old Rear-Admiral Sir Cyril Fuller, the Third Sea Lord and Admiralty Controller, who seemed destined for the top when he was promoted to lieutenant at nineteen, commander at twenty-nine and captain at thirty-six. Fuller and Captain H.O. Reinold, the *Hood*'s new commanding officer, were a colourless partnership. Fuller seldom made contact with the men and knew little of lower deck conditions.

For the next two years the *Hood* slipped into a routine of showing herself to home ports and resorts, punctuated by spring and autumn cruises and gunnery exercises. The summer of 1925 she spent at bases as diverse as Portland and Invergordon. The spring cruise to Gibraltar and Majorca relieved monotony.

On 4 May 1926, after another two months of repairs at Rosyth, the *Hood*'s crew awoke to find Britain at a standstill. The General Strike, triggered by the long-standing coal dispute, had begun. Everyone was recalled and the *Hood* sailed at midnight for the Clyde. She lay at the Tail of the Bank for a week as landing parties guarded Princess Docks, and her transmitter was used to jam any Russian attempts at interference. The strike ended after nine days, and the *Hood* retreated to Portsmouth, soon to become her home port.

In the next year she was still a familiar visitor to Scottish waters, for she was at Invergordon in September and October and at Cromarty in May 1927, when Fuller handed over to Rear-Admiral Frederic Dreyer, a brilliant gunnery officer and as flamboyant as his predecessor was grey. Dreyer, of the large head and larger brain, as a contemporary described him, had attracted the Admiralty's attention as a lieutenant when he invented a complicated range-finding machine which computed the course and speed of the attacking ship, together with that of the enemy, to produce a plot which was fed to the director and guns. It became known as the Dreyer Table.

Like Fuller, Dreyer was a distant admiral and rarely bothered about the men, but he had the fortune of acquiring as his flag captain in the *Hood* Wilfred French, who made up for this default and was affectionately known as 'Winnie the Pooh', because of his close resemblance to A.A. Milne's bear, when wrapped in his 'British warm' on the bridge.

Dreyer, the gunnery genius who had outshot the *Hood* in exercises when captain of the *Renown*, was always ready to show off his inventiveness. For the visit to Portland of King Amanullah of Afghanistan, the fleet put on a fifteen-inch full-calibre shoot, which Dreyer helped to plan. It was at a towed target, with the *Hood* and the squadron passing in line ahead on an up-Channel course. Simultaneously the battleship *Nelson*, with commander-in-chief Admiral Sir Hubert Brand and the King aboard, was to steam through a designated point on the *Hood's* starboard quarter and on the same course. With four warships nearing position, visibility thickened. Dreyer reorganized quickly and used only three-pounder blanks, with the *Nelson* training her searchlight dead ahead. 'I then increased to 25 knots,' Dreyer reported later: 'We sighted the *Nelson's* searchlight when it was expected and passed her at a distance of 1,000 yards, opening fire with three-pounder blanks ... Admiral Sir Eric Fullerton, the Naval Secretary, who was with the First Lord and King Amanullah and suite in a special position built on top of the *Nelson's* B turret wrote and told me that it was a tremendous sight when the three huge battle cruisers suddenly rushed out of the mist at 25 knots at close range, firing blanks – apparently engaging the fleet flagship.'[1]

The gunnery antics of Dreyer and the *Hood* became a fable, but not always to the credit of the admiral or the ship. In 1928 Jellicoe, now sixty-nine, went on the so-called 'autumn gunnery cruise' with the *Hood* from Cromarty. Dreyer impressed the old admiral by staging fifteen-inch firings at night. Then came shame. Harry Smith, a communications rating, who was on the flag deck, relates: 'We were sounding our siren when it jammed open and filled the North Sea with noise. It took engineers several minutes to fix. There was panic in the fleet because a prolonged blast meant "I am in distress." We had just got over this when our bearings ran hot and we lost speed to a point where we only just about had steerage way, but we made Invergordon.'

Dreyer also found himself caught between his passion for gunnery and his hobby of bird-watching. At the height of a complicated exercise, a shout came from the voice-pipe to the compass platform, where the captain stood. 'French, French,' cried Dreyer. The captain dashed to the voicepipe. 'Yes, sir, what is it?' he shouted back, believing the ship was in danger. A small, precise voice answered: 'Can you see that flight of guillemot passing across the bows?'[2]

During his two years, Dreyer proclaimed that the *Hood* was in first-class order and admitted that this was because of astute handling of the men by French and Commander Arthur Power, who both ruled firmly and without favour. The boy seamen and midshipmen were indoctrinated in the *Hood* tradition of immaculately maintained boats and splendidly drilled crews.

For spring cruises the *Hood* took a full complement of boats, but one, the twelve-oared cutter, was never used except in races. In it a Royal Marine crew had won the Rodman Cup for three successive years. Once a racehorse and a donkey were embarked, but the line was drawn at a motor cycle and sidecar. Ex-Able Seaman E. Thomas, who was on the quayside at Plymouth when it was about to be swung aboard, reminisces: 'Along came Commander Power and shouted: "What the hell is that? Take it off my ship." So it was dumped on the dockside. It belonged to a commissioned gunner, whom we called "Clicketty Click".

Later he started up the motorcycle and ran it over the dock into the water. Many years later a Plymouth newspaper reported it had been picked up by a ship when tying up.'

The *esprit de corps* was high again, and *Hood*'s reputation for winning engendered jealousy among the fleet. Officers and men rose to take up any challenge, like the one the renowned commentator Lieutenant Stephen King-Hall, of the *Repulse*, threw down at Gibraltar in 1929. In a spoof fleet circular he suggested a race for lieutenant-commanders in twelve-oared cutters – after studying the Navy List and discovering that there were at least two hundred in the ships at Gibraltar. He announced that the *Repulse* would put up a trophy – a miniature brass hat – and in his challenge stated jokingly that it was well known that a high proportion of lieutenant-commanders were sodden with drink and led vicious lives, so the strain of rowing would produce a considerable number of casualties from heart failure and hernia, which would reduce numbers. Although the race was frowned on by Brand, the commander-in-chief in the *Nelson*, and the battleship's officers did not enter, the *Hood*'s lieutenant-commanders trained fervently. It was rowed on a Saturday morning with hundreds of amused sailors cheering the contestants as they pulled for a mile between anchored vessels. The *Hood*'s crew were first past the finish, which was strategically arranged opposite the *Nelson*.

This elitism had its disadvantages, too. Often the men were in brawls ashore because the *Hood* was given preference over ships which had seen wartime service. Cambell had this cause for complaint: 'When I was returning in a launch at Cromarty, an egg was thrown and burst at my feet. Then a voice yelled from a nearby ship: "Yah! And what did the mighty 'ood do in the bloody war!" '

By the beginning of 1929 Dreyer was informed he would not end his appointment in the *Hood*, due for her first comprehensive refit in the May, but would transfer to the *Renown*. But there was no resounding farewell for him when his barge left for the last time at Spithead on 29 April. 'The three cheers by the ratings seemed very perfunctory,' says Cambell.

On 17 May the *Hood* paid off into Portsmouth Dockyard, and French handed over to Lieutenant-Commander W.M. Phipps-Hornby, in whose charge she would be for a two-year refit. The primary alterations involved new Admiralty thinking about air power. Two Mark VIII eight-barrelled pom-pom aircraft guns – soon to be christened 'Chicago Pianos' after the reign of American gangsterism – were fitted each side of the boat deck, which was also enlarged. Eight years earlier a two-seater Sopwith Panther had taken off successfully from B turret, and now an aircraft catapult was to be put on X turret's roof. A mock-up was constructed before recommissioning but was removed because it was considered that a catapult and crane would be more feasible on the extreme end of the quarterdeck for a Fairy Walrus III F seaplane.

The refit, which cost £687,074, was due to be completed by 10 March 1931, in time for trials off Portsmouth, and she was expected to be recommissioned in May, but at the beginning of the year she was still in a deplorable state. Vice-Admiral E.W.L. Longley-Cook, then a lieutenant-commander, recalls: 'I was thrilled when I was appointed to her, but then came the shock of finding her in such a state. Fortunately, the *Valiant* was just completing a refit and her captain, B.G. Washington, took one look at her and told the admiral's superintendent he refused to accept the *Valiant* in this state and he would tell their Lordships. There was a quick reaction by Portsmouth Dockyard to clear the *Valiant* and also the *Hood*. For the next four months trainloads filled with dirt and scrap left daily from alongside us.'

The refit also meant that the *Hood* would no longer be a 'Westoe' ship. 'Guz' (the slang for Devonport) had not the facilities to repair her bulk, and so Portsmouth became her home port and she was recommissioned by a 'Pompey' crew on 12 May 1931. For a month from 15 June she worked up off the south coast. A fortnight before Rear-Admiral Tomkinson was due to hoist his flag, the new Fairey seaplane came to grief. A few seconds after take-off at Weymouth it lost speed when only two feet above the sea. The port wing touched the surface, and it cartwheeled. The plane broke up and sank in thirty seconds. The crew of three were thrown clear and were picked up unhurt by the ship's boats. Next day divers salvaged the plane. The commission had begun with a catastrophe; it was to continue disastrously and end in ignominy.

6

A Stain on the Navy ...

Rear-Admiral Tomkinson had initially set foot on the *Hood* as her first captain – and a popular one at that – in 1920, so the ship's company were expecting a warm welcome when she rejoined the battle cruisers in Torbay on 10 July 1931. Instead he castigated them. The first sign of his displeasure came when she took station astern of the squadron. Longley-Cook explains: 'I was on the bridge and expected the admiral to signal from the *Renown* something like "Glad to see you back." But he signalled "Manoeuvre badly executed." From tails up we were nearly tails down.'

At 8 a.m. on the Sunday Tomkinson's flag fluttered to the masthead, and an hour later he boarded her. He walked around divisions and did not like what he saw. The men were dismissed, and then came the pipe: 'Clear lower deck; all hands aft.' From the capstan the angry Tomkinson told them: 'I was the first captain of this ship and until you reach something like the standard in which I left her I shall not be satisfied and until then I have not much use for you.'[1]

This insult did nothing to endear Tomkinson to the lower deck, who, according to Longley-Cook, had 'worked very hard to get her from dockyard condition to fleet condition'. Within two months Tomkinson was to regret his maiden speech, for soon the *Hood* would be bound for Invergordon, where his career would be put on the block in the maelstrom of mutiny.

On the eve of the fleet's cruise to Invergordon, the commander-in-chief, Admiral Sir Michael Hodges, had thrombosis and pleurisy and was rushed to hospital from the flagship *Nelson*. It was too late to cancel the fleet sailings, and Tomkinson, the senior officer, took command. Before leaving Portsmouth in the *Hood*, he went to the commander-in-chief's office in the *Nelson*, which was to stay behind to await Hodges' possible recovery. There he was handed all the documents of command by Rear-Admiral R.M. Colvin, chief of staff. Among them was a confidential warning signal about reductions in pay, which were agreed by the Cabinet and Admiralty to help offset an adverse budget balance of £170,000,000. Tomkinson studied the telegram, which read: 'For the Navy the sacrifice involves the acceptance of the recommendations of the report of the Committee on National Expenditure and these include placing all officers and men at present in receipt of pay on 1919 scales on the revised scale introduced in October, 1925 and reducing all standard rates of pay of officers by 11, instead of eight per cent, as previously decided to come into force in July last. The new regulations are to come into force from October 1 next ...'[2]

Neither Tomkinson nor Colvin realized the impact the cuts would have. To hundreds of married seamen it would mean a reduction of 25 per cent in pay, yet single sailors would lose only 10.5 per cent.

The telegram had been sent to nine commanders-in-chief; only the Atlantic Fleet had not replied. In Hodges' absence Colvin wrote two draft letters and locked the final one, which made no reference to pay, in a safe to await Hodges' endorsement. Tomkinson approved it. But he was unaware that the Admiralty considered that the twenty per cent cut, proposed hurriedly by Ramsay MacDonald's National Government after only a week's life, would have a 'deplorable affect on the Navy'.

So suddenly Tomkinson, the admiral who because of his links with Keyes had rarely been entrusted with a truly independent command, was rushed into a position of great responsibility, without the necessary rank to carry it out. For with him in the fleet were two officers with almost similar seniority – Rear-Admiral E.A. Astley-Rushton, commanding the Second Cruiser Squadron, and Rear-Admiral French, the former captain of the *Hood*, in charge of the Second Battle Squadron's Second Division.

Yet there was pride in Tomkinson's heart as the *Hood* steamed from Portsmouth on Tuesday 8 September to lead the fleet to Invergordon – and to his unjustified disgrace.

On 10 September, while the ships were in mock battle, Phillip Snowden, the Chancellor of the Exchequer, revealed his emergency budget and announced the expected deficit of £170,000,000. To balance this, sixpence was put on income tax, twopence on petrol and a penny on beer. The pay economies were published in a White Paper. Six days earlier the Admiralty had the foresight to print a Fleet Order which warned of sacrifices the Navy were about to make. But this was regarded as a 'leak' by the Treasury and was cancelled. As a substitute, after the Budget speech, the Admiralty issued another warning of the cuts. This was sent by signal to all the fleets, except the Atlantic, still at sea. Instead it was duplicated and despatched through normal postal channels. The *Nelson*, still officially the flagship, although dockbound, received the first letter. It was put in the pigeon-hole of Admiral Hodges, who was still in hospital, to await delivery to him.

Official records state there were illegal meetings among *Hood* ratings to discuss the sacrifices they were asked to make. There is little doubt that they knew of the pay docking, which would have been heard on BBC broadcasts, but there was nothing definite, although it was believed to be as high as twenty-five per cent. If there were organized meetings, they were not reported to Captain J.F.C. Patterson, nor to Tomkinson.

The *Hood* arrived at Invergordon on Friday afternoon, 11 September, the day after the Budget. She anchored a mile away from the pier with the northern line, which included the *Rodney, Centurion, Dorsetshire, Norfolk, Warspite, Valiant* and *Malaya*. Soon the waters of Cromarty Firth were dotted with boats, collecting mail, newspapers and provisions. During the dinner hour papers were on sale in the *Hood*'s canteen. The *Daily Express* and *Scottish Daily Record* revealed that the lower 1925 pay rates would apply to everyone, with pensions restricted to 1930 grades, while the *Daily Mirror* confused readers by quoting the reduction as from ten to twenty per cent. Commander A.F. Paterson, who at that time was an able seaman in the *Hood*, describes the reaction: 'In large headlines we saw our pay had been cut by twenty-five per cent. The basic of an able seaman was reduced from four to three shillings a day, without any

Ship's company 1937–39 at Malta.

Left: The size of the quarterdeck is illustrated by this game of hockey played on it and around the aft turrets.

Right: Joey the Wallaby aboard the *Hood*

Far right The *Hood*'s successful boxing team after the 'Brazilian Games' in Rio de Janeiro. They include Stoker Petty Officer Spillar (top right), who was knocked out by an American before his bout started.

Below right: Fancy dress time for ratings during the spring cruise to Gibraltar in 1928.

Below: Pay day – and for an able seaman during the war it was just over £1 a week.

Above: The chapel — the most peaceful compartment of the ship.

Left: One of the engine-room throttles.

Above right: King Haakon and Queen Maud of Norway (centre) visit the *Hood* during her Scandinavian cruise in 1920.

Right: George V inspects divisions during a visit to the *Hood* in 1922. On the right is Admiral 'Tich' Cowan and behind the King is Captain Mackworth.

Above: *Hood*'s quarterdeck awash as she crosses the Tasman Sea during the World Cruise in 1924.

Left: Going through the Panama Canal in July, 1924.

Above right: Not an inch of space is left on the dockside at Melbourne, as crowds wait to board during the World Cruise.

Right: X and Y turrets blasting off during a speed trial in 1926.

Above: The *Hood* in full glory of
peacetime days when she was with the
Mediterranean Fleet two years before
the war began.

Right: Admiral Sir Frederic Dreyer
who had a passion for gunnery and
bird-watching.

warning. There was widespread shock. We wondered whether the *Daily Mail* was running the Navy. Or were the Press just being sensational? Officers and petty officers had no answers, so a communication barrier between the leaders and the led was set up.'

Tomkinson did not seem aware of the enmity being bred in the messes. Neither did he realize that every commander-in-chief now knew of the pay controversy through the second warning signal. His copy was still in Hodges' office. But a new Admiralty Fleet Order was on the way. It arrived at 7 p.m. next day, when Tomkinson's office was closed, as was normal on Saturdays. Because there was no preliminary signal about it, the AFO was pigeon-holed until after the weekend. There were not enough copies anyway to pin on the *Hood*'s many notice-boards. Distribution through the rest of the fleet was not completed until the Sunday. Across the water Rear-Admirals Astley-Rushton and French and the captains of the *Rodney* and *Adventure* received the warning letter as soon as they anchored. Tomkinson had yet to study it because his personal copy was wrongly addressed to the *Renown*, which he had left two months earlier.

On the Saturday afternoon most of *Hood*'s off-duty watch went to the Invergordon Highland Games, where the ship's marine band played. In the early evening the custom for most was to drink in the canteen building, and it was here that the first talk of a 'stop work' campaign began. But the late Len Wincott, one of the self-styled mutiny leaders, who was then a twenty-four-year-old able seaman in the *Norfolk*, later maintained that he had instigated the idea and that of a mass Sunday evening meeting by circulating the suggestions around the fleet by boat crews.

Next day there was more disturbing news in the Sunday papers about the cuts. In the *Hood*, Lieutenant-Commander Harry Pursey, who had won promotion from the lower deck and who was to become Labour MP for East Hull for twenty-five years, went to his executive officer, Commander C.R. McCrum, and warned: 'If the cuts are not reduced there will be trouble. And if there is trouble, it will be on Tuesday at 8 a.m.'[3] Pursey predicted it would be 'tailor made' for a mass protest at the end of the breakfast hour, just before the ships sailed for exercises. McCrum thought

Pursey was being over-dramatic and ignored the warning.

Patterson and McCrum went ashore in the afternoon to settle in their own minds that nothing untoward was happening and made a detour to the canteen, which seemed orderly and quiet. A few hours later the often-irascible Rear-Admiral Astley-Rushton passed by and was worried by the tone of speeches which were being made to more than six hundred ratings inside. One of the first fiery speeches was made by Able Seaman Bond, of the *Rodney*, which was to be lead ship of the mutiny. Wincott, who was carrying his hat, so he could not be identified by the ship's ribbon on it, then jumped on to a table and incited the men to strike 'like the miners'.

Meanwhile Astley-Rushton had contacted the officer of the shore patrol, which that evening was the responsibility of the *Warspite*, and suggested he send for reinforcements to break up the meeting. Then he took a boat to the *Hood* to inform Tomkinson. The main patrol went to the canteen, where glasses had been thrown, and quietened the men. When the second patrol arrived, at 8 p.m., the bar was closed, but not before ratings had agreed that another meeting should be held there next evening.

Many of the *Hood*'s men returned in the drifter *Horizon*, singing and shouting 'We're not yellow bellies', but this was ignored by the officer-of-the-watch because it differed little from the normal rowdiness of leave at any port.

Later that night Tomkinson discussed the unruliness with Astley-Rushton, Captain Patterson and Commander W.H.G. Fallowfield, of the *Warspite*, and concluded: 'No importance need be attached to the incident from a general disciplinary point of view.' At 9.15 p.m. the *Nelson*, which had left Hodges in hospital, arrived. It was only then that the Admiralty's warning letter was passed to Tomkinson. 'On arrival of *Nelson* I first became aware of the letter,'[4] he wrote later, although Astley-Rushton and French had ample opportunity of making him aware of their copies of it. Tomkinson did not signal the Admiralty that night about the unrest. He preferred to wait for a 'sign' the next morning, when *Warspite*, the flagship of the Second Battle Squadron, and the *Malaya* were due to sail for exercises.

Tomkinson was on the bridge at 8 a.m. to watch their

going, with the crews drawn up in perfect order on the forecastle and quarterdecks. He also surveyed the other ships and was reassured by the appearance of their men carrying out normal harbour drill. Next he saw Rear-Admiral Colvin, the chief of staff, who came over from the *Nelson*. Together they studied the three foolscap sheets of the Admiralty letter and decided that certain sections of it should be explained to the men by junior officers. There were not enough copies to be fed to every ship, so extra ones were typed. Most were completed that evening but were not delivered to some vessels until next morning.

The *Hood*'s WT office then began transmitting a series of signals, which built up in urgency in the next three days. At 10.02 a message was sent to all ships that as soon as copies of the Admiralty letter were received the cuts were to be 'explained without delay'. Just over twenty minutes later Tomkinson composed this 'Important' signal to the Admiralty: 'There was a slight disturbance in the Royal Naval Canteen, Invergordon yesterday, Sunday, evening, caused by one or two ratings endeavouring to address those present on the subject of reduction in pay. I attach no importance to the incident from a general disciplinary point of view, but it is possible it may be reported in an exaggerated form by the Press. Matter is still being investigated.'[5]

At 11.45 a.m. Patterson was the first captain to clear the lower deck and explain the cuts to the crew. Because of the financial structure, based on dates on which a man received his full rating, it was difficult to analyse individual cases, but one example was that an able seaman on a 1919 rate was to have his basic slashed by a shilling a day to three shillings. Patterson ended by telling them: 'You will not improve your chances of any revision of the proposed rates by any irregular, concerted action, but should put representations forward through me.'[6]

Similar assurances were given by captains to the rest of the fleet, but they did nothing to temper the feelings of those who gathered again in the canteen that evening. Many carried copies of the *Daily Worker*, which was trying to inflame the crisis by publishing a spurious scale of cuts which put able seamen at twenty-five per cent, petty officers at twelve per cent and officers at only nine.

In plain clothes, Patterson and McCrum went ashore again, ostensibly to watch a soccer trial. Before they disembarked, they arranged for an extra patrol, under Lieutenant-Commander L.G.E. Robinson, to be standing by, but it was not detailed by name, so suspicion would not be aroused. Patterson and McCrum left the football field at 6.15 p.m. and walked by the canteen. The doors were closed, but inside they saw a crowd speaking animatedly.

The *Valiant* had guard duty that night, and Lieutenant Elkins, who had written so graphically about the voyage to Brazil when he was a midshipman in the *Hood*, was in charge of the shore patrol. He was instructed that if there were subversive talk in the canteen he should try to arrest the ringleaders. He landed at 5 p.m. and posted six men at the canteen, five in the town and similar numbers at the centre pier and dockyard pier. Because it was quiet, he went to the officers' club, but he had been there only fifteen minutes when he was warned that a meeting had begun in the canteen, that doors were locked and the chief petty officer of the patrol could not get in.

What happened after this is recorded by Elkins in his report. He looked through the window and saw a three-badge man, with red hair, talking in an 'inflammatory nature'. Elkins persuaded a rating inside to open a door. As he strode in with the patrol, there were cat-calls of 'Get out. Get out.' When Elkins could make himself heard, he said: 'I will remain until I am satisfied that what is being discussed is not to the prejudice of discipline.' The jeers continued, until Elkins noticed two civilians trying to leave. He went to talk to them but was hit in the back by a beer mug, which ricocheted off a seaman. Elkins then claimed: 'I was pushed out of the canteen by some sailors and marines, who crossed hands and bent down in the shape of a rugger scrum. The door was shut and locked behind me.'

Elkins was able to return, however, for the patrol's chief petty officer was still inside, and he unlocked the door again. By then the meeting had broken up and men were streaming on to the Black Field soccer ground to continue it. Elkins left the 'chief' in the canteen and sent a message to the patrol office for reinforcements from the *Hood*. Meanwhile he went to Black Field, where speakers included a marine from the *Hood* and Wincott. After referring to the cuts, the marine yelled: 'What are we going to do about it?' The crowd roared: 'Pack up.' The marine asked: 'When? Tonight or tomorrow?' Someone replied: 'After breakfast.'

Then the men dispersed again, some returning to the canteen. By now Elkins had joined the *Hood*'s patrol of thirty, in the charge of Lieutenant-Commander Robinson and aided by Lieutenant T.A. Pack-Beresford. The main entrance to the canteen was barred, but all of them got in through the petty officers' room at the rear. Robinson reported later: 'About 300 men were present and many of them drunk. Speeches of a mutinous nature were made.'[7]

The ringleaders ranted: 'Are we going to take our pay cuts lying down?' and 'Is the fleet going to sea tomorrow?' To both questions they received a resounding 'No.' Pack-Beresford persuaded Robinson to address them, so he jumped on the bar and gave a blast on his whistle to obtain silence. He was shouted down for several minutes, but then many of the men insisted he should be heard. 'You're going about it in the wrong way,' he told them. 'Complaints should be made in a service-like manner.' Pack-Beresford and Elkins reassured and calmed other ratings. 'I was approached by men who had recently served with me on the East Indies Station,' Pack-Beresford recalls. 'They promised they would stand by me whatever happened.'

After it was announced that there would be no more speeches and the canteen would close, the men filed away peacefully. Only one argued, and Robinson took his name.

But earlier Wincott had walked among them, repeating quietly: 'Don't forget – six o'clock tomorrow morning.'[8] Soon this was being shouted from boat to boat as four thousand libertymen returned to their ships. From drifters came the strains of 'The Red Flag'. In the *Horizon*, the *Hood*'s drifter, there were 130 men, cheering, singing and shouting. The din was so great that officer-of-the-watch Lieutenant J.S. Gabbett ordered the midshipman in charge of the boat to lay off and not to approach until there was silence. After quietening, the men were allowed to climb on board and go to their messes. Some attempted to do this without having their names ticked off by the quartermaster, but this was stopped by Gabbett.

At 9.15 p.m., thirty minutes after the libertymen's return, Lieutenant-Commander J.F.W. Mudford, who was exercising the searchlight operators, reported to Commander McCrum that there was a 'large gathering in the eyes of the ship'. McCrum went there with the master-at-arms and saw a rating inciting between 100 and 150 men. When the man noticed the commander, he slipped into the crowd.

In his cabin Tomkinson, who had been told of the canteen disturbance, was dining three admirals and ten captains in an effort to get to know these senior officers who had been placed under him so peremptorily. The party broke up at 9.30 when McCrum reported to Captain Patterson and then to Tomkinson that there had been trouble on board. By this time Elkins had arrived also to inform Tomkinson of the rowdy meeting. He was convinced the fleet was about to rebel. Tomkinson was inclined to believe it was 'a lot of drunken sailors shouting their mouths off' but, after turning it over continually in his mind until 11.15 p.m., he considered the situation serious enough to warrant signalling the Admiralty: 'Further disturbances took place among libertymen landed at Invergordon this evening. Libertymen have all returned on board but there is considerable unrest among a proportion of the lower ratings ...'[9]

Astley-Rushton returned to the *Hood* before midnight for more consultations with the admiral, who by now had received reports of disturbances from all ships. For the first time Tomkinson realized that dissension was widespread, and at 1 a.m. he sent an 'Immediate' signal to the Admiralty, which stressed his fears: 'Having received reports from flag and commanding officers, I am of the opinion that it may be difficult to get ships to sea for practice this morning, Tuesday. I have made the following general signal to the Atlantic Fleet in company. Begins: "The Senior Officer, Atlantic Fleet, is aware that cases of hardship will result in consequence of the new rates of pay. Commanding officers are to make a thorough investigation and report to me typical cases without delay, in order that I may bring the matter at once to the notice of the Admiralty." '

He was up at dawn, for, as his report stated: 'I decided that it was preferable to adhere to the arrangements already made and carry out the programme, if possible. It appeared probable that certain ships would proceed and it was anticipated that if they did, others would follow.'[10] The admiral was half right – and half wrong.

The morning dawned golden bright and crystal clear, with the waters of the firth calm and unruffled. It was perfect for exercises and also for a mutiny. The turmoil to Tomkinson's mind eased when he was told that the hands had fallen in for work on the *Hood*'s forecastle as normal at 6 a.m. and that the decks were being scrubbed. His spirits rose when the *Repulse* weighed anchor half an hour later and left. But unknown to him, mutiny had already begun. In the *Rodney* only seventy-five out of a complement of twelve hundred reported at 6 a.m., while in the *Dorsetshire* nearly a hundred were absent.

Those in the *Hood* could see that work was not being carried out on the nearby *Rodney* and that seamen were massing on the forecastle. At 7.31 the *Valiant* unmoored and was ready to sail, but she could not proceed because there were not enough stokers in the engine-room. Captain C.A. Scott scribbled a message to Tomkinson and sent it by boat to the *Hood*, because he could not rely on the *Valiant*'s signalmen. At 7.45 'Clear lower deck' was piped in the *Hood*, and the men assembled on the forecastle. Commander McCrum sensed they were loath to work and from the grumbling around him deduced they were 'obviously determined not to go to sea'. He spoke to them, but their attitude did not change. McCrum reported to Captain Patterson that the men were stubborn and advised: 'No good purpose will be served by your addressing them, sir.'[11] Patterson heeded the advice.

Rodney's mutineers were now jeering at the *Hood*, where it was apparent some ratings were working. Soon after, the order to clean guns was piped and immediately ignored by about two hundred *Hood* seamen, who remained at the fore end and exchanged cheers with the *Rodney*. At 8.30 preparations were made to go to sea. 'Both watches for exercise' was sounded, but only a third of the crew responded. Some were told to hoist boats; others were ordered to haul in the lower boom. Both commands were obeyed. But when Lieutenant-Commander Mudford, who was in charge of the cable party, his 'doggie', Midshipman Kenneth Aylwin, later to become a captain, and a petty officer went to the cable locker flat, where marines normally worked, there was no one there, so Mudford's small party uncovered the navel pipe and the cable lockers. On the forecastle they ran into opposition. Demonstrators were sitting or standing on cables; the hawse pipe cover was still in place. Mudford strode towards the cables but was hemmed in by the crowd, who did not jostle him but stood respectfully a yard or two away. One shouted: 'What's the use of trying to take the ship to sea like this, sir?' Mudford replied: 'What about it? If I give the order to heave in, are you going to stop me?'

'Yes, sir,' they yelled. 'We'll have to.'

Aylwin was impressed by the respect the men had shown the first lieutenant and by the fact they did not omit to call him 'sir'. Mudford sent a messenger to the captain. The reply he received was: 'Leave things as they are and make no further attempt to unshackle.'[12]

By wrapping a $4\frac{1}{2}$-inch wire hawser around sections of the cable, the mutineers now made sure the ship could not be slipped easily. Then they dispersed.

Patterson was prepared for mutiny in other sections but was surpised to find that normal work went on after this and divisional drills proceeded, although there was cheering as other crews refused to put to sea. Into the signal office, which remained operative throughout, came a stream of messages to Tomkinson: Mutiny in the *Rodney*, mutiny in the *Nelson*, the *Dorsetshire*, the *Norfolk* and his own flagship. Tomkinson could hear the cheering, which was echoing around the firth, and at 9.16 he reported to the Admiralty in a signal labelled 'Immediate': 'Situation at 0900 today – *Repulse* has proceeded to sea for exercises, other ships have not proceeded and considerable portions of ships' companies have absented themselves from duty. Attitude of all ratings towards their officers is at present correct. I have recalled the ships not exercising and stopped leave of officers and men. Chief of Staff leaving here today, arriving Admiralty early tomorrow evening.'[13]

It was another three hours after Tomkinson's signal before their lordships replied. Meanwhile the mutiny was polarizing in the fleet, with the unexpected centre the *Norfolk*, where Wincott had drafted a manifesto which was to become infamous world wide. This declared:

> We the loyal subjects of His Majesty the King do hereby present to My Lords Commissioners of the Admiralty our representations to implore them to amend the drastic cuts in pay that have been inflicted upon the lowest paid man of the lower deck.
>
> It is evident to all concerned that this cut is the forerunner of tragedy, misery and immorality amongst the families of the lower deck, and unless we can be guaranteed a written agreement from the Admiralty, confirmed by Parliament, stating that our pay will be revised, we are still to remain as one unit, refusing to serve under the new rate of pay.
>
> Men are quite willing to accept a cut which they, the men, consider in reason.[14]

This demand was left in the cabin of Wincott's divisional officer, who took it to the *Norfolk*'s captain. It was claimed to have been smuggled to other mutineers by normal boat traffic. There is no record of Tomkinson's receiving a copy, nor any indication of whether one was circulated in the *Hood*. News of it was revealed by a *Daily Herald* reporter who was given a copy at Invergordon and then passed it on to his editor, who in turn handed it to a Member of Parliament.

Around the *Hood*'s messes it was agreed that if arguments against the cuts were vented through the usual channels there would be no decision before 1 October, when the economies were scheduled. The opinion was crystallized by a rating labelled as 'the *Hood* mutiny leader', who told the *Herald*: 'We are fighting for our wives and children. Cuts cannot hit us on board ship any more. We have cut our luxuries long ago. We can't live on less than five shillings a week. Our wives, after the rest is paid, have no more than a pound. How can you stand a cut of 7s 6d?'

As that fateful morning of Tuesday 15 September continued, a system of signalling was established by the men cheering hourly, or lowering the jack on the forecastle staff, by secret signs from boat crews – folded arms meant a ship was not working – and even through telephone exchanges. To keep up their spirits they sang 'The More We Are

Together', but it was not always a case of 'the merrier we shall be'. Paterson says: 'The cheering became boring, until the *Rodney*'s crew hoisted a piano on to a turret. Then "The More We Are Together" was intermingled with the latest music hall hits, old war songs and sea shanties.'

The mutineers were not to know that their lordships, who met at 10 a.m., were split. There was even a suggestion by some Cabinet members – later disclosed by Vice-Admiral Dreyer, Deputy Chief of Naval Staff – that guns should be turned on the men to make them obey.

Hood's officers were surprised they had not been asked to take a firmer line. Yet the men remained polite, saluted and stood to attention for colours or similar ceremonies. At first petty officers showed signs of joining the junior ratings, but later they went on with their duties and made few attempts to persuade them to work. As all leave was cancelled, the ship's annual deck hockey tournament was advanced and played on the upper deck. A concert party was also organized.

There was no relaxation for Tomkinson, however. In a long signal to the Admiralty he itemized the three main causes for complaint and then added: 'I do not consider that the men will feel they have received justice unless reductions are more in proportion to their pay, e.g. the pay of an able seaman to be reduced by sixpence, instead of a shilling.' He underlined in the final paragraph: 'I would urge a very early decision should be communicated by their lordships. Until this is received I regret that, in my opinion, discipline in the Atlantic Fleet will not be restored and may still further deteriorate.'[15]

Yet discipline in the *Hood* had not deteriorated further, and to let the men know that efforts were being made to end the hiatus, Tomkinson announced he had sent Colvin to confer with the Admiralty Board. It seemed to have no effect, and Tomkinson was told: 'The men just remained silent.'

Although there was a great deal of discussion five hundred miles away in Whitehall, the Admiralty also remained silent in their communications. For six hours Tomkinson waited patiently for advice. Then it came, at 7.10 p.m., in this form: 'The Board of Admiralty will give their earnest and immediate consideration to representations of hardship. Meanwhile you should impress on ships' companies that existing rates of pay remain in force until 1st October and their lordships confidently expect that the men of the Atlantic Fleet will uphold the tradition of the Service by loyally carrying out their duty.'[16]

Tomkinson boiled with indignation because all this had been explained to the men already. His chagrin was exacerbated thirty-five minutes later when a long, complicated signal arrived, comparing rates and allowances and reminded him that similar reductions were being put into effect in the Army and the RAF, although fewer were affected.

Their lordships' dilemma was underscored within an hour by another signal – at 8.35 p.m. – which countermanded the previous one. It stated: 'Pending investigation and subsequent consideration by the Admiralty of representations as to hardship caused by new rates of pay, the board have approved the temporary suspension of Atlantic Fleet programme.'[17]

Tomkinson mulled this over during dinner and for the rest of the night, until just before 1 a.m., when the signal office sent this caution to the Admiralty: 'I must emphasise that the situation at Invergordon will not be met until definite decisions have been communicated. A continuation of the exercise programme is out of the question in the present state of mind of a considerable proportion of the crews.'[18]

The silent and polite deadlock continued in the *Hood* early next morning, with the men carrying on with routine work, but at the 'stand easy' at 10 a.m. two factors altered the situation. The arrival of newspapers inflamed the men, because in them was an Admiralty statement – or understatement – about the mutiny, which merely indicated that 'reduced rates of pay has led to unrest among a proportion of the lower ratings'. As they were taking their break, the tide turned and the *Hood* and *Rodney* swung parallel. This led to another demonstration of cheering, yells of 'Blacklegs' and 'Yellow' from the *Rodney*, and signals being exchanged accusing the *Hood* of not supporting the cause with sufficient enthusiasm. All routine jobs stopped on the *Hood*'s upper deck. The mutiny was raging into momentum again like an epidemic, and as the *Hood* caught the fever, she passed it on to the nearby *Dorsetshire*, which had been working normally.

At 11 a.m. Tomkinson conferred with Astley-Rushton and French, who told him that their efforts to talk to the men of the *Norfolk* and *Adventure* had failed. As they were discussing the latest reports, the Admiralty signalled that they had 'been engaged since early this morning in considering' points raised by Colvin, who had arrived in London overnight. It revealed that Admiral Field, the First Sea Lord, was locked in discussion with the Cabinet. 'You will receive earliest possible announcement of their decision,' the message ended.[19] From the shouting, which they could hear rolling around the fleet, the three admirals in the *Hood* were painfully aware that the mutiny was close to flashpoint.

So Tomkinson was forced to compose a 'Most Immediate' signal – the highest possible priority category – to Whitehall. 'I am of the opinion that the situation will get entirely out of control unless an immediate concession is made,' he wrote at 11.48 a.m.[20]

During dinner, when the rum issue was ladled out in the *Hood*, tempers worsened. There was a deep-rooted fear that the Admiralty had formulated harsh punishment for the fleet – that they would be isolated at Scapa or separated into single units to sail for Spithead, where marines would take over, or ordered to home ports for close arrest. Two leading seamen reported to Commander McCrum that the feeling was growing stronger in favour of a complete stoppage and that 'life of those against it was being made difficult'.[21]

Just before the end of the break Engineer Commander J.D. Sturrock informed McCrum that stokers were not going into the engine-room. It became evident to Captain Patterson that the majority would not turn to, so at the suggestion of Lieutenant-Commander Pursey he ordered a 'make and mend', or half holiday. Patterson wrote later: 'It took the men by surprise and resulted in their going down to sleep, instead of cheering on the forecastle.'[22] This ploy was passed on and used with success in the *Repulse*, *Malaya* and *Dorsetshire*.

Tomkinson was still attempting to stir the Admiralty. At

2.06 p.m. he roused the board with this signal: 'Situation 1400 – fleet informed Cabinet meeting at noon. More ships have ceased ordinary harbour work and men are massing on forecastle at intervals.' Tomkinson also indicated his fear that the men might sabotage machinery or break out of their ships. It had the effect of rousing their lordships, who for the first time attached a 'Most Immediate' priority to their reply, which directed the fleet to sail to home ports 'forthwith to enable personal investigation by commander-in-chiefs and representatives of Admiralty with a view to necessary alleviation being made'. There was the rider that 'any further refusals of individuals to carry out orders will be dealt with under the Naval Discipline Act'.[23]

It took ten minutes to decode, then Patterson sensibly allowed the statements in it to filter through the *Hood* as a 'mess-deck buzz'. At 4.45 p.m. he ordered the men to assemble on the forecastle. The pipe was obeyed and they formed up silently. Standing on top of A turret, Patterson explained that the ship had been ordered to return to Portsmouth, where grievances would be investigated. He did not refer to mutiny, disobedience or a breakdown in routine; neither was there any criticism of the crew's disruption. His last words were: 'I can guarantee that any rumours as to this being a ruse to divide the fleet are entirely unfounded and that any further refusal on your part would do still further harm to your cause.'[24]

In his official report Patterson stated that his address was received in silence and the men dispersed, but as soon as he had gone aft, those silent men became raucous and were shouting 'No, No, No.' Ex-Able Seaman Paterson, who was among them, recalls: 'Within five minutes a two-badge able seaman convinced nearly everyone the signal to sail was a trick to get the ships to sea and to separate them, so they lost mutual support, which would lead to the arrest of the leaders. He claimed the cuts would be made and money never restored. He then called for a vote, with a show of hands. Those in favour of not putting to sea were overwhelming. Only four hands were raised in favour of weighing anchor.' One of those four hands belonged to Paterson. After this demonstration of solidarity the meeting broke up, and roars of 'No, No, No' restarted just before 6 p.m.

This new revolt undermined Tomkinson's confidence that the fleet would obey. As soon as he received the Admiralty's last signal, he asked Astley-Rushton and French to the *Hood* to draw up sailing orders with him. About four hours were needed to raise steam, and the capital ships also required slack water, which would be later that night. It was decided that the squadrons should sail independently, with the cruisers leading the way, at 9.30 p.m.

The orders went to individual captains by boat, but Captain J.B. Watson, of the *Nelson*, preferred to discuss the situation with Tomkinson and Captain Patterson personally in the *Hood*. He was concerned that the cable parties would not turn-to, or men would sit on cables again. But with the agreement of Patterson it was decided they would unlink the massive anchor cables at a suitable point below, which would mean the weight and power of the engines would cause a tremendous whiplash that would be deadly to anyone sitting on them.

At 6 p.m. it appeared that the *Hood*'s mutiny had ended, when the engine-room watch reported for lighting boilers. Seamen also 'fell in' for preparatory duties. At 7.45 p.m., however, Tomkinson was still pessimistic and signalled the Admiralty: 'I am not sure that all ships will leave as ordered.'[25] If he judged the situation from that in the *Hood*, he had good reason to be cautious. When the cable party was piped to the waist, only Able Seaman Paterson arrived to report to Lieutenant-Commander Longley-Cook. Paterson relates: 'As we came through the forward screen of the forecastle, we were greeted by loud cheers and laughter from what seemed to be most of the ship's company. Several sailors, who were sitting on the lashed cables, eyed us suspiciously. One glance by us was enough to decide the anchor couldn't possibly be weighed without a full party. Longley-Cook was politely informed they had no intention of moving without the use of force. Longley-Cook did not argue and withdrew to report to the captain.'

Captain Patterson was prepared to stand by his word and ruthlessly part the cable, but to his relief it was not necessary. Tomkinson signalled the remainder of the fleet to sail independently. The impasse was broken. The sight of the *Warspite* steaming out weakened the will of the insubordinates in the *Hood*; gradually in groups they returned to duty, and the battle cruiser got under way with the rest of the fleet.

Hood's captain remained loyal to his men for their sudden change of mind. According to the Admiralty warning, anyone who disobeyed was liable to be punished, yet he reported to his superiors: 'Precautions were taken to prevent any further assemblies on the forecastle, where the cable officers remained until the ship was under way.' There was no mention of any disruption or threats.

Just before the day ended, Tomkinson and the Admiralty, who had been crossing words during the last forty-eight hours, finally crossed signals. At 11.50 the Admiralty, who by now had sent intelligence agents to Invergordon, signalled: 'Unofficial reports received that fleet have sailed. Request report forthwith.' But Tomkinson had foreseen their anxiety and five minutes earlier sent this message: 'Atlantic Fleet ships have all sailed from Invergordon ...'[26]

The mutineers might have left Invergordon, but it was a name which was to remain a stain on the Navy's reputation and an episode which even fifty years later most officers and men preferred not to resurrect.

7

... Red Stain on the *Hood*

As the *Hood* steamed south on Thursday, 17 September, news of the mutiny spread worldwide, and it made a bigger impact in the United States and France than in Britain. For the Royal Navy *was* Britain and its Empire, and as Ramsay MacDonald had declared two years earlier: 'Our Navy is us.' Navies had been the hubs of revolution in Germany and Russia. Was Britain on the brink of Communism, too? With the devaluing of the Navy came the devaluing of sterling and a run on gold reserves. The previous day £5 million had been withdrawn; now on this day the figure doubled. And as the somewhat sullen sailors of the *Hood* obediently went about the lighter tasks which had been devised, lip service to them, to the fleet and to Tomkinson was being paid in the Commons. Sir Austen Chamberlain, the First Lord, had papered over the cracks which were appearing in the Admiralty's walls, but his 'general amnesty' and praise of Tomkinson had gone further than their lordships had intended.

Tomkinson, who was preparing his report of proceedings, signalled he proposed to visit the Admiralty after the *Hood* docked. But he received this snub from First Sea Lord, Field: 'Although I shall be glad to see you at any time, I suggest you remain at Portsmouth so far as necessary to assist C-in-C Portsmouth in his investigation.'[1] Two hours later – after listening to speeches defending the mutineers in the Commons – Field cancelled his earlier message and indicated he would be pleased to see Tomkinson.

At 5.30 a.m. on Saturday 19 September the *Hood* and the other Portsmouth ships returned home, weeks earlier than expected.

As soon as the *Hood* moored alongside, Tomkinson

disembarked, bound for the Admiralty. Among mail taken on board was a letter from Field, to whom he was about to report. It ran: 'My Dear Tomkinson, I congratulate you on the very able way you handled a most difficult situation ... . well done! All the board consider you handled the job with great ability and tact.'²

Because it was a Saturday, leave was granted from 12.30 p.m. to 7 p.m. on Monday, and waiting ashore for the crew were agents from two diametrically opposed organizations – the Communist Party and Naval Intelligence. The Communists were surprised by the mutiny but tried to exploit it in the home divisions once the fleet returned. Two agitators were unmasked and imprisoned in an under-cover operation by Able Seaman Bill Batemen, who crewed the *Hood*'s drifter.

Many men were 'talking big' around the pubs that first weekend ashore and elaborating on the mutiny, knowing intelligence agents and Scotland Yard detectives were listening. Two focal points were the 'Red House', Church Street, Landport, and the 'Sailors' Rest', where a disrated leading stoker, an avowed Communist from the *Hood*, was believed to have made inflammatory speeches, according to an MI5 report. Shadowing agents warned that, if there was a recurrence, it would break out in three capital ships – and the *Hood* was thought to be one of them. Credence for this fear came with an interview with a *Hood* seaman, who said: 'It's no good us trying to do anything because we have not been able to get at the "natives". We have four good members in our ship that belong to the "society" but we can't do much until we get the fleet together again.'³

It was believed that the mutineers had an executive committee, composed of representatives from all ships at Invergordon. The *Hood* had three on it, but intelligence records do not give proof. The *Rodney* was reputed the 'reddest' ship, with their leader code-named 'Gandhi', and held under-cover discussions during meetings of the Royal Antediluvian Order of the Buffaloes in the ship. There is no evidence that the *Hood*'s Buffaloes held similar clandestine conferences. Further executive meetings were anticipated in Portsmouth, and this led to the assumption – again without proof – that the fleet was about to revolt again.

A few hours after the announcement that Britain had been

forced off the Gold Standard and that the value of sterling
had plummeted by four shillings in the pound, the Atlantic
Fleet heard they had won. All ships and establishments were
informed that the 'simplest way of removing just grievances'
was to limit reductions on the three services to not more than
ten per cent.[4]

Interviews with ships' companies by commanders-in-
chief about their dispute had already begun and were to end
within twenty-four hours. The Admiralty would have
preferred to hold boards of inquiry or court-martials, but the
amnesty to which Chamberlain had agreed made this
impossible. However, they were determined there should be
an inquiry of sorts and on 6 October appointed fifty-nine-
year-old Admiral Sir John Kelly, the former Fourth Sea
Lord, as commander-in-chief of the Atlantic Fleet, with a
special brief to conduct his own investigation with a view to
restoring discipline. His singling out for this unpopular task
was at the behest of the King. Kelly was a dispassionate
admiral, who spoke the language sailors understood. He was
determined to instil into them confidence in their officers,
but before taking over, he asked Tomkinson to draft the
mutiny ringleaders to barracks. Within days of his
appointment, Kelly was making his rounds of the fleet. At
one huge gathering in an aircraft carrier, he assembled
almost every man who was off duty. The *Hood*'s contingent
was the biggest. In a two-edged speech he did not deny that
their 'action' at Invergordon had caused incalculable damage
abroad to Britain, but admitted: 'All the mistakes were not
on one side.'[5]

On 7 October, the day before the *Hood* sailed out of
harm's way to Rosyth, ten of the crew were discharged to
Portsmouth Barracks for interviews with intelligence officers
to decide whether their services were still required. At the
barracks were a total of 121 mutiny miscreants, so the
Hood's ratio was not high in relation to her size. The
Admiralty issued the strict instruction that no one was to be
discharged 'services no longer required' until after the
General Election, which was on 27 October. A week later,
after a National Government was returned, Chamberlain,
who did not want to be First Lord, was replaced by Sir
Bolton Eyres-Monsell. The way was now clear for the

discharge of twenty-seven men, who, it was alleged, had attempted to subvert their shipmates after the mutiny and amnesty. The clear-out began in November, and only three of the *Hood*'s accused escaped. They were an able seaman, who, despite confessing he would 'make further trouble' and wanted to join the Communist Party, was allowed to re-engage; a stoker, who, although a good worker, 'appears slightly mad and would like to cut down senior officers and Bluebell [polish] to save money,'[6] and a leading seaman who had spoken in the Invergordon canteen.

An able seaman, with three good-conduct badges, who was said to be 'a fanatic under Communist influence and unbalanced when faced with a grievance, but a good, very cheerful working hand',[7] asked to be discharged because he felt that if there was more trouble he could not stop himself being implicated. But he was not released until the following April. Later he unsuccessfully protested about his discharge through a solicitor and even went to the length of boarding the *Hood* more than a year after the mutiny to try to persuade the captain to take him back.

The sacked ratings left barracks immediately. They were given back pay, 13 shillings for a suit, and a travel warrant to their homes. Several from the *Hood* claimed that their mates would 'down tools' because of the victimization. Their expectations were never fulfilled. Another 'polite mutiny' was not contemplated.

On 8 October the *Hood*, in company with the fleet and with Kelly in charge, sailed for Scotland again – but not to Invergordon. At Rosyth, Kelly began to put them through rigorous exercises. Ex-Able Seaman Paterson says: 'One evolution meant the *Hood*'s marine band lowering a boat, putting their instruments in it and pulling to the flagship to play a popular tune. The bandmaster led them in to "Anybody Here Seen Kelly?" The c-in-c was not amused.'

On the last day of Kelly's three-day inspection, the ship was exercised at general quarters. Aylwin's midshipman's journal reveals: 'The bridge personnel were "killed" in the first five minutes ... The admiral inspected every action station. A message, warning he was on the boat-deck, was misinterpreted by the starboard 5.5 inch guns' crews as "Enemy is on the boat-deck." Whereupon they rushed to draw side-arms and the admiral was met by fixed bayonets to repel boarders.'

On 19 November the *Hood* returned to Portsmouth, where Kelly was able to report that the fleet were at a high level of efficiency. Tomkinson recommended that the *Hood* should be paid off and recommissioned with a different crew, but his request was rejected. Instead, Christmas leave began in the middle of November.

Tomkinson took his leave believing he had ridden out the tempest, but the Sea Lords, who were studying Kelly's highly controversial report, had not dismissed him from their thoughts. Tomkinson's future was discussed by them from New Year's Day 1932 through most of January, although on 6 January the admiral and the *Hood* were on their way with the *Repulse, Delhi, Norfolk* and *Dorsetshire* to the West Indies. The gale which battered them off the Lizard that day presaged the storm ahead for Tomkinson.

It was a wet start, with the quarterdeck continuously under water. Because of her dampness the *Hood* was acquiring the reputation for being rife with tuberculosis among ratings and midshipmen. The Navy's death rate from TB in the 1930s was twice as high as among civilians. This caused Lord Bridgman, a former First Lord, to complain to the Chief of Naval staff that there were 'rather disquieting' reports about the *Hood*'s ventilation, which might induce TB. He wrote: 'The gunroom and sleeping accommodation are said to have been affected by some extra plating which has been added.' Although £5,000 was spent on improving living-conditions during her last refit, neither the gunroom nor the messes had benefited. But the Admiralty replied that there had been no ventilation complaints and that in the previous ten months only two cases of TB – or 1.8 per cent – had been notified.[8] The ratings could have given a different answer about the damp conditions.

Bad weather dogged the *Hood* to the Azores, where even at anchor she was 'taking it green' on the forecastle. Morale was low, but on passage to Barbados it warmed to the strength of the sun, and by the time she arrived in Carlisle Bay on 21 January the men were in a fit state of mind and body to join in the jollifications arranged ashore. The West Indies idyll came to an end for Tomkinson in Trinidad on 16

February, when he read a transcript of a BBC broadcast picked up by the communications department. This revealed that he had been superseded by Rear-Admiral Sir William James as commander of the squadron. Tomkinson had no prior warning that he was to be relieved, and from the broadcast he was unable to ascertain when it was to occur. He could only assume he was about to become the mutiny's scapegoat.

For the next two days Tomkinson was in the limbo of not knowing if the report were correct or false; then he received two Admiralty letters, both marked 'Personal and Secret' and both bearing the date 2 February. The first was a mixture of good and bad news. It informed him that he had been promoted to vice-admiral five days earlier, but also that he would be reappointed for only another six months as squadron commander, which meant that his original two-year term was shortened by eight months. The second was virtually the announcement of the end of his peacetime career, as the brunt of the blame for Invergordon was shouldered on to him. The censure read: 'After making every allowance for the difficult and unusual circumstances in which you were placed, Their Lordships are unable to relieve you of responsibility for a serious error of judgement in omitting to take any decided action on the 13th and 14th September, when dis-satisfaction had begun to show itself amongst the men. If the situation had been well handled on those two days, instead of being allowed to drift, Their Lordships consider it improbable that this outbreak would ever have occurred.'[9]

The air was heavy with tropical heat and retribution that day in the *Hood* at Trinidad, for Captain Patterson had been told bluntly that he was to be relieved at the same time as Tomkinson, although this blow was lessened because the commanding officers of the *Rodney*, *Valiant*, *Adventure*, *Nelson*, *Norfolk* and *York* were also to be superseded. Invergordon had scythed through the senior officers.

Yet the wear and tear on Tomkinson's nerves did not affect his health. He survived their lordships of this period and the Second World War and died in 1971, aged ninety-three. After his obituary in *The Times* there was a spate of letters defending his actions at Invergordon.

8

Another 'Mutiny'

The *Hood* was a challenge to Rear-Admiral Sir William James, Tomkinson's successor, just as the rest of his life had been. He had the doubtful disadvantage of being a grandson of the artist Sir John Millais and of becoming the model for the famous 'Bubbles' of the Pears' soap advertisement. As a golden-haired boy he had sat for his grandfather for the portrait, which was bought by the *Illustrated London News* and then sold to the soap company. Unfortunately he could never hide the fact that he was the gorgeous Bubbles, and complained forever after: 'The life of a small boy whose portrait is on nearly every hoarding in the country, in nearly every theatre and station lavatory and on vast numbers of postcards is unlikely to be a bed of roses. Mine certainly was not, though I more than once succeeded for a time in hiding my awful "crime" for a few blessed weeks after entering a new community of other small boys.'[1]

Nevertheless, by the age of fifty-one, when he came to the *Hood*, he had developed the ability to surmount great hindrances and a tougher image than the one which still simpered at him from the hoardings. The First World War had exploded him into naval prominence, first as commander of the battle cruiser *Queen Mary* and then as commander of the *Benbow*, flagship of the Fourth Battle Squadron at the Battle of Jutland, after which he was wrongly reported among the 'missing presumed dead'. He escaped to a quieter role as a code-cracker with Admiral Hall's famous, but originally clandestine, Room 40 staff and then successively as director of Greenwich Staff College, captain of the *Royal Sovereign* and *Royal Oak*, assistant to the First Sea Lord and chief of staff to Kelly with the Home Fleet, the new name for the Atlantic force. It was Kelly who had requested that James should take over from Tomkinson.

At the end of the summer leave for *Hood's* men, James, or 'Bubbles' as he was inevitably to be called by them, joined on 15 August at Portsmouth, just before *Hood* sailed for a tour of east coast ports. Longley-Cook, still in the *Hood*, despite Invergordon's repercussions, compared James's taking over with that of Tomkinson, because the lower deck was cleared again on a Sunday to introduce the ship's company to their admiral. 'How different it was from fifteen months earlier,' he says. 'James told us "I am proud to have joined you." For the first time in my eighteen years at sea I was told that the peacetime job of the Navy was to train for war, in order to keep the peace. To show the flag and in home waters to show the public what they were paying for abroad – a good ambassadorship for Britain. From then on it was tails up for us.'[2]

The crew had James's sympathy, for he admitted that the condition of the ship was 'far from satisfactory' and that he had never encountered a 'more unhappy party'. He found Tomkinson and Patterson 'at daggers drawn' and that Commander McCrum had 'lost all interest through being hunted by Tomkinson, whose habit was to find fault with everything'.[3]

James had confidence in the men, however, and although Kelly was again toying with the idea of complete recommissioning, James persuaded him to cancel it. He also badgered the Admiralty into appointing as commanding officer forty-eight-year-old Captain Thomas Binney, who had completed his sea-time captaincy earlier in the *Nelson*, because 'knowing that the *Hood* was still under the weather from the effects of the Invergordon mutiny, I thought it imperative that her new captain should be endowed with the gift of drawing loyal service from his subordinates.' Binney, who was with James in HMS *Hawkins*, soon discovered that he had a first rate wardroom. The officers responded eagerly to his new lead. 'A few months later the ship won the Home Fleet regatta, which is perhaps the best test of morale of a ship and the enthusiasm of her crew,' said James.[4]

But there was a long way to go, and before the *Hood* was a 'depression cruise' along the east coast to show masses of unemployed and the public that she was still the world's greatest warship, despite Invergordon. The first stop was Southend, where sleeping sailors prevented the lifeboat going out on an emergency call. Lieutenant F.J. Revell, then an able seaman, explains: 'We had all-night leave, and many of us slept in the pier railway carriages. When the lifeboat crew were summoned, they couldn't get to the end of the mile-long pier, where their boat was, because the train which normally took them was packed with sleeping matelots.'

At Hartlepool the problem was reversed when the *Hood* had to put up with unwanted guests. The form at all stops was to hold children's parties, but at Hartlepool a fog enveloped the ship when it was time for three hundred mothers and their offspring to be put ashore. The lighthouse at the harbour entrance was obscured, so no boats went out. Camp-beds were put down for the partygoers, and they stayed the night.

The *Hood* was never considered a great gunnery ship, but now she began to develop into the fleet's most accurate, under her 'guns', Longley-Cook. 'We smashed the battle practice target, which was unheard of,' he says, 'and then won the anti-aircraft competition.' During the spring cruise in 1933 the AA crews demonstrated the new multiple pom-poms to the Army and surprised the 'pongos' by shooting down the towed aircraft sleeve with the first burst.

James was delighted by these performances, but the smear of mutiny was seldom far from his thoughts. On the way to Gibraltar the squadron stopped at Vigo, and he was called to the *Nelson* by Kelly to be informed of the 'latest threat to the fleet', which was expected to be at the Rock in March. Kelly had received intelligence warnings that there was a plan to fan up trouble by ratings who were restive again because their pay had not risen in line with Britain's improving economy. James thought this nonsense but sounded out his senior officers, who also did not believe the rumours, which were triggered by Major Sam Bassett, of Naval Intelligence, who flew to Gibraltar to investigate.

Nevertheless, Kelly decided to board the *Hood* and all other ships to address the men again. Making much use of colloquial and pungent language, linked with flashes of humour, he cautioned potential trouble-makers of the consequences of insubordination. They were spellbound by his eloquence, according to James, and there were no signs of unrest when the fleet arrived.

The fleet's spirit changed to one of complete accord, and by the time the summer cruise arrived, Kelly thought it opportune to return to Invergordon, although the *Hood*'s amateur poet, Lieutenant John Shrimpton, the chief staff officer's secretary, moaned in verse: 'And we must sail to the far northern sea to InverG – for three or four weeks of monotony.'

On her return south on 30 August the *Hood* at last paid off, to be commissioned entirely by men from Portsmouth. This also brought a change of command. Binney, who was to join the Colombian Navy, rejoin the Royal Navy in wartime and then become Governor-General of Tasmania, had successfully transformed the battle cruiser into a unit again, and one which could hold its head up high. Departing officers considered she was at her peak, but the new captain, 'Tommy' Tower, who had been the *Hood*'s first gunnery officer and was an old friend of James, and his commander, Rory O'Connor, brought a different kind of drive.

Bachelor O'Conor's revolutionary ideas were to become a legend. He was one of the first 'management officers', and managing meant cementing a bond between the wardroom and lower deck. O'Conor, whom James described as being 'a born leader', had no doubts about his aims, and on the very day he joined he cleared lower deck to make sure the ship's company knew, too. Able Seaman Hector, who was among the assembly, remembers: 'He insisted we were going to be the smartest ship in the world, that we would win not only the Regatta Cock but every cup in the fleet – for boat-pulling, sailing, soccer, rugby, boxing, swimming, tug-of-war and running. He predicted we would not have a man under punishment and we would become the Navy's cleanest ship. But we all had to work together like brothers to achieve this and become the happiest ship afloat. His speech was the joke of the mess-decks for days afterwards, but within twelve months we did everything he prophesied.'

O'Conor was a remarkable commander, whose sayings became unwritten fleet law, and later he was to write a Navy 'Bible' entitled *How to Run a Big Ship*. The door of his office was always open to anyone who needed a father confessor, and his methods of running the ship were through a happy blend of supreme efficiency and great humanity. His axiom was: 'Always approach a man's faults through his virtues.'

James, who was in the *Renown* temporarily, rejoined the *Hood* on 6 September for her work-up at Rosyth before the autumn manoeuvres off Scotland in which eighty-five RAF aircraft were involved for the first time. Three weeks later he heard of his advancement to vice-admiral.

James's love of dreaming up jokey exercises and drills brought the Sea Lords close to panic during October, 1933. He devised a practice called 'the Pirates of Cromarty', which entailed two drifters, representing steamers, being captured by buccaneers. This duly took place, and the Hood's 'pirates' in four cutters landed and took to the hills near Nigg Golf Course, ten miles from Invergordon. The captain was then required to put ashore marines and seamen to round up the renegades and take them back. 'It was a good drill and great fun,' said James. 'One of the signals I received was "Have captured a pirate, but can get nothing out of him, except that his handicap is plus two." '[5]

Almost a week later the *Daily Mail* published a report of rioting and unrest in the *Hood* again, with many seamen taken off in destroyers. The startling story was also picked up by United Press of America and used under banner headlines around the world. It was 'splashed' in the *Japanese Times*, in the *Buenos Aires Herald* and in Russia's *Pravda*. British ambassadors in all these countries sought confirmation.

The Admiralty reacted swiftly by demanding to know from James whether there was any truth in the allegations. As seven days had elapsed since his pirates' exercise, he was at a loss to understand what had inspired the libels and signalled the Admiralty: 'My flagship having made splendid start to her new commission and the officers and men all working hard in complete harmony to make a name for the ship in all activities, I hope that the source of this unfounded and malicious story will be traced.'[6]

Neither the Admiralty nor James realized how the rumours had circulated. So seriously did the Admiralty take them that they ordered a special investigation, while First Lord Sir Bolton Eyres-Monsell broke off a shooting-party to issue the following denial on 12 October: 'Their Lordships state that these rumours are an entire fabrication and greatly regret that they should be forced to make this denial on a baseless rumour reflecting on a splendid ship's company.'[7]

Naval Intelligence and MI5 agents were alerted in Portsmouth and spied on a Communist meeting in the town's Guildhall Square, but all they heard was criticism of Fascism and not a mention of the *Hood*. Eventually the 'buzz' that stokers were in cells after a mutiny was traced to a rating in HMS *Dolphin*. From him it had reached the WT office of the carrier *Courageous* and the *Champion*. Then a *Daily Mail* correspondent picked it up from petty officers in Fort Blockhouse. The rumour also reached the *Portsmouth Evening News*. It was checked with the Commander-in-Chief, Portsmouth, immediately denied and killed before publication. The *Mail's* reporter did not check and was sacked for his slackness.

When the *Hood* anchored at Banff, a few days later, the provost boarded her and asked James about the 'unrest onboard'. The admiral by now realized that his 'pirates' had triggered the libel and related the incident to the provost, who in turn revealed it when he went ashore. The real story was telegraphed round the world, and the original one became regarded as the hoax of the year. Even the London *Times* could not resist aiming a barb at the *Mail* by publishing the correct version under the headline 'Hood-winked'.

James's love of playing war games was unrequited, however, for during the 1934 spring cruise and combined exercises with the Mediterranean Fleet he was mixed up in another incident. The voyage began with an accident again, when the flagship *Nelson* grounded off Fort Blockhouse. James signalled for instructions from Admiral Sir William Boyle, commander-in-chief Home Fleet, on whether he should continue and was informed that the *Hood* should take over and carry on with the exercises. She proceeded and encountered gigantic and terrifying seas in the Bay of Biscay.

Able Seaman Hector records: 'We were battened down but she was like a floating match-box with thirty-foot waves head on. The seamen's, stokers' and marines' messes were a deck below the upper deck and leaked every time a big wave hit. There was a foot of water sculling around, and the boot-racks were afloat. For nine days it was like this.' Men went seasick in battalions, Lieutenant Shrimpton reported in rhyme.

There was time for recuperation when the *Hood* visited Madeira, but by the end of January she was in Gibraltar, where James was senior officer for the next month for another exercise, which brought trouble again.

He was requested by the governor, Sir Charles Harrington, to stage a seaward attack on the Rock because, when this manoeuvre had been attempted before, the Navy had entered Government House and managed to 'capture' the governor. Sir Charles was certain this could not happen again, and James decided to take up the challenge.

With Captain A.L.G. St G. Lyster, who commanded the Home Fleet's Fifth Destroyer Flotilla, he concocted a plan in which sailors were to be landed under cover of a smoke screen. Once ashore they slipped on armlets, normally worn by naval patrols, and walked slowly along the streets to Government House. There they hid in the grounds and when the sentry's back was turned darted into the dining-room, where Lady Harrington was entertaining women friends. All were taken prisoner and escorted to a destroyer, which put to sea. Next morning Sir Charles received a signal that his wife and friends would be sold next morning in Tangier slave market. James joked later: 'The prisoners thoroughly enjoyed their adventure, particularly the bacon and eggs and coffee in the wardroom.'[8] The 'rag' was the talk of Gibraltar, but when the Admiralty got to hear of it, they were shocked, and James was 'unofficially reprimanded'.

At sea again the *Hood* was not so successful. In the final 'battle' against the Mediterranean Fleet, James was required to rendezvous with Admiral Sir William Fisher, his opponents' commander-in-chief. But the exercise was ruined by tumultuous seas, and the *Hood* could not find the flagship *Queen Elizabeth* on the first day. The weather worsened next day, when the battle cruisers were still alone and taking a sickening pounding. The messes were flooded again, the admiral's office was awash, and damage was done to the bookstall. When James returned to Gibraltar, he was adjudged to have lost. 'The *Hood* was sunk,' umpires told him. The shame of defeat in front of three knights – William Fisher, William Boyle and Roger Backhouse – did not worry him, for on the way home he was given command of the Home Fleet, for what was to be his last cruise with them. James left on 14 August 1934 to become Deputy Chief of Naval Staff under Admiral Ernle Chatfield.

Those whom he left went from strength to strength and the next year won all the principal fleet events. With them was Bubbles' son, Midshipman C.A. James. He had left Dartmouth a fortnight after the admiral's departure to join the *Hood* for a 'grand start' – his father's words – under the protective wing of Commander O'Conor.

9

On a Collision Course

The custom of a new admiral bringing a captain and chief of staff to the *Hood* and the squadron was broken – with calamitous results and a subsequent scandal – when Rear-Admiral Sidney Bailey succeeded James in August 1934. Captain Tower remained, and when Bailey arrived he found the ship seemingly at its peak for efficiency, smartness and 'pot-hunting',˙ thanks to O'Conor. Tower was prepared to stand aside and let his commander take the full glory, and to many it appeared that O'Conor was captain in all but name.

Bailey came as the protégé of Chatfield, the First Sea Lord, and with the reputation of being one of the Navy's premier gunnery officers. He had been with Chatfield in the *Lion* and followed him to the *Iron Duke* and *Queen Elizabeth*, as chief of staff to the Commander-in-Chief Mediterranean in 1932. He had captained the *Renown*, the other half of the squadron, and was appointed to the *Hood* in Chatfield's words as 'one of the most promising young flag officers'. Admiral Dreyer thought him a 'first rate fellow, extremely able and competent,' while most of the Admiralty's senior officers regarded him as a 'charming chap'.[1] Yet there was a weak streak in Bailey, which did not reveal itself until several months into his new job, when he was confronted by the strength of character of Tower, who in turn bowed to O'Conor's way of running the ship.

For the remainder of the year the *Hood* cruised peacefully in home waters; then came the 1935 fleet spring exercises and an informal conversation between two officers, which was to end the sea careers of Bailey and Tower.

Again the cruise started tragically when in the Arosa Bay anchorage on 19 January O'Conor ordered a shipboard search for Boy Jim Brown, a seventeen-year-old from Portsmouth who had joined only nine days earlier. He had not been seen since getting out of his hammock when the boys were called at 5 a.m. He was presumed to be lost overboard, a fact which was subsequently proved correct when his body was washed ashore at Villagarcia.

While the fleet were at Arosa, the *Hood's* wardroom entertained officers of the *Renown*, and during a chat between Commander E.V. Lees, the squadron navigating officer, and Lieutenant-Commander G.M.S. Stitt, the *Renown's* navigator, they briefly discussed a minor collision earlier that month between the *Frobisher* and *Renown* off Sheerness. The talk then turned to squadron exercises, and Lees told Stitt that at the end of the manoeuvres, when the ships were a mile apart, the *Hood* would turn 180 degrees to enable the *Renown* to form station astern. Stitt later reported the conversation to his commanding officer, Captain H.R. Sawbridge, who duly noted how the two vessels would rejoin.

The day before the exercises Admiral Bailey issued this signal: 'On Wednesday, January 23, the Battle Cruiser Squadron will pass through position two miles 148 degrees from Salvory Island Light. On passing this point *Hood* is to steer 192 degrees and *Renown* 254 degrees at 12 knots. At 10.50 ships are to turn 223 degrees when inclination exercises will be carried out. On completion *Hood* and *Renown* are to steer 254 degrees and 192 degrees respectively to close. Course after rejoining will be 180 degrees, speed 12 knots.'[2]

The day was ideal – clear and with a light sea – for the manoeuvring of heavy warships. The Second Destroyer Flotilla left harbour first to exercise independently and were followed by the Second Submarine Flotilla, who were to test the battle cruisers' anti-submarine defences. They were tracked by the *Hood* and *Renown*, who, on approximately parallel courses but more than ten miles apart, carried out individual inclination tests at 10.50, as ordered the previous day.

At 11.35 completion was signalled by Bailey. The *Hood's* helm was put over to 254 degrees at a constant speed of 12 knots, and the *Renown* steered 192 degrees, with the intention of closing. The distance between the two diminished at the rate of 400 yards a minute. On the starboard side of the bridge Bailey and Tower watched the *Renown*'s approach unconcernedly; Commander A.C. Allen, staff operations officer, thought the manoeuvre so commonplace that he went into the charthouse and did not bother to watch. In the *Renown*, Captain Sawbridge and Lieutenant-Commander Stitt were waiting for the *Hood* to execute a turn to 180 degrees, so that their ship could slide in behind her stern. The minutes went by with both battle cruisers holding course.

After forty minutes, with fourteen hundred yards separating them, Bailey considered that the *Renown* was slow in carrying out the manoeuvre which would have put her aft of him. 'Surely she can't expect the flagship to make way for her,' he thought.

On came the *Renown* and, although showing no anxiety, Bailey signalled by Flag: 'Form single line ahead in sequence of fleet numbers on course of 254 degrees. Guide of squadron is to proceed at 12 knots.' It took approximately a minute for the 'bending on' of the flags, for this to be seen in the *Renown*, but Bailey was still convinced that there was time for Sawbridge to alter course.

On the *Renown*'s bridge, with the *Hood* fourteen hundred yards away, the captain was told by Stitt: 'She ought to turn now, sir.' As the distance narrowed to twelve hundred yards, Sawbridge cried: 'I don't like this. Stop both; wheel to starboard 35 degrees.'

Still the *Hood* came on, and half a minute later Sawbridge ordered: 'Full speed astern both.' Three short blasts of the *Renown*'s siren alerted the admiral's bridge that the *Hood* was on collision course. Now the fate of both ships was in the hands of Captain Tower, for Bailey wisely decided that he would only confuse the situation with further orders. Petty Officer J.W. Lyons, who five minutes earlier had taken over *Hood*'s wheel, was given a string of instructions in the next two minutes, while to the engine-room went six different orders.

'Port 25, 98 revs,' commanded Tower. This swung *Hood*'s stem in towards the *Renown*, which was still approaching, despite being put in 'reverse'. To correct it, Tower barked:

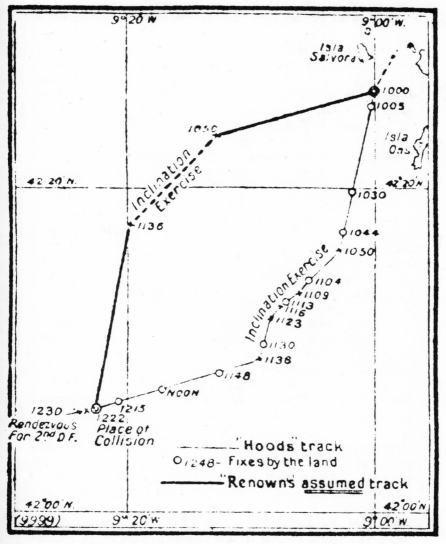

The collision path with the *Renown* (*The Times*)

'Starboard 25, hard to starboard, full speed ahead.'

Shouts were going up all over the *Hood* now: 'Close all watertight doors ... All hands to clear starboard side.' Yeoman of Signals Ned Johns remembers: 'There was a jam on the boat-deck at the passageway by the funnels, caused by ratings who knew they shouldn't be there and the nosey few who wanted to see what was happening on the starboard side. The crowd cleared as soon as someone shouted "Bugger off! The bloody *Renown*'s coming inboard!" '

Able Seaman Hector was taking the captain's lunch to his sea cabin on the bridge when he heard Tower roaring through a megaphone to clear the starboard side. 'Looking round, I saw the *Renown* coming at us,' says Hector. 'It seemed as if we were leaping forward to avoid being hit amidships.'

When the crash came, the *Hood*'s stern was swinging rapidly away, but the *Renown*'s bows ran along her A bracket amidships, bounced off and then was caught by the *Hood*'s starboard propeller. In the *Hood*'s engine-room the telegraph signalled first: 'Stop both,' then 'Half speed, astern both, full speed astern both' and finally 'Stop both.'

The armoured sides had resolutely withstood the ramming by 32,700 tons of iron and steel. But the aft guard-rails were concertinaed, and several deck planks were sprung. It was the third collision – and the worst – the *Renown* had been in since 1934. On neither ship was there casualties. Half an hour later Sawbridge reported to Bailey the *Renown*'s damage as being 'Hole in stem, about three feet square, seven feet from just above the water line upwards. Below water, stem and ram are displaced about two feet to starboard and there are at least two large fractures. Side plating is badly buckled and distorted in the vicinity. Ship is dry abaft number ten bulkhead, which is being shored up.'[3]

Other ships were waiting to open the submarine exercise, but Bailey abandoned it and ordered the *Renown* to proceed independently to Gibraltar. Two days later the *Hood* was the last to arrive at the Rock, and as she entered harbour, polite gun salutes were exchanged with the *Renown*, but soon the crews, officers and captains were to be in direct conflict in a feud which was to worry the commander-in-chief and the First Sea Lord.

When reports of the collision were studied by Admiralty experts, it was obvious that there was collusion between Bailey and Tower on one side and Sawbridge and his officers on the other. In fairness to all, their lordships decided that the three should be court-martialled.

The decision to make Bailey face trial was controversial in itself, as this was the first time an admiral had been court-martialled since the First World War, but the order of the hearings also caused controversy. Bailey was to be arraigned first, followed by Sawbridge and then Tower. If Bailey were found guilty of the charge of hazarding the *Hood* and *Renown*, it could be assumed that Sawbridge and Tower would be cleared of hazarding their ships.

In all three sittings, which were crowded with high-ranking officers, the main issues were basically similar. Sawbridge's defence, put by his 'friend', Captain R.B.T. Miles, relied on these factors:

1. Bailey's signal before the exercise stipulated a definite course for closing, something which he had never ordered before.

2. Stitt, the *Renown's* navigator, had been 'officially sent for' by Lees, the squadron navigating officer, to discuss the manoeuvre, and because of this the captain regarded the appraisal of the situation as emanating from the admiral and thus expected the *Hood* to turn away when the *Renown* rejoined.

3. The *Hood* was the overtaking ship and should have obeyed the 'law of the road' and given way.

Throughout the trials officers on opposite ships gave widely different times at which signals were made, although Sawbridge emphasized that when he stopped engines he ordered everyone on the bridge to make a note of times. Those in the *Renown* insisted that the signal to form line ahead was made when the ship's engines stopped, at least two minutes later than the time estimated by flag staff in the *Hood*, and this meant that the *Hood* was only five hundred yards away. It was alleged by Sawbridge that if Tower had held his course and called for full power there would not have been a collision.

Rear-Admiral J.A.G. Troup, who prosecuted all three, countered these submissions by stressing that Bailey's original signal had ordered a course of 180 degrees 'after rejoining' and not before. He argued that if Sawbridge had made 'bold use of the engines at port ahead and starboard astern to turn the ship' it would have been preferable to stopping and putting the wheel to starboard.[4]

Bailey, who was defended by Vice-Admiral James, his predecessor in the *Hood*, insisted that his signal was not ambiguous, because, in his view, ships of a unit had not rejoined until they were on station – and the *Renown* was not at line ahead with the *Hood*. He maintained that after his flag signal Sawbridge had at least four minutes to react. The *Hood* was also steering as fleet guide and should not have been expected to alter course.

Troup put these two questions to the court in Bailey's trial: Should the admiral have made a stationing signal earlier to the *Renown*? When the ships were not less than fourteen hundred yards apart, should he have directed Tower to turn away and to increase speed?

Tower, defended by the erstwhile Commander O'Conor, had another defender in Bailey, who said he approved all his captain's actions, which minimized the collision and 'went within an ace' of avoiding it. Bailey also stressed that he had told Tower of his 'line ahead' signal before it was made, with the intention of impressing on the captain that he did not expect him to take action because he anticipated the *Renown* would carry out the necessary turn.

It took the first court-martial, headed by Vice-Admiral Astley-Rushton, second in command at Invergordon, two hours to decide that Bailey was not guilty. Next day, 27 February, after an adjournment of seventy-five minutes a freshly composed court returned a guilty verdict on Sawbridge, because he had 'continued at 12 knots when risk of collision was present'.[5] He received the harsh sentence of being severely reprimanded and dismissed his ship, which was practically the death warrant for his career. Having exonerated Bailey two days earlier, the third court could do little except decide that Tower was also not guilty.

A week later the *Hood*, with two new propellers and a jubilant Bailey and Tower, left Portsmouth to rejoin the Home Fleet, which was at Malta. But there were unfavourable signs for them in the *Renown*, now at

Portsmouth. The verdicts still had to be confirmed by the Admiralty, and although Sawbridge had been dismissed his ship, he was still living in the *Renown*. He had told his officers: 'My conscience is clear. I reckon that I have saved the country about £10,000,000 and 1,000 lives.'[6]

There were consciences at the Admiralty, however, when the courts-martial minutes were being perused for confirmation. Admiral Kelly, who 'had the King's ear', wrote to him: 'How ACQ [Bailey] could stand up and feel blameless himself is beyond my comprehension.'[7] The King shared this opinion, and it was soon the view of their lordships, including Chatfield, who had to do some deep soul-searching before he could blame Bailey, his protégé. Not until 18 March, when the *Hood* was in the Mediterranean, were Bailey and Tower informed that the Admiralty dissented from the findings, blamed all three officers and softened Sawbridge's sentence. Their statement read:

Rear-Admiral Bailey adopted an unusual procedure in directing *Hood* and *Renown* to steer definite courses to close. Since he had given that order, responsibility for the manoeuvre rested on him and it was incumbent on him at the proper moment to make a further signal to reform his squadron. His not doing so left in doubt his final intention. The signal for *Hood* and *Renown* to form single line ahead was made too late. For these reasons Their Lordships are unable to absolve Rear-Admiral Bailey from all blame.

Their Lordships agree to the findings of the court martial held for the trial of Captain Sawbridge, but they have decided to reduce the sentence to a severe reprimand. Captain Sawbridge will therefore resume command of *Renown*. Their Lordships consider that Captain Tower should have taken avoiding action earlier and to that extent they are unable to acquit him of all blame.[8]

The Admiralty had clearly decided not to make one scapegoat on this occasion, because there had obviously been anomalies during the trials. Captain A.F. Pridham, a member of the court which tried Sawbridge and soon to command the *Hood*, revealed many years later that Sawbridge had 'produced a fake chart of the movements of his ship, but this did not go into the minutes because it was held behind closed doors'.⁹ He also disclosed that Bailey instructed Vice-Admiral James, his defence 'friend', not to make any statement which might embarrass Sawbridge.

But this was not known to the men of the *Renown*, nor the *Hood*, and for the years up to the Second World War there was hostility whenever the two were in port together. James knew of the 'lack of good fellowship' in the squadron and, although he disliked criticizing an old friend, he wrote to Chatfield:

> I do feel Bailey failed from the outset to realise the importance of fostering, by every possible means, a squadron spirit. He did not like Sawbridge ... an unusual type, but a man who responded at once to any lead. The collision accentuated this lack of good feeling between the ships and, as far as I know, no attempt has been made to improve matters. After the court martial would have been just the moment for the admiral to have gone onboard *Renown*, or better still, after the Admiralty decision was received, and show a big, generous spirit. If he had followed this up by a sustained effort to bring the officers and men of the two ships together all would have been well, but bitterness over the collision was allowed to exclude these bigger and more generous thoughts.¹⁰

There were other rivalries which needled the crew of the *Renown*, regarded as the 'royal yacht' after taking the Prince of Wales (later Edward VIII and then Duke of Windsor) on an Empire tour in 1919 and his father, George V, on a world voyage in 1927. Those rivalries were sporting and resulted in the *Hood*'s regaining the 'Cock' with a record points total during the Home Fleet Regatta at Rosyth in June 1935. Their thirty-five boats achieved eighteen victories, six second places and five thirds in winning nine trophies. No ship had ever monopolized the regatta to this extent. Congratulations poured in from all sections of the fleet, except from the *Renown*. The *Hood*'s exultant reply to all was: 'Cock-a-doodle-do'.

These were effervescent days, and none was savoured more than the King's Silver Jubilee review of the fleet, with the *Hood* the centrepiece at Spithead on 16 July. But they were also the last months of the showmanship of

Commander O'Connor. The Abyssinian crisis and the Fascist threat from Italy, Germany and Spain loomed. Soon the *Hood* would be at war-readiness.

10

English Captain's Woman

From autumn 1935 until the end of 1938 the *Hood* was the Navy's bluff ship in the Mediterranean, as Britain gambled on a game of blind brinkmanship with the dictators Mussolini and Franco. Whenever international relations became strained, the diplomatic question was: 'Where is the *Hood*?' The ship, now fifteen years old, was still a symbol of Britain ruling the waves, for the doubts about her inadequate armour had never been raised in public.

When the Italian threat to invade Abyssinia came in September 1935, Britain played for time during secret talks with France and decided that, if economic sanctions were imposed by the League of Nations, they must be applied cautiously. By 18 September, when a conciliation committee reported back calling for administrative reforms in Abyssinia and recognition of Italy's economic interests there, the *Hood*, *Renown*, three cruisers and six destroyers had been rushed to Gibraltar. Mussolini was incensed by this sudden move of the Home Fleet, and on 20 September the British Ambassador, Sir Eric Drummond, reassured him that the build-up was not to be interpreted as an aggressive act but merely the consequence of the anti-British stance of Italy's Press. For the rest of the crisis the heavy hand of the Foreign Office was to stay any impulsive action.

The job of Rear-Admiral Bailey in the *Hood* was to bottle up the Straits of Gibraltar with his hastily assembled force. This posed no problems, and the ship's companies settled into a peace-time lethargy that belied the activity and concern in Whitehall. Commander O'Conor was determined that for the four months the *Hood* was operating from the Rock there would not be boredom. Sometimes his insistence on 'comforts' for matelots caused raised eyebrows.

To combat the attractions of bars and brothels ashore, he turned the catamarans between the ship and the mole into a lido for sunbathing and swimming. The catamarans were covered with coconut matting, and garden seats were set out on them. With the aid of buckets of whitewash and church pews, he converted the South Mole coalshed into a cinema. Lieutenant-Commander William Harding comments: 'The Naval Film Service was in its infancy, but new films were made available because of O'Conor's idea.'

The ship's exterior was so smart that Gibraltar residents reckoned she looked more like a yacht than a warship, but beneath the main deck the atmosphere could be appalling, despite Admiralty assurances about TB to Lord Bridgman three years earlier. Surgeon Commander Bill Wolton, who was the ship's dentist, says: 'Air conditioning was very poor. There were several deaths from tuberculosis. At Gibraltar a rating sat up in his hammock, coughed up a lot of blood and was dead in a few minutes.'

O'Conor knew too well what it was like below decks in hot climates, and during a week at Las Palmas in the Canaries he decreed there should be 'holiday routine'. This meant that all work ended as early as 8 a.m., except for the duty watch. The rest of the day was free for the men to spend ashore, with picnic lunches packed by the galley cooks. O'Conor was so proud of the *Hood*'s standing that often for an important fixture he would delay drafting a star soccer player or athlete. This 'spoiling' of the crew became a talking-point in Gibraltar, and many officers outside the *Hood* wondered what Captain Tower was doing.

Unfortunately, there were counter-attractions for him ashore, too, which developed into a scandal that reached the ears of Backhouse, Commander-in-Chief of the Home Fleet, who relayed the gossip to Chatfield. The relationship between Bailey and Tower was under scrutiny since the *Renown* collision, and when Backhouse arrived at Gibraltar, he claimed that the colony was 'abuzz with rumours that Tower kept a mistress at the Rock Hotel and this had led to trouble between Bailey and Tower'. Backhouse disclosed this in a personal letter to Chatfield, although he admitted he 'risked libelling' Tower.[1]

Chatfield began his own investigations and asked Admiral

James to report on his former captain. James replied: 'Gibraltar is a gossipy place and it is possible that a friendship may have been magnified into something more and that an injustice is being done to Tower and the resident at the Rock Hotel.' There was a certain amount of chivalry in all the correspondence about the 'English captain's woman', for not once was she named. James admired Tower and pointed out to Chatfield that two years earlier the *Hood*'s captain had been the most prominent officer for flag rank. 'I feel he is too good a man to lose through gossip,' James declared.

Backhouse was continuing his snooping, however, and reported back to Chatfield: 'As regards the lady at the Rock Hotel – that is correct, but there is no evidence that the conduct was scandalous. He spent much time in her company, but he slept in his ship. Bailey would not ask her on board and I believe she was not asked either to Government House, when it was known about her. I gather that Tower has a wife and three children, but that he does not go home.'

Backhouse also questioned Bailey about why he 'did not have it out with Tower about her'. Bailey's answer was that he 'wished to avoid a row at the end of Tower's time and because of all the bother there had been before'. Backhouse considered that Bailey's leniency with Tower had engendered continued animosity with the *Renown*. He told Chatfield: 'Bailey [is] prejudiced strongly for Tower and against Sawbridge ... I found that he [Bailey] did not know for certain to what extent Tower handled his ship. He said he was sure he was in charge of her, but that he usually gave his orders through the navigator without cross-examining *Hood*'s officers.'

While the gossips of Gibraltar delighted in tittle-tattle about the *Hood*'s captain, the situation in Abyssinia deteriorated and the British Government were using the ship as a bargaining power. On 3 October 1935 Italy invaded, and four days later the Council of the League of Nations decided on economic and military sanctions. Trade embargoes were not operated until 18 November, and the military sanctions were never invoked. The naval balance of power was still in Britain's favour, and at the end of October feelers were put out by Mussolini suggesting that, if Britain withdrew the *Hood* and the *Renown*, he would bring home one division of troops from Libya. The Cabinet were prepared to listen to this overture and agreed to send back the *Hood* to Britain, as long as France gave an assurance of naval support if there were war.

The decision for the *Hood*'s 'retreat' dovetailed tidily with the relief of Tower, who had already been commanding officer for five months longer than the usual term. His intrigue with 'the lady in the Rock Hotel' was not public knowledge, but this affair, coming on top of the court-martial, convinced the Admiralty that he was no longer suitable for sea service. Duly promoted to rear-admiral, Tower left the *Hood*, to Backhouse's amazement, with a perfect confidential report of 'all nines' from Bailey. The Admiralty had still to decide how to use his services, but nearly a year later he was appointed Director of Naval Equipment. He was to stay in Whitehall in this capacity until the outbreak of war, when he was promoted to vice-admiral and became deputy controller. The stigma of the affair left him unscarred in society, for in 1942 he was knighted, and he remained as deputy controller until the end of the war, when he retired.

The Admiralty also dealt leniently with Bailey, who was to be allowed to finish his two-year appointment as squadron commander. But there were to be drastic changes of the old order at the behest of the new ubiquitous commanding officer, Captain A.F. Pridham, who revealed the seamy side of the *Hood* and seemed to relish it after his experience as a member of the collision court-martial.

Pridham, who joined the *Hood* as soon as she arrived back at Portsmouth from Gibraltar, was horrified at her condition. 'It took me some time before I could believe my eyes,' he said. 'Between decks she was the dirtiest ship I had ever seen. I could find no signs that good ship husbandry was within the knowledge or competence of her officers.'[2] He blamed this unsatisfactory state on Commander O'Conor, hitherto the paragon of fair play. Pridham was obviously jealous of his executive's reputation and set out to prove that, although O'Conor's methods might be popular, he was just a 'first class showman' who knew little about seamanship, nothing about ship husbandry, and was obsessed with spoiling the crew by not working them fully and rarely awarding punishment.

On his first inspection he discovered that the *Hood*'s smartness was due to unlimited coats of paint on top of dirt and rust. He had one section of the quarterdeck chipped down to bare metal and found a quarter of an inch of paint on top of almost as much filth and rust. He described the messes as 'disgusting' because of swarms of cockroaches and ordered O'Conor to have them free of the pests in six weeks. Pridham's opinion was that many officers and petty officers were frustrated in their efforts to make her a fighting ship. This was supported by Lieutenant-Commander Harding, who remembers: 'The warrant shipwright persuaded the boatswain to convince the commander to operate again the bower cable holder, which was not used because it spoilt the paintwork. It took two days and a fire around the spindle before the shipwrights freed it. The torpedo gunner was also given permission to work the above-water tubes. This entailed spoiling the side paintwork and it took almost a week to get the doors open.'

Pridham went through the ship minutely and was astounded to find that many of the seven hundred hull compartments had not been entered since she was built. He instigated examinations and checks of all. There were more surprises when he took the *Hood* to sea. 'I was shocked to see evidence of ignorance of elementary details of lowering and hoisting boats at sea,' he said. 'The commander expected me to stop the ship's way before he gave the order to slip. I had never dreamt of such slovenliness. The boats were hoisted lazily at a slow walk; I ordered them to be lowered and hoisted again. The sailors soon realised that the new, tall broom on the forebridge was no silent ornament and quickly adopted a new and enthusiastic demeanour to seaboat drills.'[3]

In the Mediterranean Admiral Fisher was expecting reinforcements, and he suggested the *Hood* should join him in Malta and then sail to Alexandria, where she should be based as a 'frightener' to Mussolini at the Suez Canal entrance. His request was considered by a sick Chatfield, who instructed Admiral James to go to the Foreign Office for approval. But Britain was in the middle of a policy of appeasement with Italy because tension over Abyssinia was still high. James described his visit: 'When I stated the object to Eden, he rang for Sir Robert Vansittart (Permanent Secretary). They told me frankly that Mussolini was in an excited state and the strengthening of the fleet at Alexandria by the *Hood* might tip the balance over to war, which was the last thing they wanted. I must have been nearly an hour with them developing every argument I could muster and in the end they agreed to the movement.'[4]

Eden, however, also sought the opinion of Sir Lancelot Oliphant, Assistant Under Secretary of State, who was handling the crisis. 'I believe that Mussolini is far more afraid of a battle cruiser than a battleship,'[5] said Oliphant, but this view was not in accord with that of Premier Stanley Baldwin's military advisers, and the orders were counter-manded.

The *Hood* was back at Gibraltar by the end of February to continue the 'watch over the Straits'. But this commitment was an embarrassment on 7 March, when Hitler denounced the Locarno Pact and German troops re-occupied the Rhineland. Chatfield's naval concentration in the Mediterranean was blatantly exposed as a bluff. He had boasted to the Cabinet that in seven days he could move the Home Fleet from Gibraltar and the Mediterranean Fleet from Alexandria so that both would be in the North Sea to meet any German threat. Yet at the same time of the Rhineland crisis there was only one cruiser, seventeen destroyers and nine submarines in home waters. The *Hood* and *Renown* were the only capital ships which could emerge quickly into the North Sea to combat three Deutschland-class pocket battleships.

With one crisis following another, Backhouse, now based at Gibraltar in the *Nelson*, was painfully conscious that many Home Fleet units were not at war-readiness. He told Pridham: 'I want you to get the *Hood* out of cotton wool. Take your time, but as soon as you think you have got the feel of the ship I want you to bring her in here after dark and in foul weather. My ships will most certainly have to do such things in time of war.'[6]

Since the collision, the *Hood* had not been handled boldly. Other ships gave her a wide berth, and she seldom moved in harbour without six or eight tugs. Pridham was determined to stop using them. He described her as 'handling wonderfully well, so long as one used engine power and treated her roughly as soon as she showed the slightest sign of taking the bit between her teeth'.[7]

When Pridham told O'Conor he would take the ship from her berth alongside without tugs, the commander doubted the sense of it and was immediately given a lecture on seamanship. To Pridham it seemed that neither the forecastle officers nor the men had any idea of how to use a wire hawser by putting their weight on it and were 'scared' stiff and stood well clear'. He commenced the manoeuvre by giving the ship a slight move ahead, checked her way and then 'washed her off' the wall by going astern on the starboard propeller. The *Hood* responded, and out she went, completely under control. That was easy enough, but Pridham could not bring her in and place her neatly alongside the South Mole. Normally he stopped her six feet from the wall and resting on the catamarans; then she had to be hauled in by using long hawsers. 'This took time and was untidy,' he complained. Pridham was determined to satisfy Backhouse, and the first chance he had of bringing her in during bad weather was in a north-westerly gale. For two hours he decided against trying to moor between the *Nelson* and the carrier *Furious*. Instead, he anchored outside the harbour. Then pride prevailed and the *Hood* made her approach. As she neared the *Nelson*, she canted sharply to port and then to starboard, like a shying horse. She suddenly pointed forty-five degrees towards the mole and was closing rapidly. Pridham ordered full speed astern and she came to rest thirty feet from the wall. By delicate use of the engines he finally nudged in astern of the *Nelson*, where he could see Backhouse watching from the quarterdeck. Dejected, Pridham went to Admiral Bailey and apologized for a poor performance. 'Don't be silly. Haven't you seen the C-in-C's signal?' Bailey commiserated. Pridham looked at a signalman's pad. It read: 'Manoeuvre well executed.'[8]

With the end of the Abyssinian war in sight as Italian troops entered Addis Ababa on 5 May 1936, sanctions began to disintegrate and demands on the Home Fleet lessened. It was just as well because, despite her outward appearance, the *Hood* was not in a fit fighting state through a tiresome defect in one of her turbines, which damaged the rotor blades. She was patched up in Gibraltar, with a full repair delayed until her return to Portsmouth in the summer. Abyssinian opposition had virtually ended, which was obvious when Bailey and Pridham showed around the *Hood* Emperor Haile Selassie and his daughter Princess Sehai, who were bound for exile in Britain. On 4 July the League of Nations lifted all sanctions against Italy, and the ship was ordered to Portsmouth for a minor refit and to recommission.

This posed a problem for Bailey, who was told by the Admiralty he would no longer be considered for sea service but would be put on full pay until another appointment. The original plan was for the transfer of his flag to his old ship, the *Renown*. Bailey was aware that her officers disliked him since the collision and that their animosity had not tempered with the going of Captain Sawbridge, for the replacement was Captain Miles, who was Sawbridge's court-martial defender. Bailey pleaded with Backhouse to be allowed to stay in the *Hood* and go on half pay for several months in preference to joining the *Renown*. This induced Backhouse to write to Chatfield: 'Bailey is greatly attached to the *Hood*. I could, if need be, arrange for the *Hood* and *Renown* not to meet here [Gibraltar] at all. It could be quite easy to keep the *Hood* away till *Renown* has left. In case of need, Bailey would move out of the *Hood* without a murmur at any notice ... I am sorry for Bailey, who I like very much, but somehow or other this command has not worked out well for him. I don't think he was strong enough to handle the situation which came about.'[9]

Bailey was allowed to remain in the *Hood* and returned with her to Portsmouth in the middle of July, when she paid off. He retired voluntarily, but his career was reactivated six months later when he took a senior officers' war course. In July 1937, as a vice-admiral, he commanded the Royal Naval College, Greenwich, and he was knighted at the end of a two-year appointment. At the start of the war he was recalled for an Admiralty desk job but did not make a complete recovery after having an appendicitis operation and died in March 1942. His naval epitaph was written by Admiral Dreyer in this letter to Chatfield: 'He was a first-rate fellow ... an extremely able and competent captain. A good many of us thought he had never really recovered from that *Hood* collision and that it broke his stout heart ... a very fine fellow has passed over.'[10]

11

'HMS *Hood* Will Be There'

Nothing suited Pridham more than the *Hood*'s recommissioning on 8 September 1936. He had been reappointed flag captain, but most officers, including O'Conor, left and 'veteran' ratings of the previous commission were drafted. The start of the Spanish Civil War on 18 July also came as a blessing to Pridham, for this inspired the Admiralty to attach the *Hood* and *Repulse* to the Mediterranean Fleet. Pridham favoured the fairer weather conditions of the Mediterranean for training a new crew and always contended that the efficiency of Home Fleet vessels was affected by operating close to United Kingdom shores.

With his new executive, Commander D. Orr-Ewing, whom he described as a 'good one', he addressed the crew, including younger members of the previous commission, and insisted: 'We are going to do things a little differently in future and I will require from you a far higher standard.'[1] The 'little differently' meant that the ship was not to be so sport-conscious and, in fact, during the next two years it was men of the cruiser *Sussex* who were to outbox, outrun, outkick and outsmart her in the Mediterranean. But Pridham had a new sport for them – sail training. He was a keen yachtsman and while re-equipping in Portsmouth he acquired from dockyard a white galley, in which he planned to teach officers and ratings, 'particularly coxswains', the art of sailing small boats, instead of pulling, at which the *Hood*'s sailors had been more than proficient.

Many newcomers were daunted by *Hood*'s reputation. Ex-Shipwright C.T. Haynes, who retired as a commander, explains: 'We had to try to "live down" the last commission. About a third of our company were in the previous commission and were always telling us it was the best ever.'

But LTO Stan Hazell says: 'She was in a bad condition and required a lot of improvements to bring her up to date, particularly in defence. Living conditions were very poor.'

The commission started ingloriously. On 1 October the *Hood* left for Malta, where Vice-Admiral Geoffrey Blake was to transfer his flag from the battleship *Barham*. When the new navigator, Commander E.D. Brooks, piloted her over a shallow off Spithead, gravel was sucked into the condensers and to Pridham's consternation the *Hood* was forced to return to Portsmouth, where it took ten days to remedy the defect.

During the fourteen-day voyage to Malta, Pridham worked the crew as hard as he dared, but it was obvious to him that another month needed to be spent on 'chamferring' them up before Blake could hoist his flag. The gunnery was abysmal, and Pridham failed to understand why many new members were frightened by the thunder of the fifteen-inch turrets. In the first full-calibre night firing he came across young seamen who were supposed to be manning the 5.5s, but so scared were they by the roar and blast of the fifteen-inch guns that they took shelter away from their weapons and slowed the rate of loading. When the practice ended, Pridham rounded them up and chided: 'You're not fit for me to take into action against even an Eyetie ship.'[2]

But the blast of the fifteen-inch turrets and the chattering of the pom-poms were unnerving. Surgeon Commander Wolton remembers: 'Everything moveable in the dental surgery had to be put on the deck when they fired. If you were caught outside, the blast was like being hit across the face with a wet cloth. The pom-poms were just outside my surgery. Sometimes no warning was given that they were about to fire, and the effect on me was shattering. But the gunners never seemed to hit any targets towed by planes.'

At Malta Pridham received detailed drawings of a massive, three-year rebuilding programme for the *Hood*, estimated to cost £4½ million. It was a complete upper deck reconstruction from B turret to X turret. The 5.5-inch and 4-inch armament were to be replaced by twelve 5.25- or sixteen 4.5-inch dual-purpose guns and six eight-barrelled pom-poms; the torpedo tubes were to be removed, new turbine machinery was to be fitted with high pressure boilers, modernization of the aircraft catapult and hangars and an extension to the forecastle deck were planned. But above all, extra deck protection and a revamp of the conning tower and bridges were scheduled.

Additional armour was to include a twelve-inch belt over the upper deck and an increase to five inches over the magazines and machinery. Pridham was delighted to see that the bridge was to be removed; it had been a source of complaint from every captain. Vision of thirty-six degrees from any position was unattainable. If the captain wanted to look aft, he had to move to the platforms on the bridge wings, and this meant he was away from voice-pipe communication. The admiral's bridge was equally inadequate. In the enclosed position in front of the charthouse, vision ahead was blotted out by the rangefinders' armoured hood above the control tower. If he wanted to look aft, he had to go on to the 5.5-inch director platforms on the sides of the bridge, and this lost him a view of the opposite side.

But there were two drawbacks to the plans. The first was that the Achilles heel of the magazines sited above the shell-rooms would not be remedied; the second was that, although experts doubted whether the machinery would last for another $3\frac{1}{2}$ years, the reconstruction would not begin until March 1942. With the international situation worsening and growing demands on the Navy – and in particular on the *Hood* – since the outbreak of the Spanish Civil War, it was decided there should be two 'first aid' minor refits in 1938 and 1939.

By 28 November Pridham considered the *Hood* ready to accommodate the admiral's staff, and Blake moved in. Nine days later the *Hood* and *Repulse* relieved the battleship *Valiant* and the *Sussex* at Gibraltar, which for the next five months became their second home from Malta, as they toured the trouble spots off Spain, now embroiled in a bitter Fascist-Communist conflict.

The increasing outside interest in Spanish affairs was obvious to Blake on a trip to Tangier, for also in harbour were the German cruisers *Königsberg* and *Nürnberg*, the German destroyer *Iltis* and Italy's *Quenton*, a cruiser, and *Aquila*, a destroyer. And when the *Hood* returned to the Rock for Christmas, she was followed in by the German pocket battleship *Graf Spee*. From then on the two met in many western Mediterranean harbours.

Accidents were always part of life, but during this spell there were two serious ones. When the fleet were exercising, a hydraulics test was carried out in the *Hood*'s turrets, and as a dummy-run ended, the gunner's mate's knee accidentally touched the hydraulics switch. A fifteen-inch shell was in the cage, and it was rammed into the gun, crushing the left arm of Able Seaman Fred Hard. 'I was conscious and rushed down the iron ladder to the sick-bay,' says Hard. 'A tourniquet was put on my arm, and the captain was told. He was given permission to leave the fleet and we tore back to Gibraltar. Gangrene had set in, however, and it was thought best to get me to Malta. The *Hood* went there at full speed and we arrived in under two days. I was taken off by tug to Bighi Hospital. I could not understand why a security man laughed when he saw my name written in the entry book. I learned later the previous patient was named Luck – then came me, Hard.'

Hard's luck was in, though. His arm was saved and so was his career. He returned to the *Hood* four months later and eventually retired as a lieutenant-commander.

The second accident was more tragic, and it was caused by Pridham's insistence on not using tugs when berthing at the South Mole. When a sudden gust blew the stern away from it, a hawser snapped and writhed like an angry snake across the quarterdeck into the cable party. Ordinary Seaman D.D. Smith died from head injuries, Marine Corporal W.J. Hayward was seriously hurt and Boy J.E. Kelly had a fractured leg.

With the British Government still insisting on a non-intervention policy in Spain, despite the incursions of Germany and Italy, the bluff of Royal Navy patrols off the north and south coasts was often being called. Admiral Blake was to find himself enmeshed in a situation which divided his three loyalties – to Chatfield's, the Government and freedom of the seas.

Blake was another of Chatfield 'young men' destined for flag rank and known as the 'B men' – the others were the deposed Bailey and Binney, former captain of the *Hood* – who had all served under him in the *Iron Duke* and *Queen*

Elizabeth. Blake, now fifty-five had won the DSO as Jellicoe's gunnery officer in the *Iron Duke* at Jutland and by the 1930s was regarded as a future Sea Lord. He was an alert intellectual, with an inquiring mind which often focused on social responsibilities. He was supremely confident yet surprisingly mellow. Sometimes he was too gentle and patient for his subordinates; conversely he was a fitness fanatic and drove himself beyond his physical capabilities. Because he was rich and not as inhibited as career-conscious officers, he rejected command of a cruiser squadron in 1935 when his wife became ill. He was also less politically biased than his superiors – Chatfield and Backhouse leaned towards Fascism as a bulwark against Communism – and surveyed the international scene with an open mind. In short, he and the *Hood* were the ideal combination to solve the maritime crisis off Bilbao, northern Spain, which was to bedevil the British Government during April 1937.

By now Franco's forces had been halted in their push to Madrid and turned to an all-out offensive against the Basques and on the Bilbao enclave. One sure way to force the besieged port to submit was to stop food supplies by sea, the only means of egress. Previously the Nationalists were able to effect a legal blockade only of war materials, but now Franco warned British merchantmen they must obey his warships' signals.

The first incident came on 6 April when the SS *Thorpehall*, loaded with food for Bilbao, radioed at dawn that ten miles off the coast she had been fired on by the Nationalist trawler *Galerna*. Commander R.M.T. Taylor, in the destroyer HMS *Brazen*, sighted the two ships, which had stopped, and signalled the *Galerna* to 'Cease interference'. As the Spanish cruiser *Almirante Cervera* approached, the *Brazen*'s crew went to action stations, and Taylor signalled that the *Thorpehall* was carrying only food. The cruiser and the trawler then manoeuvred between the cargo ship and the coast to prevent her proceeding to Bilbao. For three hours they lay like this, and then the Spanish vessels moved in on the *Thorpehall*. By now other warships had picked up the signals and were homing in. First the *Graf Spee* nosed in, followed by the destroyer *Blanche*, carrying Commander C. Caslon, senior officer of the British flotilla. The *Graf Spee*'s captain appreciated the tenseness of the situation, and the German warship steamed off. But the confrontation grew with the arrival of a third British destroyer, the *Beagle*, and a sudden turn of speed by the *Almirante Cervera* towards the *Thorpehall*. Caslon ordered all the destroyers to interpose between the Spanish cruiser and the merchantman. This effectively screened the *Thorpehall*, which was able to slip into the three-mile limit, where the Nationalists had no legal jurisdiction.

Caslon had kept his nerve, yet afterwards he became strangely obtuse about the crisis and reported to Backhouse that it appeared the Bilbao blockade was a reality, because his flotilla of four destroyers would be unable to combat the Nationalist forces of a battleship, cruiser, light cruiser, destroyer and armed trawler. The next day Caslon bolstered the blockade by advising all merchant ships in the area that if they were bound for Bilbao they should put into St Jean de Luz, the tiny French harbour just across the border.

Although the captains of the blockade-busters were to become swashbuckling heroes in British newspapers, the Government regarded them with a jaundiced eye as highly paid adventurers, employed by shipping companies bent on making huge profits from the Basque government.

Caslon's report of superior Spanish naval forces had alarmed Sir Samuel Hoare, now the new First Lord, who was a persistent pacifist, and Chatfield, who was given misleading intelligence about Franco's ships. The battleship to which Caslon referred was in fact the coal-burning *España*, which had twelve-inch guns but had been constructed before the First World War and not commissioned until 1921. Nevertheless, Franco's threat had to be countered, and after a special ministerial meeting on 10 April, the Government decided that the *Hood* should be used as a frightener again and be despatched from Gibraltar with all speed to Bilbao.

At 2.48 that afternoon an 'Immediate' signal was sent to Blake to take over as senior officer off northern Spain and to get the *Hood* there as fast as he could. The crew were on shore leave, it being Saturday afternoon, so Commander Orr-Ewing formed special patrols which toured the bars, cafés and haunts of the sailors, ordering them to return immediately. While they were being rounded up, the *Hood* was refuelled. It was essential she should be fully loaded, for Backhouse had informed Chatfield she could remain off Bilbao for a week 'if not much activity was needed'.[3]

The *Hood* was able to clear Gibraltar at 8.45 p.m. and was soon working up to twenty-seven knots with WT silence. To confuse the many informers ashore, Pridham steered an easterly course and then tracked back through the Straits and into the Atlantic. It was a ploy to be used many times during the Second World War. The Government's orders had been kept secret, but that night the crew heard from a BBC news bulletin that they were on their way to ensure the safe passage of a coaster loaded with potatoes from St Jean de Luz to Bilbao. Lieutenant-Commander Harding relates: '*Hood*'s movements had been kept under wraps all day, and many people were upset at this disclosure on the news. We put the leak down to John Reith, the director of the BBC. He had been Blake's guest in the *Hood* and left at Gibraltar, where we believed he phoned the news to the BBC.'

As the *Hood* raced towards Bilbao, the Cabinet met on the Sunday to discuss a new caveat by Franco that he would use force to sustain the blockade. It brought this statement from them: 'His Majesty's Government cannot recognise or concede belligerent rights and they cannot tolerate any interference with British shipping at sea. They are, however, warning British shipping that in view of conditions at present prevailing in the neighbourhood of Bilbao, they should not, for practical reasons, and in view of risks, against which it is at present impossible to protect them, go into that area, so long as these conditions prevail.'[4] Yet at the same time the Admiralty informed Blake and all ships off Spain that, if merchant skippers ignored advice and made a run for Bilbao, all naval protection would be withdrawn.

Despite assurances from Captain R.R. MacGrigor, that the passage was safe, Prime Minister Baldwin told the Commons that it was 'dangerously mined'. But the Government were having second thoughts and performed an about-turn. Late that night in the *Hood* at St Jean de Luz, Blake, who had conferred earlier with Caslon, was handed this Admiralty message: 'If a British ship proceeding to Bilbao, in spite of Government advice, calls on you for protection in a particular case, you should render protection on the high seas.' It confused Blake, and later he admitted he found the order 'lacking in clarity'.⁵

The massive battle cruiser off the coast 'electrified the Basque countryside by her majestic appearance', according to David Scott, *The Times* correspondent at St Jean de Luz,⁶ and great crowds watched her anchor four miles off shore, but early on the Tuesday a violent south-westerly and squalls lashed the inadequate anchorage and forced Pridham to take the *Hood* to sea and out of sight of land. This caused Blake to ask the Admiralty for permission to withdraw from the area because of lack of a base, unless force was to be used.

Blake had already observed enough to convince him that the blockade was a myth. He had seen not more than one insurgent warship at a time and informed the Admiralty on the Wednesday that the Navy had sufficient forces to shield British merchant shipping and that the blockade was not working. The Admiralty were inclined not to believe him and quickly asked for more details because the Government's ploy was founded on contrastingly different information. The Admiralty might have been groping for intelligence, but the Labour Party were not – and it was ironical that they obtained it through forty-six-year-old Commander Harry Pursey, who had been in the *Hood* during the Invergordon mutiny and had retired from the Navy a year earlier to take up journalism and politics. He went to Bilbao with a committee of investigation into the working of the Non-Intervention Agreement to find out whether the blockade was as complete as had been claimed.

Pursey discovered that many of the Nationalists' old mines were defective and that the majority had been cleared from the harbour and territorial waters by a daily patrol of sixteen Loyalist minesweepers. Bilbao was also adequately defended by shore batteries high on either side of the mouth of the River Nervion. These could keep insurgent warships well outside the three-mile limit. There were also two destroyers, a submarine, six armed trawlers and a squadron of aircraft available for the port's defence.

Pursey lost no time in divulging the results of his mission to the Labour Party, and around the time Blake was telling the Admiralty there was no blockade, Clement Attlee, the leader of the Opposition, was telling the Government similar facts in the Commons.

The eyes of the world were directed now to St Jean de Luz, where it appeared that a convoy of six merchant ships and four destroyers were waiting for the right moment to make a dash to Bilbao. On Thursday 15 April the *Hood* arrived at La Rochelle, where Blake and three of his staff landed in the late afternoon. They motored 175 miles to St Jean de Luz, where for half an hour they conferred again with Commander Caslon, whose flotilla were due to be relieved by Captain V.H. Danckwerts with five B-class destroyers. Afterwards the admiral's party visited Hendaye, where the British Ambassador, Sir Henry Chilton, was in residence. He warned that hot-headed insurgent naval officers were likely to open fire on merchantmen if they ventured into territorial waters. They discussed the problem for several hours, dined and stayed the night. Next day Blake informed the Admiralty that there was a definite indication the insurgents might shell freighters inside the legal limits. He asked what he was to do if this happened. The Admiralty reply was to 'intervene if a ship had been fired on, once it had submitted'.[7]

On the same day in St Jean de Luz, Captain Danckwerts, who had arrived in the *Faulkner*, accompanied by *Firedrake*, *Forester*, *Fortune* and *Fury*, heard a rumour that the tramp *Seven Seas Spray* was leaving at 10 p.m. to run the blockade. Blake was notified and tried to dissuade Captain W.H. Roberts from sailing but ordered the destroyers to give protection if necessary. The *Hood* also left her anchorage and kept station off Bilbao to watch all night.

The *Seven Seas Spray* moved out at the anticipated time, with Captain Roberts at the helm and Thomas McEwen, one of the owners, on board to take responsibility. To show their contempt of the blockade, they had with them two women, the captain's twenty-year-old daughter, Fifi, and Mrs B.M. Docker, wife of the chief engineer. Roberts ignored a Morse light signal from the shore, which said he should not sail. All through the night the *Seven Seas Spray* dawdled towards Bilbao. At 6.30 a.m. the *Faulkner* spotted her and asked by light: 'Where bound?' Roberts made no attempt to conceal that he was heading for Bilbao. From the *Hood*, the reply of the *Faulkner* could be made out. It warned: 'Enter at your own risk.' Roberts signalled: 'I accept full responsibility.' The *Faulkner* answered: 'Good luck.'[8]

And luck was with Roberts, for the *España* and *Almirante Cervera* were fourteen miles away, and the *Seven Seas Spray* slipped past them into Bilbao at 9 a.m.

Twenty-four hours after this easy passage, Blake, who had returned to St Jean de Luz in the *Hood* at 4 p.m., was perplexed by another Admiralty signal seeking further details about the Bilbao situation. He had appraised it fully nearly a week earlier and still believed that, if a merchant ship were escorted to the territorial limit, she was virtually certain to complete the trip without interference because of the 'insurance' of the shore artillery. He cautioned, however, that there was a risk a Nationalist warship outside the three-mile limit might fire on a British vessel, which was inside territorial waters. Now he reaffirmed this view but added that, as long as the Navy were there in sufficient strength, the insurgents would not prey on merchant ships outside the limit. He still would not give a definite opinion on what might occur inside territorial waters.

To test the insurgents, the blockade and their lordships' nerves, he disclosed that three merchantmen at St Jean de Luz were preparing to enter Bilbao on 23 April and he proposed to help, because it would embarrass the Government and the Navy 'if an incident took place outside territorial waters with no adequate protection at hand'. He signed off dramatically: 'HMS *Hood* will be there.'[9]

With the euphoria of the tiny *Seven Seas Spray*'s exploit still in the Press, and with the master, crew and Fifi still being fêted in Bilbao, the Admiralty were aware they had to commit the mighty *Hood*. They approved Blake's 'testing convoy' but at the same time administered a minor reproach because 'such measures would scarcely be practicable or desirable on every occasion that a British merchant ship wished to enter Bilbao'.[10]

Blake had written the scenario for calling Franco's bluff. The heroes, in the shape of the steamers *MacGregor*, *Hamsterley* and *Stanbrook*, were in the wings at St Jean de Luz; the villain, the *Almirante Cervera*, was hissing through the sea; the star, the *Hood*, was waiting to perform with a supporting cast of destroyers – and the production was patriotically premièred for 23 April, St George's Day.

Not a hammock was occupied in the *Hood* as dawn broke off Bilbao. Everyone was up watching, waiting or listening, for they had been told the convoy was to attempt a break-through. The battle cruiser left her anchorage at 11 p.m. after the darkened *Hamsterley* (Captain Still), *MacGregor* ('Corn Cob' Jones) and *Stanbrook* (Captain Prance) slipped out of St Jean de Luz. The three masters had spread the rumour they were going to French ports to coal. They had consulted Blake, who could not promise to escort them but gave the undertaking that, if they arrived off Bilbao at a given time, destroyers and the *Hood* would be close. The *Hood*, therefore, did not accompany them but steamed on a wide northern sweep, which would bring her back to Bilbao, while the steamers crept along at about six knots. Blake timed his move cleverly, for the non-aligned nations had agreed that a system of placing observers in merchant vessels bound for Spain should be instituted from midnight – but all the blockade-runners had sailed before it could be invoked.

As a light mist drifted seawards to screen the convoy partially, the merchantmen steamed to within five miles of Bilbao. But at 5.45 came the enemy. Blake and Pridham had their binoculars focused on the *MacGregor*, half a mile ahead of the other cargo ships, when out of the mist chugged the armed trawler *Galerna*. As the insurgent buffeted to within hailing distance, her commanding officer ordered the *MacGregor* to stop. 'Corn Cob' Jones did as he was instructed, and as the ship lost way, he sent an SOS to the *Firedrake*.

Blake signalled the *Firedrake* at 6.39: 'Follow in and report immediately any action by insurgents when merchant vessels outside territorial waters.'

The destroyer was veering in to help when the cruiser *Almirante Cervera*, which had been standing off, cleared for action and steered in towards the *Galerna*. By light her captain, Manuel de Navio don Moreu, signalled at 6.45: 'Please tell steamers not to enter Bilbao.' In unison Blake and Lieutenant-Commander J.M. Rodgers, *Firedrake*'s skipper, snapped back: 'Stop interfering.'

There was difficulty in reading the insurgent signals because they were in Spanish, but Blake gathered that the *Almirante Cervera* was claiming jurisdiction within territorial waters extending to six miles and not to three. Rodgers anticipated this and answered rapidly: 'Please do not interfere outside territorial waters.'

For forty-five minutes these laconic conversations by light went on; then the insurgents lost patience. At 7.17 a shell from the *Galerna* screamed across the *MacGregor's* bows as she attempted to sail on, after being told by Blake: 'Proceed on your voyage if you wish.' She was still two miles outside the official limit, and Rodgers, who had discussed this possible emergency earlier with Blake, ordered the *Firedrake's* guns to be aimed at the *Galerna*. It was the first time the Royal Navy had ranged on an insurgent, and this brought immediate reaction from the larger vessels on either side. The *Hood* began to close, and the *Almirante Cervera* steamed slowly by the *Firedrake* to show her eight six-inch guns, which were ready for action. But Moreu, her commanding officer, chose next to communicate with Blake. His streams of light in Spanish confused the *Hood's* signalmen again, but they were able to make out: 'I have the right to prevent entry of these ships to Bilbao.' The rest was garbled but signified that Britain had no justification to intervene.

Another twenty minutes of erratic and erroneous signalling followed, in which Blake reiterated that he did not recognize the six-mile limit. These delaying tactics gave the merchant ships time to move closer to the harbour amid the circle of warships. At 7.56 they were within range of the Galea Point battery. True to their word, the Basques opened fire on the *Galerna*, but every shot splashed harmlessly in the sea. The *Galerna* took heed, however, and turned away to the north-west.

Thirty minutes later the tiny convoy was approaching the harbour entrance when Commander I. Black, of the *Fortune*, which had been aiding the *Firedrake*, signalled Blake that the *Almirante Cervera* had her guns trained on the British. Blake refused to reciprocate. Instead he ordered that the *Hood's* fifteen-inch turrets be swivelled round to Green 30 in a broadside towards the Spanish cruiser, but twenty degrees off target. This command was misunderstood. The menacing turrets revolved straight towards the *Almirante Cervera*, and for the first time Blake showed his annoyance. The mistake was effective, however. The insurgents remained outside the three-mile section, and Moreu, who was aware the *Hood*'s guns were trained on him, held his fire as the three merchantmen entered the legal zone and were welcomed by the harbour pilot boat.

As the *Firedrake* gave way and steamed parallel to the Basques' craft, she was cheered by the crew. Then during a turn towards the *Hood* a sudden succession of explosions rang out. The *Firedrake* was being shelled accidentally by the Loyalist armed trawlers *Bizkaya* and *Ipareko Izarro*, which were aiming at the *Galerna*. To Blake it was ironic that the only danger to his ships had come from the friendly side. From the admiral this signal went to *Firedrake*: 'Duty well executed.'[11] In harbour the blockade-busters were being greeted hysterically by great crowds.

That night Blake made a personal report to Ambassador Chilton at Hendaye. Afterwards a watered-down account of the episode was issued to the Press, but there was no mention of the *Hood*'s having trained her guns on the insurgents. Overseas newspapers were varied in their comments. Russia's *Izvestiya* had earlier charged the *Hood* with helping Italian and German warships 'starve out the gallant defenders of the Basque country'. Now Germany's journals were complaining. *Deutsche Allgemein Zeitung* screamed: 'Breach of non-intervention.' *Volkischer Beobachter* headlined the incident: 'Business before loyalty to principles.' The pro-Franco *Diario Vasco* ranted: 'Flagrant violation of international law by Great Britain.'

The *Hood*'s officers also had their principles. In spite of the subsequent trumpeting of the exploit in British papers, few of them were proud of their part in the relief of Bilbao. Pridham said: 'We in *Hood* felt that we had been a big bully, the Spanish cruiser being only a rather ancient, old ship.'[12]

Three days later Blake was relieved of any further anxieties, when Rear-Admiral C.G. Ramsey, commander of the Second Battle Squadron, in the battleship *Royal Oak*, accompanied by the *Resolution*, arrived to take over as senior officer, Northern Spain. As far as the public knew, the *Hood* was sailing to Britain for the next month's Coronation Naval Review at Spithead. Her return served a dual purpose, however, for the day after she arrived, Blake was summoned to Whitehall with Chatfield to relate his delicate mission and give his recommendations to the Cabinet's Committee on the Protection of British Shipping (Spain). His report was, however, suppressed by the Admiralty.

The *Hood* was the first of the Mediterranean Fleet to arrive for the review, and the short trip back brought her a new record, thanks to Pridham's confidence. She was the first capital ship to approach Portsmouth through the Solent, instead of taking the normal route past the Nab Tower and through Spithead. Haynes tells of how, 'there was very little room to spare under the keel, and it was significant that a full anchor crew were ready to let go on the forecastle.'

During the waiting days off Spain, side-parties had preened the ship with special, light Mediterranean grey enamel paint. This enhanced her graceful, symmetrical lines as she sparkled in the sunlight when going by Spithead. So impressed was the captain of the nearby USS *Arkansas* that he signalled: 'You sure do look swell.'

She was definitely the 'swellest' ship at the review by George VI on 20 May, when Blake was knighted in the *Queen Elizabeth*, the fleet flagship. Backhouse had wanted Chatfield formally to decorate officers and men for 'valorous services off Spain', but this was rejected for fear of exacerbating relations with Franco.

As Blake bent his knee and bowed his head, he reached the pinnacle of his seagoing career. Within a year this quiet, thoughtful admiral would be out of the Navy.

12

The Admirable Admirals

With the 'naval war' against the Spaniards flaring again, the *Hood* rejoined the Mediterranean Fleet in June 1937, and Blake was given the new title of Senior Officer, Western Basin of the Mediterranean. The *Hood's* frightening capacity was to become a symbol of safety for both sides in the Spanish conflict, for irrespective of which port she lay off, there were no air raids during her stays.

The ship's immediate destination when she left Britain on 1 June was Malta, with calls at Gibraltar and Tangier.

It was at the North African port that Pridham suspected that Blake's health had deteriorated because of the demands of the anti-blockade patrol. The admiral still pushed himself in a fitness campaign of rowing, squash and swimming, but after playing polo at Tangier he complained of a pain in his left leg. He put it down to a muscle strain and forgot about it, for ahead were four days of rigorous evolutions with the fleet. Blake did not spare himself, and at the end it was obvious to Pridham that the admiral was extremely fatigued.

The *Hood* was anchored outside the breakwater at Malta in preparation for firing practice the next day, and again the schedule was to be an exhausting one, so after dinner Pridham persuaded Blake to go to bed and not to get up early next morning for his accustomed hour's rowing. Blake awoke refreshed, however, ignored his captain's advice and telephoned the officer-of-the-watch to have a skiff ready for him. He changed into his kit, gulped down his customary tumbler of Apenta water, which had been iced by mistake in the admiral's pantry, and ran down the quarterdeck gangway to the skiff.

After rowing for a short distance, his senses became fuzzy but he put it down to the coldness of the Apenta. Instead of returning, he decided to swim to push off the giddiness and slipped from the boat into the sea. But the admiral, who was used to handling big ships, did not make allowance for the vagaries of his small skiff. He swam to the windward, not realizing that his boat would drift fast down wind. As he turned back, it was going away from him, and he had to swim swiftly to catch it. He was out of breath when he managed to clamber on to it and collapsed. The officer-of-the-watch was concerned about his plight, and as the skiff was caught by the wind again, he sent out the motor-boat's crew to help. Blake was bundled into it and carried back to his cabin.

Pridham decided that the admiral should be examined by the Fleet Medical Officer, and by the time the doctor arrived he had recovered partially and it was agreed he should remain in the *Hood* for the day's full-calibre firing but should stay in his cabin. Pridham was still worried about him and banned the shooting of all the aft guns near the admiral's cabin.

Next morning the captain cancelled seagoing orders and signalled Admiral Sir Dudley Pound, the commander-in-chief, that he would like to see him at Admiralty House. Pridham did not wait for the courtesy of a reply, which was received in the *Hood* as he was on his way by boat. The message stated that Pound was too busy to grant him an interview. (This was not surprising, because Pound was still smouldering over a gunnery *faux pas* a few days earlier: he had been in the destroyer *Shikari*, which was controlling the target ship *Centurion*, during a practice shoot, when in a signals mix-up the *Hood* straddled the *Shikari* with fifteen-inch practice shells. *Hood*'s officers found the incident somewhat hilarious, for the next day their gunnery expert, Lieutenant-Commander S.H. Carlill, was promoted to commander. It led to a cartoon being drawn about the blunder, but Pound was not amused.) So when Pridham arrived at Admiralty House, he was greeted by a frosty flag lieutenant, who repeated the message and said Pound was unable to see him. Pridham stood his ground and refused to leave without talking to the commander-in-chief. Eventually he was ushered into the study of the cold, aloof Pound, who thawed when he heard the news and agreed that Blake should go to hospital.

At first Blake was thought to have had a mild attack of

pleurisy, but early next morning he had a heart attack, which was swiftly followed by another. But Pridham's urgent action had saved him, and he began to pull round.

Blake was not to return, however. A specialist was sent from London to examine him, and in August he went back to Britain as a 'cot case' in the cruiser *Arethusa*. Two years later he was retired 'medically unfit'. Yet he was to serve the Navy still, for during the war he was recalled to the Admiralty as 'shadow First Lord'. His war service brought reward with his appointment as Black Rod at the House of Commons. He died at the age of seventy-four in July 1968.

Meanwhile, Chatfield wrongly anticipated that Blake would need only four months before re-assuming command, and a temporary replacement was available – Vice-Admiral A.B. Cunningham, who had been in charge of the Mediterranean Fleet's destroyers just over a year earlier. He was now ashore and did not expect another appointment until 1938, but when the call came from Chatfield to take over temporarily, Cunningham, in his own words, 'naturally leapt at the opportunity'. There were many legends and stories to be written about the mercurial Cunningham, now fifty-two, who was to become Britain's foremost admiral in war, and his arrival in the *Hood* on 15 July led to the telling of the first.

Cunningham, who disembarked from a liner at 7 a.m., preferred to relate it this way: 'I was met by Blake's flag lieutenant, James Munn, a young officer I had known well in the *Coventry*; in spite of his persuasions I went aboard the *Hood* at once, whereby I was not at all popular, as they had hoped I would not appear before 8.30. The captain was still in his bath, for which no one could blame him.'[1]

But Commander Haynes' version is that Cunningham arrived on board unnoticed, in 'civvies', asked a boy to direct him to the admiral's cabin and then sent his compliments to Pridham and the commander with the request that they 'attend' him. 'Although Cunningham later indicated his private amusement when he wrote it up for his book, his amusement was far from apparent at the time,' Haynes insists.

It did not take long for the crew to adjust to 'ABC' – his initials – as everyone knew him. They found him friendly voiced, even in anger, yet resolute and relentless. He was seldom pessimistic, exuded confidence and inspiration and was fully aware of the needs and needlings of lower-deck life. When he appeared on the bridge, he would ask: 'Are there any dirty stories this morning?' Or he would end a stormy encounter with staff or ratings with a peace-offering from a tin of sweets he kept by him. Sympathy was never lacking in Cunningham, and one of his first actions endeared him to the wardroom, if not to Pridham. The berthing accident several months earlier, which had killed an ordinary seaman, was blamed by a board of inquiry on the quarterdeck lieutenant-commander and he was 'disciplined', but Cunningham studied the minutes and decided that the accident was the responsibility of 'those on the bridge'. He had the board's decision reversed and cleared the name of the officer.

The *Hood*, her officers and her ratings were to become involved in new dashing roles at sea and ashore under Cunningham, who after twenty-four years in destroyers expected the battle cruiser to be handled like a destroyer, too. In one operation, however, his liking for the greyhounds of the sea flashed back on him. He decided the *Hood* should refuel the *Cossack*, a new Tribal-class destroyer, although she was not properly equipped for it. After completion, the admiral's bath was mysteriously half full of oil. Lieutenant (E) C.F. Kemp, who was later to attain flag rank, was ordered to appear before Pridham. He explains: 'As we were not fitted for this type of operation, we used a boiler-room fire-and-bilge pump, discharging from our oil fuel filling main. There was concern, however, that there was a discrepancy between the amount of oil discharged and that received by the *Cossack*. I was shattered on being sent for and told there was oil in Cunningham's bath. The evaporators were in the engine-room, for which I was responsible, and I had visions of being court-martialled.'

The mystery was solved by the discovery of a large dead rat, which had been sucked into the boiler-room fire-and-bilge pump and lodged in the overboard discharge valve. Consequently a lot of oil intended for the *Cossack* was pumped into the sea. The escaping fuel followed the bilge keel and was sucked back in by the evaporators; some had run into Cunningham's bath. The main and turbo generator condensers were also contaminated. 'Pink gins in the wardroom had a paraffin flavour for about a week afterwards, despite all our endeavours to clean out the oil,' says Kemp.

Ashore the men became the lifeblood of Malta, now in the middle of a social whirl which has never been equalled. At the centre of the social scene were Pridham's three attractive daughters, Anne, Elizabeth and Joan, known as 'the three Graces', who had a host of admirers. For Anne the *Hood* became a match-maker.

Commander Gould, who as a midshipman had served in the ship when she was involved in the miners' strikes, was now skipper of HMS *Thames*, which with the *Severn* and *Clyde* was the Navy's largest submarine. Early in 1937, when the *Thames* was anchored close to the *Hood*, he tried to photograph the two to compare the submarine's length of 345 feet with that of the battle cruiser's 860 feet. It was then that he met Pridham, and later he was introduced to Anne. A rapid romance followed and Pridham was given permission to hold their wedding reception in the *Hood* on 27 July 1937, the ship's first and only marriage celebration.

The honeymoon was over now for Cunningham's squadron, which consisted of the *Hood* and *Repulse*, the carrier *Glorious* and the repair ship *Resource*, for they were to alternate in a mission of vigilance and a showing of strength in the triangle formed off Barcelona, Majorca and Valencia. The ship was darkened in all ports for fear of air raids by both sides, and tin hats were worn on the upper deck. After ten days of being confined, the ratings were allowed shore leave in Marseilles.

When the squadron returned to Malta to re-victual, Cunningham joined Pound in the *Barham* on a mission to Oran, where they discussed details with the French Admiral Esteva for the Nyon patrols, named after the conference of neutrals who devised a system of protection for non-belligerent vessels off Spain. In the autumn of 1937 British ships were being sunk without warning. At first it was believed to be the work of Spanish Nationalist submarines, but Cunningham had no doubt that the Italians were responsible, and this belief was given substance when

Mussolini did not send delegates to the Nyon Conference.

Most of Cunningham's time during his second Spanish sortie was spent gathering eye-witness reports of incidents, arranging destroyer patrols and protesting to the Spanish Admiral Francesco Moreno about the 'high-handed treatment of some British ship or another'. Quick trips were made to Valencia and Barcelona to visit British consuls and to allay their fears. Cunningham boasted about *Hood*'s prestige by claiming: 'Almost every day we spent at Palma squadrons of Italian S.79s roared overhead to bomb Valencia or Barcelona, though when we lay off these ports the bombers never came, so the inhabitants were glad of our arrival.'[2]

The *Hood* arrived back in Malta during the first week of November for festivities to mark the visit of the French commander-in-chief Admiral Abrial, in the cruiser *Algèrie*, and for Christmas leave. There were four days of heavy wining and dining of the French, with Cunningham entertaining most of the time in the *Hood* because he and his wife had only a small flat ashore. Just before Christmas his appointment was confirmed as permanent. In his moment of celebration he also felt for Blake, his predecessor, and wrote: 'He was another serious loss to the Navy and undoubtedly one who would have risen to the very top.'[3] For the third time an admiral's sea career had come virtually to a standstill in the *Hood*.

Another 'anti-piracy' patrol off Spain brought the opening of mysterious submarine attacks on shipping. Five months earlier the Admiralty had authorized counter-attacks against any submarine which interfered with British vessels, and this led to destroyers depth-charging the Italian submarine *Iride* after a torpedo missed HMS *Havock*. The *Iride* was severely shaken but escaped. Since that day at the end of August 1937, submarine piracy had died down, but when the *Hood* was patrolling the coast between Barcelona and Valencia from 11 to 14 January, news came of the torpedoing of the Dutch freighter *Hannah*. On 16 January the *Hood* was in Palma, and Cunningham had to go through the courtesy of dining the Italian Admiral Conte Alberto Marenco di Moriondo and his staff. Cunningham took the chance of bluntly asking his guests whether an Italian submarine might have sunk the *Hannah*. Moriondo promised an investigation, but this did not materialize, and Cunningham was forced to warn the Italians that the sinking was too close to a British patrol zone for his liking.

Attacks continued. On 31 January signals streamed in to the *Hood* of the plight of the British steamer *Endymion*. She had been torpedoed by an unknown submarine – the third transgression against British ships in eleven days – and had sunk sixteen miles south of Cape Tinoso. There were only four survivors out of a crew of fifteen. This time Cunningham took action. He ordered three destroyers to sweep the area but stressed they must keep outside the three-mile limit. It was purely sabre-rattling by the admiral. There was no chance of making contact, but after this show of strength he set up a policy of regular patrols ten miles off this now dangerous coast.

On 3 February he handed over and thankfully headed in the *Hood* for Malta. 'I was not at all sorry when an admiral from the Home Fleet relieved me at Palma,'[4] he said. Soon Cunningham heard he was to be relieved of command of the squadron, too, and was to become Deputy Chief of Naval Staff.

The admiral in the *Hood* might have been in favour with his superiors, but the captain was falling out with them. For the third time in six years the Invergordon mutiny repercussions resounded around the *Hood*. The Admiralty had already published its *Notes on dealing with insubordination*, which underlined that officers must indicate 'unmistakably that they intend to retain or regain control' and that 'shooting to kill should only be resorted to as a last extremity'.[5] But times had changed; the climate was cooler, and old wounds were not to be re-opened: in 1938 the Admiralty issued another confidential memorandum entitled *Disaffection*, which they required to be read to all officers. Pridham took a violent dislike to its title. He considered it should have been called *Mutiny* and prepared his own memorandum under this heading, which every officer joining *Hood* had to study. It veered from original Admiralty advice and instructed officers to isolate ringleaders in a mutiny. As a senior captain, Pridham brought his memorandum to the Admiralty's attention but did not receive a reply. Now, in order to avoid confusing his officers, Pridham chose not to make them aware of the new memorandum and relied on his own policy document.

Nevertheless, he told Admiral Pound, the commander-in-chief, that he was ignoring Admiralty guidance. Unfortunately for him, he did not know that it was Pound, as Second Sea Lord, who had composed the memorandum. After this Pound, who was to become First Sea Lord in June 1939, never spoke to Pridham again. The incident was to affect Pridham's career: he was one of the most senior captains and, although promised command of a cruiser squadron, he was never to receive a sea-going commission again and was to spend the war ashore, first in the inferior appointment as Flag Officer, Humber, and then as vice-president, and finally president, of the Ordnance Board.

Back in Gibraltar the *Hood* became involved in a fortnight of niceties during what was called a 'stand easy' period. There was a scare during the 'holiday', however. It was rumoured that the Italian Navy, who were experimenting already with frogmen, had planted a pernicious spreading weed in harbours and on the sides of ships to block their openings. Ex-Able Seaman Hard, a diver who had recovered from the shock of nearly losing an arm in the gunnery accident a year earlier, says: 'This fantastic story was received while we were in Gibraltar, and I was sent down to inspect the sides of the *Hood* for this weed. After several dives I couldn't find a sign of any.'

When Cunningham in the *Hood*, accompanied by the *Repulse*, arrived at Majorca on 28 March for another month of Nyon patrols, it was obvious that a Nationalist victory could not be denied long. From the beginning of April the *Hood* became involved in a series of evacuations, as the plight of the Loyalist government in Barcelona became irretrievable. She was supply ship for the embassies as she landed much-needed stores; she was a mercy ship as she picked up more than a hundred evacuees; she was spy ship as Cunningham reported military movements.

Rear-Admiral Kemp recalls the evacuation of senior members of a convent from Barcelona: 'The mother superior was concerned that there was no key available for her cabin in the *Hood*. It was mislaid and she protested: "I have guarded my chastity for eighty years – and I'm not going to take chances now." But the key was found and she slept soundly.'

In Barcelona, where two thousand had died in air raids, citizens went about their business with 'remarkable stoicism', according to Cunningham. He was surprised to find the Rambla 'crammed with stalls with every imaginable spring flower'.[6] Yet again it was stressed to him that the *Hood*'s frightening size and power could act as a peacemaker, for once more the sky raiders stayed away.

For twenty-four days the *Hood* shuttled from Palma to Caldetas, Valencia and Barcelona, and then on 21 April she sailed for Golfe Juan in the South of France for a 'rest cure' and what the Admiralty earlier would have termed a mutiny. During the ten-day stay the townsfolk queued for boats to the ship, attended dinners on board and enjoyed a *thé dansant*. In return the crew were hailed as heroes and drank their leave away in the bars and cafés. On their last 'liberty', ratings were due back at 7.30 a.m., but when boats arrived to collect them, there were only a handful of men waiting. The remainder were spending their last francs in nearby bars. When their money ran out, the café owners supplied drinks 'on the house' because the men had been big spenders. The *Hood* should have been under way at 8 a.m., but half an hour later the bars were still full of revellers. Among them was Stoker Harry Holderness, who remembers: 'No one was interested in returning until a stoker petty officer, who had drunk his fill, said he was going aboard – and soon we were all following him.

'When the boats arrived at the *Hood*, which was three miles out, the officers were furious because the ship had not sailed. Most of us were singing and waving long French loaves. Commander Orr-Ewing called for us to be quiet and ordered the coxswains to take the boats round the ship until we were silent. But that set us singing "Side, Side, Jolly Ship's Side". Once round, however, we all quietened and filed aboard.'

There were too many drunks for the commander to put in cells, and most were due on watch, so they were allowed to change into their working rig and resume their duties. 'The stoker petty officer, who had drunk too much, got a recommend for getting us all aboard,' says Holderness.

Both admiral and captain were about to leave. On 20 August the *Hood* returned to an empty Grand Harbour at Malta. Pridham was to be relieved within a few days, and he was determined to mark his farewell by speeding the great ship into Bighi for a breath-taking finale. The cable parties knew their skipper wanted to put on a show and were at their fastest and smartest. As the *Hood* came in backwards, Pridham ordered full speed ahead on all engines to bring her to a halt before reaching shoal water. 'The ship's company handled the bridles ahead and the two six-and-a-half inch hawsers astern admirably in record time before the commander-in-chief,' he later wrote in his unpublished memoirs. 'The captain of a P and O ship in harbour told the Admiral Superintendent of the Dockyard he had never seen a more spectacular piece of ship handling.'[7]

But Pound did not convey his compliments. His animosity to Pridham over the *Disaffection* memorandum continued, and he refused to see him for a courtesy farewell. Nevertheless, Pridham, who handed over to Captain H.T.C. Walker, made a triumphant exit. He left in his beloved white galley with the crew pulling the traditional 'disappearing stroke' and the ship's company lining the rails to cheer him to the shore. The day after, he visited hospital, where his daughter Anne had just given birth to her first son.

On 22 August came the end of the other half of the partnership which had 'chamferred' the ship and her crew into a feared, fighting machine. Cunningham could not delay his return to Britain any longer, for the Admiralty expected him to take up his new appointment as DCNS on 17 October. With regret he struck his flag and left command of the squadron to Vice-Admiral Geoffrey Layton. With him went a young leading hand, Percy Watts, whose ability and seamanship Cunningham had noticed in the *Hood*. Watts was the epitome of discreetness and was to be with him in all his future exploits.

The Admiralty, world acclaim and a chest full of medals awaited Cunningham. His fame was to promote many yarns, and a host of them emanated from his *Hood* days. There was that of his flag lieutenant James Munn, who disclosed that one of Cunningham's after-dinner pranks was to make guests lie on the deck and throw ping-pong balls into an electric light bowl hanging from the deckhead. Or that of Captain J.S.S. Smith, who swore that Cunningham climbed the *Hood*'s gangway without his trousers, which he had soaked when fishing. Or that of Surgeon-Commander Wolton, who, in his dental surgery in the *Hood*, filled two holes in Cunningham's upper molars only to find that secretly the admiral wore a small denture which fitted into the cavities he had just blocked!

With a new team on the bridge, blunders in seamanship and gunnery began to dog the *Hood* again. Neither Admiral Layton, a submarine hero of the First World War, captain of the *Renown* and former commodore of the RN Barracks, Portsmouth, nor Captain Walker took a firm enough hand in control. This was understandable because Layton knew he was to transfer his flag to the *Barham* soon, while Walker would relinquish the captaincy when she went into dockyard for six months at Portsmouth during the New Year.

A major navigating mistake came on her first cruise under the new partnership to Gibraltar, where she grounded. The port side around the bulge and buoyancy spaces was damaged and there was a slight leak. This did not impair efficiency, but she was not fully seaworthy. The date was 20 September 1938, and it could not have happened at a worse time, for, with Hitler on the brink of invading the Sudeten-German districts of Czechoslovakia, war seemed inevitable. Instead of going into Malta's floating dock, the *Hood* was placed on wartime readiness, like the rest of the Navy. On 28 September the crew were roused early at the Rock and told they were to put to sea because within twenty-four hours it could be war.

The Admiralty ordered the *Hood* to steam into the Atlantic under cover of night and shadow the German pocket battleship *Deutschland*, which had been in Tangier and was presumed to be tracking the liner *Aquitania*, carrying RNR and RNVR reservists to various outposts. 'Full battle stations' was piped, which meant duty around the clock, until a temporary stand-down. There was confused apprehension throughout the ship. She still had to be fitted with a tannoy system, and Captain Walker passed the information by word of mouth through the different departmental heads. Because of her size, the *Hood* was an ideal talking-ground for the rumour-monger, and on this mission the gossip was wilder than ever. Ex-Shipwright Haynes writes: 'As chippies we were responsible for the very meagre damage control and repair arrangements, so we spent the first few hours checking equipment, tools and shoring timber. None of us had any experience of war. There was one thing which we did understand – if war came, the first naval action could well be between us and the *Deutschland*.'

For twenty-four hours the *Hood* steamed on in the darkness of speculation, not making contact with either the *Deutschland* or the *Aquitania*. Then came the dramatic announcement on the radio that Prime Minister Neville Chamberlain had signed the Munich Agreement and that appeasement was to take the place of war. Cheers went round the *Hood* as the news was circulated. An immediate reversal of the ship was ordered by the Admiralty, and soon she was back in Gibraltar, preparing for another Spanish patrol. A day later the captain of the *Deutschland* was given permission to enter Gibraltar to re-store. Extra shore patrols were landed that night by every Navy ship for fear of brawls between British matelots and the Germans. 'But there was not an angry word, nor a scene between the two sides,' says Haynes. 'Jack' and 'Jerry' got on famously for ten days, and the battle at sea which did not materialize became a contest on shore, with the *Hood* beating the *Deutschland* at soccer.

On 24 November, after Layton had transferred to the *Barham*, the *Hood* was taken into floating dock at Parlatorio, Malta. It was designed to hold sixty thousand tons, and by removing four thousand tons of oil it was assessed that there was ample margin for lifting. But as she was raised, the straining dockside structures leaned inwards. After this experience the dockyard superintendent refused to accept the *Hood* again, unless she was de-stored, defuelled and de-ammunitioned.

The opportunity was taken to carry out part of the refit and to add extra AA guns. Ordnance workers sweated in vain, for within six months the AA system was to be revamped again.

On 10 January 1939, the day Commander Orr-Ewing was

relieved by Commander William Davies, who had been fleet torpedo officer in the *Nelson*, the Maltese said farewell to the *Hood*, whose crew had bolstered the island's economy for nearly three years of intermittent visits. She arrived at Portsmouth on 18 January 1939 for her first major refit. Malta was never to see her again, although in the years of siege ahead she was to help the beleaguered island.

PART II

The Frightened

by Ted Briggs

13

A Boy Goes to War

There she lay – the 'Mighty *'ood'*, as sailors called her, the world's most famous and powerful warship, which had been the impetus of my ambition to join the Royal Navy. It was 29 July 1939, early, bright and sunny. The *Hood* was to be my home for the next two years, and the war, which was to bring her disastrous demise, was just thirty-six days away.

I had signed on as a signal boy just a week after my fifteenth birthday, on 7 March 1938. During sixteen months in the whitened sepulchre of HMS *Ganges*, the boys' training ship at Shotley Gate, Ipswich, I had hardly dared to hope that I would be sent to the ship of my dreams at the end of my 'apprenticeship ashore'. Then came the joyous listing of my name with twelve other boys from *Ganges* as a draft to the *Hood*.

We were packed off to Portsmouth, where disappointment awaited us. The *Hood* had just completed a six-month refit and apparently could not accommodate in her bulk thirteen eager, bumbling amateurs. Instead we were dumped on board the old battleship *Iron Duke*, which was acting as a depot ship. For a fortnight we were cooped up in this veteran of the First World War, and with each day our enthusiasm drained away. But then, at 8 a.m. on 29 July, we were decanted, like immature, tangy wine, into a three-ton lorry, which was to take us to the South Railway Jetty – known to sailors as 'Farewell Jetty' because it was usually the last berth of a capital ship before leaving for a foreign commission of $2\frac{1}{2}$ years. As the lorry dawdled along the wharves, cruisers and destroyers came into view, and we chanted out each name as we passed them. Then ahead there loomed a long forecastle with three gigantic gun turrets at the end. 'There she is,' cried my closest friend, Signal Boy Don Proctor. Ship

131

identification had not been of paramount importance in our training: this was HMS *Nelson*. We cheered as we went by her.

The excitement was making me queasy; my stomach seemed empty, although I had just breakfasted, and my lips were dry where I had been biting them in expectation. And then we saw her. This time there was no mistaking her. That enormous forecastle could belong to no other ship. She was awe-inspiring. She dwarfed everything around her. I had never felt so small and insignificant, yet at the same time there was an immense surge of pride and patriotism through me. I truly believed that at sixteen I had achieved my lifetime ambition. I was staring at my destiny, obviously unaware of the part that this grey, gargantuan creature of beauty, grace and immaculate power was to play in my life. 'Beauty' and 'grace' may seem ludicrous to describe a vessel whose primary function was destruction, but to me there was no menace in the huge A and B turrets from which one shell could blast a destroyer out of the sea. She epitomized pride – pride of the Royal Navy, of King and country and Empire, to a boy who had yet to have his ideals blown away in two devastating minutes.

The rough reality of Navy life was bawled back at us as we were ordered to jump down from the lorry and 'fall in' on the jetty with our kitbags and hammocks. Then we were marched up the long gangway to be swallowed by this whirring monster. Everything seemed twice as big as normal. The mess decks were colossal; a series of scrubbed wooden mess-tables reached out at me like massive conjuror's fingers; mess-kids gleamed in imitation of sterling silver; even the overhead hammock bars glinted, while the faint whiff of fuel oil and the constant humming of the air vents engulfed me. This sense of space and clean-cut lines did not diminish in the boys' mess deck, where we were deposited to make ourselves at home.

One of the first tasks of a newcomer to the *Hood* was to find his way about the thousand-plus compartments, although to my knowledge no one had ever seen all of them! There were horrendous stories on the mess decks about lost boys, particularly of a youngster who became seasick and crawled into a funnel casing on the upper deck. He was found dead several days later by a stokers' repair party after he had been reported lost overboard to the captain. My only official tour around the ship was conducted by one of the petty officer instructors. Again, I was too overawed to take it all in.

Yet we soon slipped into the routine, which included long sessions in the schoolroom, studying for educational tests, washing down the long passages of cortecene and sprucing up the paintwork and brass. In addition we were required to keep watch with the rest of the communications branch, which included the yeoman, leading signalman, two signalmen and two boys, or ordinary signalmen. To me it was all a delight in these early days, because the *Hood* always had a friendly family atmosphere about her, something which was unusual for a capital ship and normally found only in destroyers and smaller craft.

Most of the senior ratings were kindly, yet firm, to us boys. On our initial visit to the flag deck my first non-commissioned boss, Yeoman 'Shiner' Wright, assembled us to ask our names. One of my pals who, like the rest of us, was used to addressing everyone as 'sir' above leading seaman at *Ganges*, replied: 'Bell, sir.' He was told immediately: 'Don't call me, "sir". I'm not a commissioned officer, and you are not under training now. You're all sailors.' It was a wonderful way of making a youngster suddenly feel ten feet tall. We had confidence in the ship – albeit, on hindsight, false confidence – and now it was beginning to grow in ourselves.

The refit which the *Hood* had just completed was mainly to improve her armament, particularly the aircraft defence. In our eyes there was not a chink in her armour. Not so in Admiralty eyes. Nine years earlier Admiral Sir Frederic Dreyer, who had flown his flag in the battle cruiser and was then Director of the Gunnery Division, had stated: 'It has become quite obvious to all of us that the improved type of armour-piercing shell with which we had equipped the Grand Fleet in 1918 could easily penetrate and detonate in the *Hood*'s main magazine.'[1] I wish he had told us, for I am certain that few officers aboard were aware of the fact that plans for extra armour for the main deck and over the magazines and machine spaces had been cancelled.

August 1939 brought the beginning of the Polish crisis, as Hitler, backed by a German Press campaign, called for the annexation of the Danzig corridor. For the *Hood* it was a month of hustled preparation and many days at sea on manoeuvres, training a green crew. We exercised with the carrier *Courageous* and the destroyer *Sturdy*, and for my colleagues it was 'darken ship' and 'light up ship', interspersed with full-calibre shoots. But I missed most of this for I contracted impetigo through a rusty razor blade and was sent to isolation in the sick-bay, which was under A turret. My purple, blistered face prevented my applying a razor to a fuzz of brownish hair, and I was reputed to be the only bearded sixteen-year-old in the Navy at that time. The quarters resembled a cottage hospital and included a main ward, composed of twenty bunks, an operating theatre, treatment room and consulting spaces. I lazed in luxury, for the bunks could be unclipped to swing freely if the ship rolled prodigiously.

I was joined in the sick-bay by my old classmate Don Proctor, who had appendicitis. Medicine did not improve his condition, and he was operated on at sea by a surgeon commander. After rapid preparations, the sick-bay suddenly became quiet. Don had died. With other patients in the ward I was ordered to assemble in the treatment room. While we were there, unknown to us, his body was carried through the ward into a nearby cabin. When we returned, I was told by the sick-bay petty officer to wash the floor of the operating theatre. I froze in the doorway. The petty officer realized then that I had been Don's pal. He took me by the arm, led me to the other end of the sick-bay, sat me down and said sympathetically: 'You should have told me, lad, that you were his mate. After you went as white as a sheet and your eyes were like saucers, I knew he was a friend of yours.' He spent the next five minutes placating me. Again it was a timely example of the family spirit in the *Hood*. This was the first experience I had had of death at close hand. The date was 21 August, the very day that Germany and Russia were signing a non-aggression pact as the Wehrmacht prepared for the invasion of Poland.

Yet there seemed no crisis in the *Hood* for me. My most anxious moments were going to the lavatory – the 'heads'. I

found it embarrassing to sit on the throne with only my
genitals covered by the tiny cubicle doors and being able to
see over the top the straining faces of my shipmates,
squatting in long rows like roosting birds. I was too shy to
have discussion with other matelots, which was the general
practice, and in heavy weather tried to contain my motions,
otherwise one risked a sudden dowsing of urine from a
neighbouring lavatory as the ship rolled. The bathroom
could be equally as wet and a trial to my modesty at peak
hours. The drains and scuppers could seldom cope with the
ablutions and laundering of scores of naked matelots, and
the result was a constant flood of four inches of murky water
on the floor. Hence the old expression: 'For you I swim the
stokers' bathroom in full flood backwards.'

Gradually we boys began to settle down to our duties and
to show we could play our part in the running of a fighting
ship, which was just as well, for Rear-Admiral Sir William
Whitworth had just hoisted his flag in the *Hood*, as second in
command of the Home Fleet. Nevertheless, we blundered on,
sometimes the faults being our own and at others those of
our superiors. One of my jobs was being 'boat boy'. This
meant keeping the officer of the watch informed of
approaching craft when in harbour, so that the appropriate
courtesies of piping or sounding bugles could be performed.
We were given binoculars and a pendant list and stationed
on the quarterdeck. I was so obsessed with my importance
the first time I did the duty that I ignored a destroyer which
was under way and about to pass the quarterdeck. At that
moment, Captain Irvine Glennie appeared on deck and
yelled: 'Boy! What's the name of that ship?' The four gold
rings under my nose and the sight of the captain's
authoritative figure brought complete panic. 'H47, sir,' I
stammered, forgetting the pendant list which had been given
me to spell out the destroyer's name. 'I can see that, you
young fool,' barked the captain. 'What's her name?' A few
minutes later a relief arrived on the quarterdeck and I,
thoroughly demoralized, was back washing paintwork.

Another of my special duties I performed more
adequately. As 'cable flags' I had to set myself up on the
forecastle whenever we moored or weighed anchor and
signal by flags to the chief yeoman on the bridge the number

of shackles of cable on deck or whether the anchor was down, away, clear or foul. To be such an important linchpin in the communications system did my ego the world of good, even though the very information which I was signalling was also being sent to the bridge by voice-pipe and telephone!

I have always had a head for heights and enjoyed climbing the ninety-two-foot main mast. Because of this it was I whom the bridge normally detailed to strike the foretop mast whenever the *Hood* passed under the Forth Bridge at Rosyth. I was also sent aloft when a halyard was 'lost' accidentally by one of my fellow 'bunts'. The masts were not difficult to scale, and only the last six feet of the main one, which was a sheer pole, had to be shinned up. One day when a halyard had been blown away on the starboard forward upper yardarm, I was ordered to go up for it. I had inched my way to the end of the yardarm to retain the Inglefield clip when the safety valves in the engine-room were blown. A large cloud of steam swirled up towards me. I clung on grimly but decided that, if the white mist spiralling upwards was hot, I would let go and drop into the sea. I preferred drowning to being boiled alive. But by the time it immersed me the steam had turned into a cold shower.

All the boys, whether they were to become stokers, seamen or signalmen, were subjected to the normal apprentice-type jokes, like getting green oil for the starboard lamps, but I was not expecting to be the target of a hoax on 31 August, the day the fleet mobilized. The *Hood* was entering Scapa Flow to join the *Repulse* and *Renown* as the Battle Cruiser Squadron. It was a serious – and for me emotive – occasion, until I noticed Yeoman Wright and Ivor Holding, a Royal Marine signalman, directing their binoculars towards the shore. 'Quick, there's one over there,' shouted Wright. 'What is it, yeo?' I asked. He handed me a telescope, put the binoculars to his eyes again and replied: 'Just look at them – they're wild haggis. They have webbed feet, a duck's bill and are covered in brown fur.' I scanned the shoreline for several minutes before the guffaws of the two men forced me to realize that I was 'being had'.

During the next twenty-four hours frivolity turned into fervour when we prepared for war, as unit by unit the biggest fleet I have ever seen gathered at Scapa. Battleships, cruisers, carriers, destroyers came and went until it was time for the *Hood* to go. We weighed anchor at 0400 on 1 September and immediately went to action stations. For the next nervous forty-eight hours we were standing down constantly and then being called back again. No longer were there great, wide open spaces below decks: the full wartime complement of just over fourteen hundred men were embarked. At night hammocks were slung in every passageway, in every nook and cranny. Sleeping space was guarded jealously, and once a claim had been staked, it was rarely relaxed. At first I slung my hammock in one of the boys' locker spaces. Later I acquired the 'luxury' of hooking up in the warrant officers' cabin flat aft. Black-out curtains were rigged, and 'darken ship' was piped at sunset. Polishing was down to the minimum, and apart from the working parts of the guns, equipment that sparkled was dulled by gallons of grey paint. The once white decks began to take on a greyish tint, and most of the other woodwork was toned down. All the hangings and 'niceties' – including the many mess pianos – were landed. The *Hood* was never to know peace again.

At 11 a.m. on 3 September, in company with the *Renown* and a group of the fleet, we were on watch with the intention of shadowing German surface raiders which might slip through the Iceland-Faroe Island Channel into the Atlantic. I was on the point of making my first signal in a warship. The flag 'E' was hoisted as a preliminary for a general semaphore message, and Chief Yeoman George Thomas ordered: 'Briggs, get a pair of hand-flags and get up to the fifteen-inch director and show up 46.' It was with a strange sort of pride and yet a sinking feeling in my belly that I spelt out to the fleet: 'Commence hostilities against Germany.' Over the tannoy to all parts of the ship came Prime Minister Chamberlain's almost somnolent, low-key announcement that Britain's ultimatum to Germany to withdraw from the invasion of Poland had expired. It seemed an anticlimax that soon after the *Hood* was ordered to return to Scapa. Our patrol to bottle up the German pocket battleships was in vain, for the *Graf Spee* and *Deutschland* had slipped out into the Atlantic before the end of August. We had been hunting phantoms.

After three days refuelling and revictualling at Scapa, the *Hood* was detailed for her first fully wartime errand. With the *Renown*, the cruisers *Belfast* and *Edinburgh* and four destroyers, we left at dawn for a sweep to the Faroes and Iceland. Our orders were to intercept blockade-running German cargo ships, but fog hampered the mission. On 8 September, the first day at sea, the destroyer *Fury* was despatched by Admiral Whitworth to investigate a false Asdic contact. Two days later the *Fearless* halted a Swedish oiler, which was allowed to proceed, while on the last day of the trip the *Fearless* was sent to search for lifeboats of SS *Kirby*, which had been torpedoed by a U-boat off the Faroes. By 12 September we were back at Scapa to refuel from the tanker *Wardware*. It had been an unspectacular, though tremulous start to the war for me.

From now on the *Hood* seemed to be operating a shuttle patrol out of Scapa. On 14 September we were *en route* to Loch Ewe, on the north-west coast of Scotland, only to return immediately to Scapa, where we rested for a week. The first real piece of excitement, as far as I was concerned, came on 22 September, when we were on patrol in the North Sea. The *Fortune* made contact with a U-boat at 1320. This was confirmed by *Firedrake*, and the bells for action stations awoke the *Hood* from her after-rum slumbers. We zigzagged at twenty-two knots for an hour and then returned to normal conditions. The next day the *Express* sighted a mine off the *Hood*'s port bow and exploded it with rifle fire.

In the boys' mess deck we prattled on about war being a bore, but despite the bravado, most of us were glad to be back at Scapa for divisions on Sunday 24 September, when Admiral Whitworth cleared the lower deck and proceeded to keep the ship's company on their guard by speaking of the necessity for the humdrum patrol work which would be in front of us. Two days later the *Hood* was to smell the enemy's powder.

14

'Look What Just Missed Me'

Our bombing baptism came on 26 September during a curious, swashbuckling foray into the North Sea by the Home Fleet. The previous day Admiral Forbes, the commander-in-chief, had learned that the submarine *Spearfish* had been depth-charged off the Horns Reef, the shoal shaped like a hand which points out from Denmark towards the Dogger. She was unable to dive and began to head for home on the surface. Forbes ordered out the Second Cruiser Squadron with an escort of destroyers to assist her. We and the *Repulse* sailed in company with the Eighteenth Cruiser Squadron to give heavy cover, in case the German capital ships were enticed out. Throughout my time in the *Hood* the captain and commanders believed in keeping the ship's company informed of what action might be ahead of them and what was expected of them. On this occasion we were well briefed on the situation over the tannoy from the moment of leaving harbour.

For most of that day we were at standing action stations – also known as 'second degree of readiness' – but the full call to arms did not come. The force penetrated deep into the North Sea to contact the *Spearfish*, and then we turned about and headed for Scapa. The way home was led by the *Nelson*, the Home Fleet's flagship, and the *Rodney* in the northern column, with the famed aircraft-carrier *Ark Royal* in the centre and the *Hood* and *Repulse* to the south. In the forenoon our group were spotted by a Dornier flying-boat, but at this stage of the war the Navy lost little sleep over the Luftwaffe, and the Dornier headed for base without a parting shot from the fleet.

Fortunately for us, only thirteen bombers from Wester-land, Sylt, could be got into the air, and four of them –

Goering's 'wonder aircraft', the Junkers 88 – were aimed at the *Hood*'s section of the fleet. They arrived in eight-tenths cloud at nine thousand feet. The attacks were unco-ordinated, and the first I saw of them was from the flag deck when the *Ark Royal* disappeared behind high walls of bomb burst spray. It was while I was 'goofing', like everyone else, at this explosive display of cascades that I heard someone yell, 'Look at that bastard.' I did – and was transfixed by the sight of a JU 88 almost overhead at about five hundred feet. A massive, black object, which seemed to be as big as a London bus, tumbled gently from it and almost in slow motion fell towards the *Hood*'s quarterdeck. A great flash, a crump and a cold clamminess unfroze me, and I found myself blown to the deck. I got to my feet, and below and abaft the flag deck I could see the crew of the pom-pom shaking from their clothes the black, dirty water spewed up by the explosion. They had not fired a shot at the bomber, which had been piloted bravely by Leutnant Storp of the Adler Geschwader (KG 30), who cost me a clean pair of underpants. In fact, not one of the *Hood*'s guns had opened up. The bomb caught us a glancing blow on the port quarter, bounced off and exploded harmlessly in the sea. Rivets were sprung in the torpedo bulge, there were minor breakages in the stokers' bathroom, and the port gash chute and boom were peppered with shrapnel. If the *Hood* had been a few yards further ahead, it was likely the bomb would have penetrated the quarterdeck. We were lucky to escape so lightly in this first encounter of the war between bomber and battleship.

It served as a warning to the ship's company to be on the alert for air attack and prepared us for stormier days ahead in the Mediterranean. The immediate effect was for Admiral Forbes, in the *Nelson*, to make a general signal of 'Negative DG', which meant 'Manoeuvre badly executed'. Later all ships were told to 'buck up' while in his official despatch he stated that the control personnel were unprepared obviously for such high-performance dive-bombing. In fact, all of our gunners had been waiting for permission from the bridge to open fire.

The next day in harbour we boys were digging out with jack-knives the bomb splinters in the lower boom. My piece of metal found its way home to my mother with the note: 'Look what just missed me.' She probably needed the assurance, for already Lord Haw-Haw was proclaiming on Hamburg Radio that the *Ark Royal* had been sunk and that the *Hood* was badly damaged. So much credence was given to later German claims of the *Hood*'s being repaired in dry dock that Prime Minister Chamberlain had to reassure Clement Attlee in the House of Commons: 'It is not true and I must repeat it once again – though by now the news grows stale through repetition – that neither the *Hood* nor the *Repulse*, nor any other capital ship has suffered the least damage.' Reports of this in most of the popular newspapers of 19 October stated that Chamberlain's reply was followed by laughter and cheers – and that in turn was echoed in the *Hood*'s mess decks.

It was in October that Winston Churchill, then the First Lord at the Admiralty, paid his first visit to us. I was on the flag deck and only saw him leave the ship in the admiral's barge, giving one of the first of his famous victory signs.

For the next six months the *Hood*'s routine became long days and piercingly cold nights at sea, punctuated with unsuccessful sorties and unfulfilled scares. We boys were being honed not only to razor sharpness but also to a keen sense of survival. When we went to our stations during the Atlantic patrols, there was a scramble for the lee side of the flag deck. It was usually very unwise to be on the weather edge for more than an hour at a time because it took a further two hours to thaw out. One unofficial punishment if we did anything wrong was to be sent to the side which caught the worst of the weather. 'Telescope soup' was also dished out as a penalty. This meant receiving a sharp blow with the leading signalman's telescope on the elbow or funny bone. The consequence was that we were guilty of few misdemeanours.

It was in the schoolroom that we did not care. Although we had instructor officers aboard, Able Seaman 'Tommo' Thompson taught us most of the elementary subjects which would push us through ET1 (Educational Test One). He was a three-badge man and one of the longest serving of the ship's company. He was highly intelligent and should have been commissioned, but strangely he preferred to remain an able seaman. Yet when my attention wandered, he would tell me: 'Look at me, son. If I had not been like you and paid attention at school, I would be a warrant schoolmaster by now.' It was these words of wisdom which gave me an education and which eventually led me to a commission. I never forgot old 'Tommo'.

The *Hood* was always held in readiness to thwart a break-out by an enemy surface raider, and on 8 October we were despatched at high speed, with the *Repulse* and the cruisers *Sheffield* and *Aurora*, to cover the Northern Approaches a hundred miles off Bergen, Norway. Over the tannoy Captain Glennie explained that a Coastal Command aircraft had spotted the battle cruiser *Gneisenau*, with the heavy cruiser *Köln* and nine destroyers, steaming north out of the Skagerrak. Admiral Whitworth's orders were to prevent any outflanking movements by the Germans.

For two days we swore and grumbled about the cold on the flag deck, while Whitworth waited for more intelligence reports. When no news of the enemy was received, he headed the *Hood* for the Butt of Lewis. In the afternoon of 10 October a signal reached us that the *Gneisenau* and escorts had retreated two days earlier and had entered the Skagerrak again. There was no quarry to chase. Later we learned that it was a ruse by Admiral Raeder to draw out the Home Fleet as targets for Goering's bombers again. Normally we would have returned to Scapa Flow, but this time with the *Rodney* and six destroyers we entered Loch Ewe, another barren naval outpost on the west coast of Scotland, facing the Outer Hebrides.

The *Hood* wasted little time at Loch Ewe. After twenty-four hours we were raising steam again to join the *Nelson*, *Rodney*, *Furious*, *Aurora*, *Belfast* and nine destroyers to help the Northern patrol intercept German merchantmen on their way back to their homeland through the Denmark Strait. The very name still chills me like the winds which knifed this barren edge of the Arctic Circle. To keep the hunt going, we refuelled the destroyers at sea and learned to curse the cold and the enemy but we had no regrets that we searched in vain. Elsewhere the Germans were hunting for us, for in an air raid on Scapa the *Iron Duke* had been damaged by three near-misses and forced to beach. Scapa was deemed to be unsafe for us, so we returned to Loch Ewe.

As Hitler's U-boat packs swarmed out of the Jade, the waters around the Orkneys were becoming more hazardous for the *Hood*, although I did not know of one particularly close call until after the war. On 30 October we set out with the *Rodney* and *Nelson*, who were 'our chummies', as part of a covering force for a convoy carrying iron ore from Narvik to the Firth of Forth. Apparently at 10 a.m., when west of the Orkneys, Leutnant Wilhelm Zahn, the skipper of *U56*, found he had penetrated accidentally our zigzagging destroyer screen. Through his periscope he was horrified to see the *Hood*, *Nelson* and *Rodney* heading towards him. Suddenly we turned through an angle of nearly thirty degrees, which put the *U56* in perfect firing position. The *Rodney*, which was the leading ship, passed out of the field of fire, and this made the primary target, the *Nelson*, which was close to the *Hood*. From nine hundred yards Zahn aimed three torpedoes at her. The first two clanged against the *Nelson*'s side but failed to explode. The third missed.

Blissfully ignorant of this escape, our force bucketed in a heavy swell towards the Lofoten Islands, Norway. Tons of water thrashed over the *Hood*'s forecastle and then boomed on to the quarterdeck. At times it seemed that the stern would never re-appear again. On the flag deck the scathing wind and spray turned cheeks numb in minutes, while in the fug below decks the groaning of her frames, plating and superstructure gave notice of the *Hood*'s age. Twenty-four hours in these seas were enough for man, boy and ship, and thankfully we put in at Greenock.

During this period of the incongruously named phoney war — at least for the Navy — the Admiralty became increasingly concerned of the danger of a break-out into the Atlantic by the *Gneisenau* and *Scharnhorst*, currently trapped in Wilhelmshaven. For this reason the *Hood* was sent to Plymouth during November. It was a welcome change from the icy blasts of the Shetlands and enabled us to enjoy the doubtful delights of Devonport and Union Street. We even began to hope that there would be Christmas leave. Then, on 21 November, the Admiralty's fears became reality. The *Gneisenau* and the *Scharnhorst*, with the cruisers *Köln* and *Leipzig* and a strong destroyer escort, swept into the Skagerrak. Without being detected, the two bigger warships penetrated the Shetland-Norway passage. Two days later the merchant cruiser *Rawalpindi*, a former P & O liner, armed with eight old six-inch guns, engaged them in her famous suicidal fourteen-minute battle, which ended in her obliteration. With the cruisers *Newcastle* and *Delhi* approaching, the German pair sped off.

The alarm bells were ringing now in most of the ships of the Home Fleet – and that included the *Hood* at Plymouth. Admiral Forbes wanted every available vessel at sea immediately.

As the *Hood* scythed out of Plymouth in heavy weather, we on the flag deck heard that for the first and only time Britain's mightiest ship was to come under the command of a French admiral, based in Brest. In mid-Channel we rendezvoused with the French battle cruiser *Dunkerque*, in which Vice-Admiral Gensoul was flying his flag, and the cruisers *Montcalm* and *Georges Leygues*, soon known to our ship's company as 'Gorgeous Legs'. Both forces had their own destroyer escorts. From the flag deck I managed to get glimpses of the *Dunkerque*, which, although smaller than the *Hood*, had a Continental rakishness about her that I admired. My fellow signalmen were scornful of the fact that she possessed only thirteen-inch guns. Even if we had been warned that in eight months time she would be an enemy and that we would be firing at her, instead of signalling friendly courtesies, none of us would have heeded. This was the first combined Franco-British naval operation of the war, and everyone was determined that it would be a success. The ship's company were fully aware that in the next two days they might be in action against the German hit-and-runners, as we ploughed through tremendous, troughing seas towards a position sixty degrees north, twenty degrees west.

In this area, just south of Iceland, was a shoal known as 'Bill Bailey's Bank', and it was here that we were to wait for an 'interpose' between a convoy and the German raiders. We were supposed to be in unison as the combined force pitched off the west coast of Ireland, but so high was the sea running that it appeared from the *Hood* that we were alone as the other vessels became shrouded in grey spray. For two days the battering continued, and then came the blessed relief of a recall. The *Gneisenau* and *Scharnhorst* were safely tied up in Wilhelmshaven. As the weather deteriorated, they had doubled back on their course, evaded the cruiser patrols and slipped far to the south before Forbes' storm-hindered battleships could arrive.

Back in Plymouth we appreciated the snugness of the haven even more. Christmas in Plymouth? We were too optimistic, for by 3 December the *Hood* had returned to Loch Ewe for refuelling in readiness for convoy protection work. I hated the place. Scapa, which was desolate enough, was a beauty spot in comparison. Few of us bothered to go ashore. The loch was being used as the Home Fleet's main base because the defences of Scapa were being improved after the torpedoing of the *Royal Oak* there two months earlier. Strangely, this switching of bases brought Admiral Forbes more trouble, and on the day after our arrival the *Nelson* was damaged by a magnetic mine as she was entering the loch. With the *Rodney* incapacitated because of serious defects, it meant that the *Hood* was the only capital ship available to the Home Fleet.

We, too, were in dire need of a refit. The maximum speed was down to twenty-five knots, rust, that creeping brown peril, was fingering up the sides, and our superstructure was caked with salt. We were putting in more sea time than any other ship in the world, and we could not, and would not, be spared.

While we were at Loch Ewe there came the 'buzz' that something big was on. Indeed, there was. Five liners carrying 7,450 men were in mid-Atlantic. This was the first Canadian troop convoy of the war from Halifax, in the care of the *Furious, Repulse, Emerald, Hunter* and *Hyperion*. The *Hood* and her destroyer escort were to provide extra cover. Our orders were to steam to the Clyde and leave there on 13 December, but twenty-four hours earlier we were heading north to lock up another suspected Atlantic break-out. This time the light cruisers *Leipzig, Nürnberg* and *Köln,* accompanied by five destroyers, had been sighted by Coastal Command aircraft and the submarine *Salmon* in the central North Sea. Admiral Forbes misinterpreted the intention of this foray, however. It was a minelaying sortie towards the west, and as soon as this was revealed, the *Hood* was ordered back to the Clyde and then out to the Atlantic with the *Warspite*, *Barham* and six destroyers to meet the Canadians. The only piece of excitement after our rendezvous came from an allied ship, when the SS *Samaria*, which was steaming in the opposite direction, steered into the convoy and collided with the *Furious* and the liner *Aquitania*. The *Hood* stood by, but we were not needed and returned to port two days afterwards.

We were now spending more time at sea than in harbour, with most of our duties involving the Northern Patrol. It was a lonely existence, for rarely did we come into close contact with convoys, but we were strategically placed to intervene if surface raiders threatened. The grey days stretched interminably before us on the flag deck. Christmas Day and New Year's Eve were almost indistinguishable from the rest. For most of February we worked from Greenock, with Clydeside a reassuring respite to Loch Ewe, to which the *Hood* was never to return.

By now I was messenger to the flag lieutenant, a plum job for a signal boy. I had to follow Lieutenant-Commander J.M. Villiers at a discreet distance, run his errands and supply him with copies of signals throughout the day. I was given the grand title of 'staff signalman' and felt extremely smug about my position – until one night on Atlantic patrol. During the first watch, at around 2230, I was given a message by the flag lieutenant to take to Commander Davies, who was in his cabin aft. I dashed down the ladder from the compass platform to the admiral's bridge and was trotting across to the ladder to the flag deck when I bumped into a soft body. There was a crash, a strangled grunt and the shout 'Yeoman!' On the deck I could just make out the stretched-out figure of Admiral Whitworth. I was escorted away from the scene by 'Shiner' Wright, who promptly blasted me for being so careless. Within the next hour I was given a 'rocket' by everyone on the bridge from Captain Glennie downwards. The admiral was about to leave the *Hood*, and I thought that this *faux pas* would be removed from my record the day he went, for rarely does an admiral remember a boy, but Whitworth, who was something of a martinet, was kind enough to remember me more than a year later when we met again in more emotional circumstances.

In March 1940, with signs of a German build-up for the invasion of Norway, the *Hood*'s operational zone was based on the east coast again, and we alternated between Scapa and the Firth of Forth. The first mission was on 2 March with the battleship *Valiant* and six destroyers. We provided assistance for a convoy from Norway. It was an uneventful five-day stint, and we returned to Scapa yawning from lack of sleep and boredom. But within twenty-four hours we had to be on the top line for another visit by Churchill. The old warrior was aboard the *Rodney*, which was prevented from entering harbour because two magnetic mines had been dropped by a German plane the previous night. I understand that Churchill was never informed that it was the *Hood*'s fault he had to transfer by admiral's barge. We had been the anti-aircraft guard ship on the night of the raid and had allowed in a 'Jerry', who circled the Flow and then let loose the mines. A week later fourteen Heinkel 111s attacked the Flow. No bombs fell near us, but the commander of the Nazi squadron claimed direct hits on the *Hood*, *Repulse* and *Renown*.

When Admiral Whitworth struck his flag on 11 March and transferred to the *Renown*, it was obvious to everyone on board that at last the *Hood* was to have that long overdue refit. Our lovely old girl was beginning to show signs of engine strain, and many times A and Y turrets had to be drained by deck tackle because the argoline oil and distilled water hydraulics systems had filled with salt water. Air raids had also proved that the anti-aircraft defences were still not sufficient. Our last trip north was around the Shetlands and down to Greenock, where we stayed for several days.

As one *Hood* moved out of Clydeside on 30 March, so another moved in. The newcomer was one of Churchill's decoys. On his third day back at the Admiralty he had revived the First World War idea of constructing dummy capital ships to fool enemy reconnaissance planes. With the approval of Admiral Pound, he had ordered six decoy frames to be set up on merchant ships, but only three were built. We considered ourselves fortunate that we had a 'double', and indeed it served its purpose because I understand it took the people of Greenock several days to tumble to it that the real

Hood had gone. My older 'oppo' on the flag deck, Marine Holding, was in trouble with his girl friend ashore because of the dummy. She, too, believed that the *Hood* was in port and thought that, because she was not seeing him, he had ditched her!

Admiral Sir Roger Keyes, the first admiral to fly his flag in the *Hood*.

Admiral Sir Frederick Field, who commanded during the World Cruise and later became First Sea Lord.

Admiral Sir Andrew Cunningham in his Mediterranean days of glory.

Vice-Admiral Lancelot Holland who went down with the *Hood*.

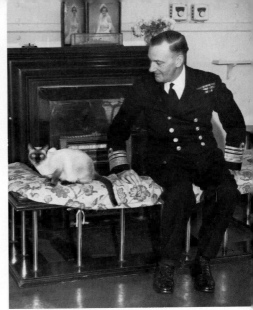

Above left: King George VI and Queen Elizabeth with Vice-Admiral W. J. Whitworth, the *Hood's* first flag officer in the Second World War, who had a double encounter with Ted Briggs.

Above right: Vice-Admiral Sir James Somerville with his cat, Figaro, which he always took on his flagships.

Below: Workmen repairing the damage after the collision with the *Renown*.

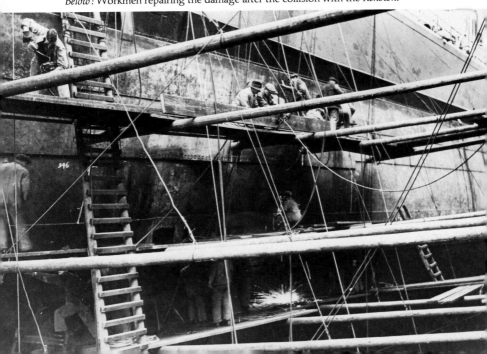

Rough seas off Spain. *Hood*'s A and B turrets are painted red, white and blue to signify her neutrality during the Spanish Civil War.

Anti-aircraft gun crews ready for action in 1939, replaced by twin four-inch dual purpose guns in 1940. Gas masks were always ready, although never necessary.

Despite the war, lessons go on at sea under the eye of the ship's 'schoolie', as midshipmen take bearings from the sun.

The *Hood* peppered with splashes from Italian bombs in an abortive foray towards Cagliari, Sardinia on 9 July 1940 – picture taken from HMS *Ark Royal*.

The *Hood* close up to *Ark Royal* (right) as the Italian Air Force strikes off Sardinia — taken from HMS *Delhi*.

The four-inch dual purpose gunners in 1940, just before the *Hood* was sent on the Oran mission.

Left: The bombardment of Oran begins. Among the shell bursts on the right are those of the *Hood.*

Right: The last picture of the *Hood* as a fighting force, just before the massive explosion which destroyed her — taken from HMS *Prince of W*

Below: The last of the *Hood* in the Denmark Strait, as seen from the *Prinz Eugen.*

Right: Ted Briggs, with his sister, Ethel (left) and mother, on survival leave, just a week after the destruction of the *Hood*.

Below: Leaving HMS *Ganges* in June, 1939, on the way to join the *Hood* as a boy signalman.

Right: Ted Briggs unveils the only memento from the *Hood* – a metal container washed up in Norway – at HMS *Centurion*, Gosport on 21 May 1981, forty years after the sinking of the battle cruiser.

15

Force H for *Hood*

Leave, which was long overdue, was given to half of the crew after we had been dry-docked at Devonport at the end of March, but 250 of those unfortunate enough to have been left on board were to be involved in a disastrous adventure, for which they were not trained.

We in the signals branch knew something was 'on' during the forenoon of 12 April when secret orders code-named 'Primrose' began to arrive in the ship. Our howitzer was swung over the side on to the quay soon after. Then came the news that 250 marines and matelots were to pack their kit immediately and prepare to go ashore that night. Three days earlier Germany had invaded Norway and Denmark, and the mess buzz kings did not take long to deduce that this sudden collecting of manpower had something to do with a mission to Scandinavia. Several boys wanted to volunteer to go – although I can't say that I was particularly keen to join them – but it was decided that only marines and senior ratings should be picked. After a day of feverish preparation the contingent boarded a special train at midnight. Some were to return a month later; others, such as Able Seamen Kelly, Harris, Thorpe and Walker, were wounded; some, like Lieutenant-Commander C.A. Awdry, Lieutenant E.D. Strand, Sub-Lieutenant Goodale, Sub-Lieutenant D.C. Salter, Sergeant J.P. Lees and Marines McPherson, Lashmar and Welch, fought on until the evacuation. Many did not leave Norway alive. One who did was my shipmate Marine Holding, and the messes heard of his and others' adventures when the *Hood* re-entered the war at 9.30 p.m. on Monday 27 May 1940.

It was at this time that the *Hood* was towed out of the Tamar into Plymouth Sound after two months of hammering and riveting at Devonport. And in those fifty-seven days Norway, Denmark and Holland had been overrun by the Nazi *Blitzkrieg*. Belgium was on the eve of capitulation, and the French Channel ports were under siege. Britain was just a week from Dunkirk.

As we slipped the towing wires of the tug and regretfully left the leisurely life of the West Country, we were cheerfully confident that the battle cruiser was in fighting fettle again. The ack-ack defences had been bolstered and a set of five UP (unrotating projectile) rocket-launchers had been fitted, in addition to other minor improvements. What we did not know was that there was another list of comprehensive modifications, which it was not intended to do. These included new machinery, the removal of both the conning tower and the above-water torpedo tubes, the fitting of an aircraft catapult and crane and, most important of all, extra horizontal and vertical armour, which the Admiralty were doubtful about now because of the extra weight of the ship.

That morning we steamed northwards, escorted by three destroyers. We were retreating from the threatened southern coast of England to Liverpool's Gladstone Dock for a fortnight of underwater repairs and painting. It was inconvenient, to say the least, that the *Hood* dry-docked alongside and the ship's company were required to use the lavatories ashore as the main heads onboard were closed. Diarrhoea swept through the mess decks, and there was an incessant stream of 'bodies' going back and forth down the gangway through the day and at night. Hardly a man was not affected by it during a forty-eight-hour spell. When the bug had run its full course, Paymaster Commander D.C. Roe, who was responsible for victualling the ship, found a heap of bad meat chained down outside his cabin the next morning. The culprits were never discovered, but the butcher was glad to be rid of the stuff.

While Britain listened for church bells which would warn of enemy invasion, our sentries were becoming jumpy about rumours of fifth columnists and spies. This led to the shooting of an innocent dockyard matey by a Royal Marine sentry. The workman was seen to approach the side of the ship and throw something into the dock. He was challenged immediately by the guard but did not reply. The marine challenged him again and this time shattered the silence by firing his .303. The workman was nicked by a bullet in the side of the neck. After he was arrested, he explained that he had merely thrown away the remains of his sandwich lunch and had not heard the sentry because he was deaf.

The possibility of more serious shooting was ahead when on 12 June the *Hood* left Gladstone Dock to rendezvous with one of the most important convoys of the war. Our escort included the Canadian destroyers *Skeena*, *Restigouch* and *St Laurent*, and we were to meet the convoy three hundred miles west of Cape Finisterre. Two days later there lumbered into view the aircraft-carrier *Argus* and then on the horizon the rest of the brood gradually appeared – first the *Queen Mary*, then the *Empress of Britain*, the *Mauretania*, *Aquitania*, *Andes* and *Empress of Canada*. It was the finest array of liners I have ever seen together at one time. On board were Anzac troops, too late for the Battle of Europe but on hand for the Battle of Britain and then North Africa. Everyone expected that this treasury of ships would bring hordes of aircraft and U-boats: instead there were just two submarine scares, and on 14 June we entered the Firth of Clyde and anchored off Greenock. Why had there been no attack, we wondered? The answer came the next day. The Germans had been too busy in France, for Marshal Pétain was asking for his 'honourable peace'.

As libertymen began to return that night, it was obvious that the ship was on the verge of another 'special mission', and just before turning in we were alerted to stand by for a broadcast by Captain Glennie. In contrast to other briefings, he did not give any indication of where we were bound. All we were told was that we were to prepare for sea and raise steam for twenty knots.

At 0230 special sea duty men were ordered to their stations. Two and a half hours later we had whisked through the submarine boom from the Cloch Lighthouse to Dunoon. From the southerly course which was set, it seemed apparent to me that the *Hood* was heading for the South-Western Approaches, and that meant we should be involved in the defence of southern England. How wrong I was! During the next afternoon – a bright and sunny one, which belied the normal storminess of the Bay of Biscay – we crossed the path of our old chummy the *Ark Royal*. It was then that Captain Glennie announced to a ship's company befuddled by rumour and counter-rumour that with the great carrier and her destroyer screen we were to make for Gibraltar, where we were to form a section of Force H for operations in the Mediterranean – just like that, for there had been no preparation: none of us had been kitted out with 'whites', and we had been issued only balaclavas and woollies!

On 23 June the *Hood* arrived at Gibraltar and berthed alongside the harbour mole. Astern lay the battleship *Resolution*, which had been waiting for us thirteen days. Soon after, the *Ark Royal* put in at the jetty on our port side.

By now we assumed that the *Hood* was to be based at the gates of the Mediterranean, just as she had been in the 1930s, to put the 'frighteners' on Italy, who had declared war on the Allies thirteen days earlier. Churchill was determined that the Mediterranean was not to become an Italian lake. That was the way it appeared to the lower deck. Again we were wrong. Our allies were about to become our enemies.

The main concern of the War Cabinet was the destiny of the French fleet, and the day after, 25 June, when Pétain signed an armistice with Germany, we were ordered to sail with the *Ark Royal* on another panic mission. The French battleship *Richelieu*, based at Dakar, had put to sea and was thought to be heading for Toulon, where she would be neutralized. We were supposed to escort her to Gibraltar, but no one seemed to have the slightest idea of what action to take if her captain refused. The policy of dealing with the defecting French had yet to be decided, and at this stage we were unaware of just how ruthless it was to be. But the *Hood* and the *Ark* were not needed in this instance. The *Richelieu* was intercepted by the cruiser *Dorsetshire* off the West African coast, and her captain was persuaded to return to Dakar. At 2200 we turned about and went back to Gibraltar. By now, after ten months of war, the ship's company were thoroughly used to these false alarms. Another followed on 28 June when the *Richelieu* was again reported to be about to make a run for it. Again we put to sea. For sixteen hours we rushed towards Dakar; then the emergency fizzled out to its normal frustrating end with a recall to the Rock.

But in London twenty-four hours earlier there had been held an emergency meeting of the War Cabinet to give the *Hood* her most murderous mission, with which few of us would be proud to be associated.

16

Shooting Fish in a Barrel

During the next few days we watched the build-up of Force H. First came the cruiser *Enterprise*, then four older destroyers of the Thirteenth Flotilla and finally the *Valiant*, a veteran of Jutland. Our main signal office was alive with messages during this period, and the messes were hives of rumour, until after divisions on Sunday 30 June, when Captain Glennie announced mistakenly that 'within a few days' Vice-Admiral Sir James Somerville would be hoisting his flag in the *Hood*.

When a new admiral is expected, it does not take long for a ship's company to form a mental picture of him through the wardroom and gunroom telegraphs. We soon knew that he was a showy admiral, with a blue sense of humour, an alert brain, a penchant for keeping his men on their toes and an impatient streak which drove his flag staff to distraction. The general opinion of the veterans of the lower deck, who had served with him when he was Rear-Admiral Destroyers in the Mediterranean from 1936 to 1938, was that he was kindly to the matelot, and since Invergordon this trait in him had helped to restore confidence in the officer class. Above all – and this was like possessing a rabbit's foot – he had a link with our ship, even if in name only, for his great-great-grandfather was Lord Hood, an admiral of the fleet. To crystallize: he was a popular admiral.

Certainly he was a hustler, as we found out when the cruiser *Arethusa* berthed nearby at 1745 that day, and not 'within a few days' as the captain had stated. I watched from the flag deck as the dazzling array of gold braid arrived. At this moment they were nameless to me, but in the forty-six days we were associated with them they all showed their little idiosyncrasies to the crew. In order of seniority they were: Captain E.G. Jeffery, the chief of staff, who had been snapped up from the Imperial Defence College; Commander Anthony Buzzard, rakish, sandy-haired and Navy tennis champion, who two months earlier had survived the sinking of the destroyer *Gurkha* – his first seagoing command – during the Norwegian campaign, for which he received the DSO; Commander Keith Walter, flag lieutenant and signal officer, Paymaster Lieutenant-Commander Bill Farrell, the admiral's secretary, who had never had this type of job before and who two weeks earlier was running Jersey Airport, and Paymaster-Lieutenant John Rennie. All looked weary from hours at sea, which had been not a cruise but a gruelling spell of thrashing out a 'rough and ready' organization to administer the new fleet. Jeffery, in particular, was showing the strain of a man who lived on his nerves – a strain that was to end tragically when he hanged himself in the *Renown* several months later.

Although it was now twilight into the Sabbath, Somerville refused to relax, and as soon as the hardware of his command had been taken inboard, he cleared the lower deck. In no uncertain terms he informed us that the objective of Force H was to hit the German and Italian fleets in the Mediterranean as hard as we could to relieve the beleaguered garrison in Malta. We believed him because there was no mention of the French fleet. Oran was still a place on the map to us, but it was a name to become linked with treachery.

For the next two days there was a succession of comings and goings up and down the gangways of the *Hood*. Never had I – a decimal in a vast permutation of naval figures – seen so much 'scrambled egg' assembled in one spot. Within hours of arriving, Somerville left the *Hood* for 'The Mount', the eighteenth-century residence halfway up the Rock, to converse with his old friend Admiral Sir Dudley North, who in effect was in command of the area but who had been superseded unofficially by his junior.

This informal get-together heralded a further 'top brass' conference in the *Hood* that evening. Our quartermasters were on the top line for vigilance as a bevy of braid arrived, until congregated in the admiral's day cabin were North, Vice-Admiral 'Nutty' Wells, commanding aircraft-carriers, who felt spurned because he was not in charge of Force H, Captain Cedric 'Hooky' Holland, commanding officer of the *Ark Royal*, the captains of the *Resolution, Valiant, Arethusa* and *Enterprise*, and the commanding officers of the Eighth and Thirteenth Destroyer Flotillas. It was a top-secret conference, and not a word of it leaked out to the ship's company. Only thirty years later, on examining official records, did I know of the full import of the briefing by Somerville, who held centre stage. In a grim atmosphere and one which lacked even the odd flashes of impromptu quasi-heroic humour, he informed his command that under the terms of the armistice France was required to deliver her fleet for demilitarization under German or Italian control. The British Government, however, were demanding that the French Navy should consider four alternatives – sail all warships to British harbours and fight on, put in to British or West Indian ports, so that crews could be repatriated, demilitarize their vessels immediately or scuttle. Somerville added menacingly, but not really meaning it: 'Should the French be unwilling to adopt any of the above measures it will then be necessary to show that we are in earnest by offensive action without endangering the French ships by our own action.'[1]

In revealing the plans for Catapult, scheduled for 3 July, he said that Holland would embark in the destroyer *Foxhound* for Oran to negotiate with the French. If they did not acquiesce, he proposed that the *Hood* should 'fire a few rounds, or the *Ark Royal* aircraft drop bombs close to, but not actually hitting the French ships'. Should these tactics not work, he gave specific instructions that the priority targets for the guns of Force H should be the *Dunkerque*, the *'ami'* of the *Hood*, with whom we had operated the previous year, and the 26,500-ton new battle cruiser, *Strasbourg*. The secondary targets were to be the older 22,000-ton battleships *Bretagne* and *Provence*, designed in 1912, and then other warships in order of size.

'If the French offer organised any spirited resistance we may need to develop a full offensive on their ships and shore batteries, with all the means at our disposal,' he warned. 'In this case the code word Anvil will be signalled to all our forces. Senior officers are then to take all necessary action to crush the resistance, ceasing fire as soon as it is apparent that the French are no longer resisting.'[2]

The next day, Somerville conferred again with Holland and Lieutenant-Commanders A.Y. Spearman and G.P.S. Davies, all of whom had been liaison officers with the French Navy.

But events were rapidly overhauling the sympathetic attitude of Somerville and his entourage. At 1425 that day an Admiralty message alerted him to ready Catapult for launching on 3 July. It also prescribed these four alternatives to be put to the French:

1. Sail your ships to British harbours and fight with us. 2. Steam to Britain and hand over your vessels. 3. Demilitarize your ships to our satisfaction. 4. Sink your ships where they are.

Somerville was more impressed by the opinions of the former liaison officers and tried to temper the Admiralty's firmness by signalling that force should be avoided 'at all costs'. As a compromise he suggested that, if the French rejected the Admiralty's first alternative, they should be invited to sail with a skeleton steaming party and allow themselves to be captured by Force H, with the proviso that at the end of the war their ships would be returned. He also wanted the third and fourth alternatives to be an invitation and not ultimatums.

The signal and cypher offices in the *Hood* were at their busiest of the war as detailed instructions went back and forth, but that evening in a long message Somerville was rebuked by the Admiralty and icily told – if the airways could be that cold – that his proposals were unacceptable. He was informed weightily: 'It is the firm intention of HMG that if the French will not accept any alternatives, which are being sent you, their ships must be destroyed.' This did signify that new instructions were being despatched, and sure enough they arrived in the early hours of 2 July in four 'Most Secret' messages, which superseded any other orders. On the face of it, the four alternatives had barely altered. The third one had been changed to 'sail their ships with reduced crews to some French port in the West Indies, such as Martinique'[3] for demilitarization under British or United States jurisdiction. A concession had been written in, however, that if it were suggested the French should disarm at their berths in Oran within six hours, this should be accepted.

Telegraphists in the wireless office did not sleep that night. A full version of the terms to be sent to Oran was transmitted, and then at 0113 came a third, longer message which outlined some of the arguments which could be put to the French. The Admiralty insisted that, although no time limit was being set for acceptance, it was imperative that Catapult should be completed during daylight of 3 July.

The next morning, 2 July, there was another parade of senior officers to the *Hood* when the final phases of the operation were thrashed out, although most were under the misapprehension still that Catapult would not become Anvil, when Force H would be expected to belch out a devastating denunciation of their reneging ally.

Even as a signal boy I had a better knowledge, although limited, of what was going on than men in other branches. We were constantly being quizzed by others with 'What's buzzing, cousin?' or 'What hunts, bunts?' It was more than we dare do to reveal classified information, and at times we smugly adopted an attitude of 'I know more than you do, mate.' But on this occasion we were all in the dark as all signals from London were in code. With the amount of fuel and ammunition that the *Hood* had taken on board during the last forty-eight hours, no one could deny that a 'stunt' was on. I genuinely believed that we were about to seek out and destroy the Italian fleet.

It seemed certain that we would leave that night, for our boilers were fully fired and around us curled smoke from the sixteen other ships of Force H. It was a surprise when the pipe came for sea duty men to fall in at 1600. Most of us expected to sail under cover of darkness, but it was a bright evening, with exceptional visibility for the many pro-Axis observers at Algeciras just across the Spanish border.

In company with the *Ark Royal*, *Valiant*, *Resolution*, *Arethusa*, *Enterprise* and screen of eleven destroyers, we cleared the Rock at 1700, worked up to seventeen knots and zigzagged. Soon after, Captain Glennie cleared the mess-deck smokescreen of speculation by broadcasting to the ship's company that we were bound for Oran – or, to put it correctly, to nearby Mers-el-Kebir – to try to persuade the French fleet to join us. He gave full details of the ultimatum and also informed us that negotiators would be conferring with our 'old friend' the stocky, fifty-nine-year-old Vice-Admiral Gensoul, under whose orders the *Hood* had been during the *Gneisenau* panic in 1939 and who was known to be 'a hundred per cent pro British'.

This announcement caused mixed feelings on the mess decks that night. The general opinion was that it would not come to the point when we would be firing on allies. For me it was a sickening idea, and I honestly thought it would never happen. Similar broadcasts were being made in other ships of the force as Somerville made a general signal explaining the mission. We had 195 nautical miles to go to Oran, and for most of that night Somerville was awake studying the signals that kept the cypher office at full stretch. Just before midnight the distastefulness of the operation was underlined in a message from First Lord A.V. Alexander. He wirelessed: 'You are charged with one of the most disagreeable and difficult tasks that a British admiral has ever been faced with, but we have complete confidence in you and rely on you to carry it out relentlessly.'[4] The midnight oil was also being burnt at the Admiralty, for at 0135 Somerville was instructed that, although a time limit had not been set for French acceptance, it was still imperative Catapult be completed during daylight hours on 3 July.

In between these signals there was a more immediate emergency. A torpedo exploded ahead of the destroyer *Vortigern*. With her sister *Vidette* she was detached to hunt for a U-boat. For more than an hour they 'pinged' their Asdics, but they failed to get an echo and returned to the escort screen. This was the only scare on the passage to Mers-el-Kebir, where we arrived at 0810. Five hours earlier the destroyer *Foxhound*, with negotiators Captain Holland and Lieutenant-Commanders Spearman and Davies on board, had been detached from Force H with orders to push on to Oran at full speed. *Foxhound* beat the *Hood* by an hour to the harbour but had to wait for another hour before being given permission to enter.

It was a shimmering hot morning, and we were at action

stations already. I was 'closed up' on the flag deck and consequently had a grandstand view of the historic events being played out before me. There were few flag signals to be executed at this stage, and it was just a question of standing and watching and trying to keep out of the stultifying sun as it turned my action rig into a cloying sack of sweat. Looking towards the dun-coloured hills cloaking Oran, the scene was tranquil enough. Three miles to the west of Oran harbour I could see a forest of masts. This then was the French fleet moored at Mers-el-Kebir. In addition to the two battle cruisers and two veteran battleships, it also included the seaplane-carrier, *Commandant Teste* and six large des-troyers. An anti-submarine net boom screened the harbour entrance. The ships themselves had a further protection in the form of a thirty-foot high mole which ran half a mile from the shore; another half a mile was still being built, but this had a stretch of anti-submarine nets on either side, with access through a six-hundred-foot wide gate. At Santon, the highest hill at a thousand feet, was a battery of four 7.5-inch guns, of which I was soon to know more.

The peace was soon broken by the buzzing of patrols from the *Ark Royal*, which could put into the air thirty torpedo-spotter reconnaissance planes and twenty-four fighters. Our entire force steamed backwards and forwards menacingly in line ahead parallel to the coast, our smoke blackening the azure sky in portent of the power we had at our disposal. The *Hood* led the formation, followed by the *Resolution* and *Valiant; Arethusa* was on the starboard bow and *Enterprise* on the port bow, with the screen of destroyers outside them. To seaward, just in sight from the *Hood*, was the *Ark* and her destroyers. Occasionally I glimpsed Somerville on his bridge. He looked pallid, drawn and haggard after a night without sleep, but I heard from the messengers that he was maintaining his usual crackling banter, although the familiar crossword puzzle he kept by his chair for solving during long spells of waiting was missing. Every now and then he would come out on to the wings of the bridge and clamp his binoculars to his eyes, as an Aldis lamp winked from the *Foxhound*. He dare not let his attention wander, for on the one hand signals were made before him and on the other was a stream of instructions from the Admiralty. As soon as a coded message came in from London, he would be informed by telephone by the WT department. He would let a few minutes elapse and then ring his secretary, Lieutenant-Commander Farrell, and Paymaster-Lieutenant Rennie, secretary to the chief of staff, for a decoded version long before one could be reasonably expected.

As the *Hood* traversed across the harbour mouth, our rangefinders twirled, while all the fifteen-inch turrets were trained and readjusted at the end of each turnabout. Until the force repeated these long sweeps, like impatient caged lions, the French genuinely believed that we were on our way to tackle the Italian fleet. Through a telescope I could see the comings and goings in the harbour, although I was obviously unaware at this stage of what was actually happening. First the admiral's barge from the *Dunkerque* arrived alongside the *Foxhound*; then the destroyer weighed anchor, leaving her motor-boat, in which were Holland, Spearman and Davies, heading for the *Dunkerque*. Halfway between the inner boom and the mole they were met by the admiral's barge again and stopped. The French boat scuttled back to its parent ship, returned again to the negotiators' craft and then went to the *Dunkerque* yet again. This little charade was played out for two hours until just before 1130, when Holland and his party climbed onboard the *Foxhound*. Reports of proceedings and eye-witness accounts have revealed since that Admiral Gensoul refused to see the British officers but considered the ultimatum which was handed over. He adamantly rejected it but assured Somerville that he would not allow his ships to become German possessions and finally resolved to 'defend himself by every means at his disposal'.[5]

The *Hood* was using her twenty-inch signal projector to keep in touch with the *Foxhound* by light, and Somerville had transmitted the intention that he would not allow the French ships to leave harbour unless the terms were accepted and that the ultimatum would expire at 1430. Again we saw the *Foxhound*'s motor-boat go in the direction of the *Dunkerque*, and then the destroyer take up a position outside the boom. Soon the motor-boat chugged back. For nearly an hour around noon there was an uneasy calm. By now the heat below and above decks in the *Hood* was of bludgeoning intensity. Although I was in one of the airiest parts of the ship, the hot deck drew my feet through the soles of thick shoes. To touch a handrail was like putting one's fingers on the handle of a poker which had been left in a fire for hours.

Captain Glennie took advantage of this lull to pipe 'Cooks to the galley'. It relieved the waiting, if little else. One rating from each position was detailed to collect action rations from the main galley on the starboard side above the boys' mess deck. Whoever devised the menu that day had little idea of the sweltering conditions we would face, for up to us came hot soup, followed by the usual great door-stepped bully beef sandwiches, or 'corned dog' as we called it. Rum had been issued, but I was not yet eighteen and 'not entitled', so I sipped the 'limers' normally served to all ratings in hot climates, which by the time it reached me was warm. The officers were barely better off. Hot stew, with rock cakes as a dessert, was their fare. While we were eating, more serious developments had been taking place in the harbour. The wisps of smoke coming from the French fleet suddenly turned into spiralling plumes; bugles sounded, awnings were furled. Lights blinked back and forth from the *Foxhound* to the *Hood*, and the number of aircraft keeping surveillance over the town increased to twenty. A sudden flurry of reports to Somerville indicated that Gensoul planned to sail his fleet.

At 1236 our twenty-inch projector flashed this message from Somerville to Holland in the *Foxhound*: 'Presume there is no alternative to Anvil.' After a few minutes the reply came: 'Am afraid not. Am waiting in V/S touch in case acceptance before expiration time.' After this Somerville's staff hurried up to the admiral's bridge. At this snap conference it was revealed that Gensoul had ordered the opening of the harbour boom to admit three tugs. It was also reported that four submarines were on the move. Somerville's response was to signal *Ark Royal's* aircraft to mine the entrance. His order was soon obeyed and we could see the splashes as four mines were dropped.

The ultimatum was due to expire at 1330 local time, and fifteen minutes before this Somerville kept his options open by making this light signal to Holland: 'Does anything you have said prevent me opening fire?' A heavy-hearted Holland, who genuinely liked the French officers with whom he was negotiating, answered: 'Nothing I have said, since terms were not discussed, only handed in and reply received. I would suggest there might be a chance of avoiding Anvil if *Foxhound* went in to V/S touch and asked if there was further message before force employed.'

Several minutes later – after the *Foxhound* had moved in closer to the harbour – Somerville tried again. 'Pass to Gensoul,' he signalled. 'If you accept the terms, hoist a large square flag at the masthead, otherwise I must open fire at 1500. Your harbour is mined.'

The ship's company were being informed intermittently by broadcasts of the situation. Two loudspeakers on the flag deck kept us up to date, but most of the signalmen were reading the light messages which were being flashed to and fro. However, when *Foxhound* relayed Somerville's last demand to the *Dunkerque*, few of us could understand. To avoid mistakes, Holland had passed it in French.

The aerial mining was regarded by Gensoul as the initial belligerent act, and by now it seemed that he would open fire first, for observers in the patrolling Swordfish aircraft reported that the turrets of the *Dunkerque*, *Strasbourg* and *Bretagne* were trained on the *Hood* and that tugs were pushing them from their moorings. Most of us watching the painfully slow proceedings were realizing now that Gensoul was playing for time. From the pacing up and down of Somerville on the bridge, we could tell that his patience was ebbing. At 1415 the *Foxhound*'s projector was active again, transferring a message from Gensoul. It read: 'I have no intention of sailing. I have telegraphed my government and am awaiting their reply. Take no irrevocable step.'

This duel of light on the nerves seemed to have been resolved without injury to either force when fifteen minutes later Holland indicated by the *Foxhound*'s projector that Gensoul was ready to meet him in the *Dunkerque* for 'honourable discussion'. Unfortunately this clashed with Somerville's peremptory warning: 'Accept our terms or abandon your ships as I must destroy them at 1530.' Holland did not think it necessary to repeat this last message to

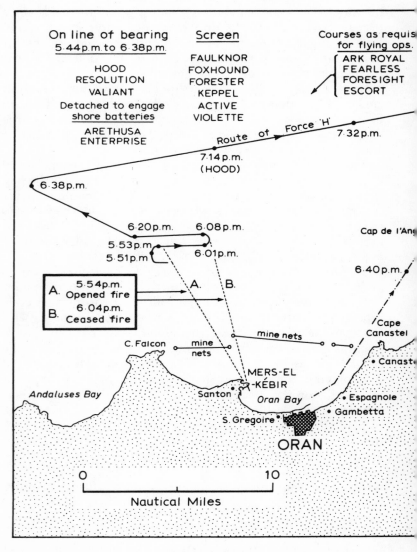

The track of Force H and the *Hood* during the bombardment of Oran

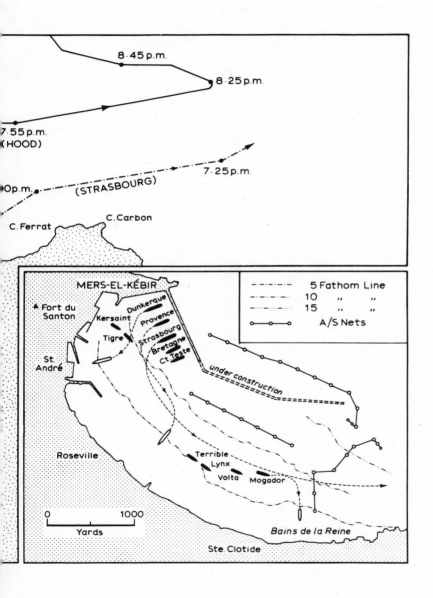

Gensoul. At 1500 I watched the *Foxhound*'s motor-boat cast off again. It was more than seven miles – or thirty minutes by boat – from the French flagship, and a strange, foreboding calm seemed to settle over Force H as the patrol was continued in line ahead.

For $2\frac{1}{4}$ hours the sun blazed down, and it was difficult not to lower one's eyelids against the glare and nod off. Boredom began to settle in for us, but Somerville was being prodded into action by Churchill. Four hours earlier Gensoul had wirelessed the French Admiralty that he was being threatened by a massive British force, and this had led Admiral Darlan to direct all ships in the western Mediterranean – especially the Third Squadron and Algiers Squadron – to steam immediately for Oran to 'meet force with force'. This signal had been picked up by British Intelligence and brought this timely reminder from Churchill to Somerville at 1646: 'Settle matters quickly or you will have reinforcements to deal with.'[6]

Of course, the average rating, like myself, was unaware of this explosive order from Churchill. During the last six hours the dilemma of opening fire had been the continual subject of an escalating debate. I gathered that most of our officers hoped that it would not be necessary. The lower deck were not so compassionate now, and the attitude of many was: 'They've chucked it in, so we've every right to sink 'em.'

With the pressure from Whitehall building, and not wishing to attack in darkness, Somerville made up his mind. Just before 1700 I saw his messenger, Leading Signalman Lewington, who spoke fluent French, scuttle to the projector, which soon blinked out: 'If one of British proposals is not accepted by 1730 BSM I must sink your ships.' The reply was sent in English from the *Dunkerque*. Eagerly we all spelt it out on the flag deck. It read: 'Do not create the irreparable.'

The flag deck was coming to life again now, and a few minutes later Chief Yeoman Thomas called down the voice-pipe to us. Leading Signalman Ned Johns answered and then turned to Marine Holding, my friend Signal Boy Bell and myself to tell us to string together and hoist the series of flags ZTH 1 – readiness for instant action. As they

fluttered to the starboard masthead, I still could not believe
that for the first time in the war our fifteen-inch guns would
be hurling tons of high explosives – and on helpless friends
at that!

As we turned our telescopes towards the harbour again,
there was a burst of searchlight activity from the
Dunkerque, then from the *Foxhound* to the *Hood*. It was
Holland's final communication, the basis of which was that
he had managed to squeeze a compromise from the French.
'Admiral Gensoul says crews being reduced,' it ran, 'and if
threatened by enemy would go to Martinique, or USA, but
this not quite our proposition. Can get no nearer.' This last
signal did not reach Somerville until one minute before the
deadline. Still the dreaded moment of opening fire was
delayed. For nearly half an hour, as the sun dipped, I
clutched the cooling rail on the flag deck, watching for any
sign that would mean a reprieve for both sides. Somerville
came out on the wings of the bridge. Outwardly he seemed
cool, but then I thought that was the difference between
myself and anyone who wore such heavy gold braid!

In Mers-el-Kebir tugs began bustling around the
wharves; there appeared to be movement among the cram of
ships; darker, thicker smoke swept skywards. Over the
town, strike aircraft circled like bull-nosed vultures, waiting
for the moment to descend and tear asunder. In the *Hood* all
guns were cleared as Force H inclined more towards the
coast. In the spotting-top there was a grotesque array of steel
helmets with binoculars sprouting from beneath the brims.
Somerville was no longer on the wings of the bridge. The
Foxhound's motor-boat emerged from the harbour.

The voice-pipe squealed. Leading Signalman Johns
answered it, listened, rapped out 'Yes, sir,' looked at
Holding, Bell and myself and shouted: 'Flag 5 – Hoist.' The
three of us took up the white and red horizontal halved piece
of bunting that signified 'Open fire – may be obeyed as soon
as seen.' My fingers trembled as I performed my task of
putting an Inglefield clip on the flag's head. Bell was working
on the bottom of it, while Holding hoisted as soon as we had
clipped on. The bunting slid easily up the halyards to the
starboard masthead.

The response was immediate. Just as I turned round to

watch, the guns of the *Resolution* and *Valiant* roared in
murderous hair-trigger reaction. Then came the ting-ting of
our firing bell. Seconds later my ears felt as if they had been
sandwiched between two manhole covers. The concussion of
the *Hood*'s eight fifteen-inch guns, screaming in horrendous
harmony, shook the flag deck violently. In line with
Somerville's original plan, the first salvoes were not intended
to land in the harbour. I found myself counting off the
seconds. First the shells from the older battleships erupted
the sea north of the harbour, and then twenty seconds later
the *Hood*'s salvoes sent up high, cascading water-spouts. It
seemed as if after all we were not to be involved in a
full-scale battle, for these shots were frighteners.

Then to my horror the thunder continued and the next
salvoes enfiladed the masts alongside the mole. The French
were trapped in the close confines of the harbour, and for the
next ten minutes the old cliché of shooting fish in a barrel
kept going through my mind, as from a range of fifteen
thousand yards Mers-el-Kebir was pulverized. We were
using GIC (Gunnery Information Centre) concentration,
with *Ark*'s aircraft spotting our fall of shot. With the line of
firing from the north-west and Force H on a steady, easterly
course, it meant that Gensoul's vessels on our starboard
quarter could not bring all their guns to bear because of
being masked by Fort Santon.

It was an awesome sight as shells continued to plunge into
the harbour area. A massive cloak of smoke hung over the
town and this would change colour as great orange flashes
sent wreckage up to four hundred feet. Intermingled with
this were sheets of water and oil. The smell of burning fuel
and cordite soured the air, even at this range. Suddenly
pinpoints of amber light punctuated the blackness. Above
the roar of our guns came the high-pitched, blood-curdling,
crescendoing, low whine of being under fire ourselves by
warships for the first time. There were vivid red flashes as a
salvo fell just short of the starboard side. Within seconds
came a series of blue flashes. Later I learnt that each French
ship's salvoes exploded in a different colour to make it easier
to judge their fall of shot. The *Dunkerque*'s were red and the
Strasbourg's green.

These first ranging shots seemed so ineffective that my

terror subsided and I watched for more. This time I could actually see some approaching, surprisingly lazily, end for end and visible throughout the whole of their trajectory. I was told afterwards that one of the French capital ships must have had defective driving bands and this was causing the slow motion and tumbling phenomenon.

In the distance I spotted Holland's motor-boat clearing the harbour and running into a barrage of gunfire as it approached the *Foxhound*. Then the destroyer put down a smokescreen, and they were lost to view. It was also becoming hazardous for the *Hood* by now. Suddenly we were straddled by one salvo. Splinters thudded into one funnel and along our starboard side. But our only casualties were a lieutenant and a rating on the boat deck, who were slightly wounded. The sea around was foaming continually now as the French bombardment heightened. This further menace came from the shore battery at Fort Santon, which the *Arethusa* and *Enterprise* were not engaging too successfully, mainly because they were out of range. There were no coloured shell bursts now, and the impenetrable pall of smoke, which the evening breeze could not disperse, marked the end of the French navy's resistance. But the shore batteries continued to bedevil the *Hood*, and our guns were turned on them just before 1810. By now 13.4-inch shells from Forts Santon, Canastel, Gambetta and Espagnole were peppering not only the line of heavy ships but also the flanking destroyers. The bombardment was becoming more accurate, and several ships were straddled without being damaged.

I was brought back to my duties by Somerville's peremptory order of a change of course to 180 degrees port. With Bell and Holding I ran up 18 Blue. At the same time every ship was ordered to 'make smoke' to obscure us from the explosive torment coming from the shore. As we turned to seaward, I looked back on the pulsating ball of fire which was once Mers-el-Kebir.

At 1812 the voice-pipe came alive again. 'Flag six ... hoist,' yelled Johns, during a gap in the cacophony of gunfire and the screaming aircraft. We grabbed the yellow and blue vertically halved flag, and it shot to the masthead. Thankfully, it was the cease-fire. Somerville had made this decision because of repeated signals by wireless from Gensoul to halt the slaughter so that the wounded could be taken ashore. The *Hood* had unleashed fifty-six rounds of fifteen-inch shells and 120 four-inchers, or more than sixty tons of high explosive. A total of two hundred tons had rained on the French ships.

For the next twenty minutes an uneasy silence surrounded the *Hood* amid the smoke she made. Then at 1835 Somerville signalled Gensoul: 'Unless I see your ships sinking I shall open fire again.' He was to admit later: 'My appreciation of the situation at this time was that resistance from the French ships had ceased and that by ceasing fire I should give them an opportunity to abandon their ships and thus avoid further loss of life. Since the French knew the entrance to the harbour had been mined, I felt positive that no attempt would be made by them to put to sea.'[7]

Admirals are mere mortals, too. In the confusion of the smoke Somerville had confused himself.

17

The Pursuit of Unhappiness

Throughout the operation, Admiral Gensoul had played for time, and in the immediate moment after more than a thousand of his men had died, he still bartered minutes and seconds to save a section of his fleet. Earlier he had visualized an escape route past Oran and clear of the aircraft-sown mines. He achieved this by ordering his marines to machine-gun the buoys mooring the anti-submarine nets. When they had sunk, a channel of more than three cables in width was created. Half an hour before the one-sided battle began, he had received the signal from Admiral Darlan that all French forces in the western Mediterranean had been ordered to rush to his aid. 'You will then take these forces under your command,' he was told.[1] With this intention Gensoul had instructed all his ships to make for the gap in the submarine screens.

Behind the chaos created by British guns, the admiral attempted to salvage a part of his fleet. The super destroyers *Volta*, *Terrible*, *Lynx*, *Tigre* and *Kersaint* were first into the open sea, and the battle cruiser *Strasbourg*, which had not suffered a single direct hit, followed them.

In his self-imposed smokescreen Somerville relaxed for a fateful twelve minutes. At 1818 he discounted a carrier pilot's report that a ship of the *Dunkerque* class was escaping and heading eastwards. Then at 1830 another sighting from the air put the *Strasbourg* and the five destroyers steaming to the east and opposite Canastel. It was only at this point that we on the flag deck realized that something was amiss. Staff officers began to rush in a hive of activity to and from the admiral's bridge and the compass platform. Somerville had made the tactical blunder of keeping to the west, instead of maintaining a watch to the north-east of Oran to cut off a break-out towards Toulon in southern France. He had also relied too heavily on the barrier of mines. There was nothing to do now but to give chase, so at 1838 the *Hood* was ordered to turn about to try to catch the *Strasbourg*, which was ten miles to the north-west, working up to twenty-eight knots and obscured by smoke. Five minutes later the *Arethusa*, the *Enterprise* and the destroyer screen shot ahead of us into the vanguard as a precaution, in case we and the *Valiant* and *Resolution* had to deal with the *Dunkerque*, which might also have slipped by the nets. It soon became obvious that the *Strasbourg*, now joined by six more destroyers from Oran, was the only big fish to have eluded the trap, and the *Hood* parted company from the two older battleships and surged ahead of Force H in pursuit.

As we emerged from the smoke and just before hitting top speed of thirty-two knots, our look-outs sighted a small craft flying the strange combination of a white flag and a white ensign. It was Holland's motor-boat, which had run out of petrol after dodging the bombardment for fifteen miles. Everyone on our upper deck cheered as we swept past.

I had been at my station on the flag deck for nearly twelve hours now, and we were still to have more action, this time the bravest I have ever seen. Where there had been six destroyers in our screen on the starboard wing, there was unaccountably a seventh, and this interloper was heading straight for the *Hood* at full speed. It was the French light cruiser *Rigault de Genouilly*, which had attempted to join the *Strasbourg* from Oran, had failed to keep up and had turned back again. She was close to the shore and making a torpedo run on the *Hood*. From twelve thousand yards the *Arethusa* opened fire; from eighteen thousand yards the *Enterprise* joined in; the *Hood*'s guns roared again, too, at this mosquito which might have a deadly sting. Three hits were observed on the lone raider, but before she veered away the *Hood* had to veer, too. The *Rigault de Genouilly* managed to unloose two torpedoes, and we swung 180 degrees off course to port to avoid them. I looked back and saw the bubbles boil by well astern of us.

It seemed poetic justice to me that this futile but gallant attempt against immense odds should end in survival as the

Frenchman eluded us – but only for a day. The *Rigault de Genouilly* regained the shambled safety of Oran only to be sunk by the British submarine *Pandora* when on the way to Algiers.

By now we were told that it was hoped to halt, or at least slow, the speeding *Strasbourg* by an air strike from the *Ark Royal*. Six Swordfish and three Skuas, carrying between them four 250-pound semi-armour piercing bombs and eight twenty-pounders, found it easy to track her down by following the involuntary smokescreen she was emitting through a shell splinter hole in a funnel. But that was the limit of their success. The French anti-aircraft barrage was of such intensity that three planes were shot down. The closest they got to the *Strasbourg* was a bomb thirty yards off her stern. But a misleading report claimed that there had been one hit, and this prompted Somerville to continue the pursuit.

We, the attackers, were also the target for the French Air Force. From 1930 French reconnaissance planes, followed by bombers, tailed us. High-angle anti-aircraft fire warded off their half-hearted attempts to bomb. A stick of four exploded fifty yards from the *Wrestler*, and surprisingly the *Hood* was not the main target.

Meanwhile the *Strasbourg* and destroyers were drawing further ahead. Just after 2000 they were plotted as being twenty-five miles in front, with the distance increasing every minute. In the gloaming I could see another exodus of officers to the admiral's bridge. Then at 2020, a quarter of an hour before sunset, came the order from Somerville to return to Oran. Somerville was sick of the whole nasty business and did not relish putting any of his ships at risk just to stop the French warships falling into German or Italian hands.

Our course was altered to the west, and the Admiralty were informed that Force H would stay in the vicinity of Oran during the night to make air attacks on ships in harbour at dawn. From this message it is apparent that Somerville had no stomach for turning his fleet's firepower on the French survivors again. He did order, however, another aircraft strike on the *Strasbourg*. It was made by six Swordfish in the dark, and although one torpedo seemed to explode under the battle cruiser's stern and another amidships, there was no sign of her slowing. The Admiralty were confused about Somerville's intentions, for as late as 2200, when I at last left the flag deck, they signalled him to race after the *Strasbourg* again, if the Swordfish had been successful, but by this time the *Hood* was off to Oran again.

It was eerily quiet as we approached the battered French harbour. Columns of smoke were still spuming up as the ship's company prepared for a night of vigilance, although at 2130 the devious Gensoul had signalled Somerville: 'Warships at Mers-el-Kebir *hors de combat*. Am evacuating personnel from ships.' Nevertheless, Somerville insisted that the *Ark Royal* must prepare for another strike on the stricken *Dunkerque*, now aground on a sandbank. Around midnight our force became shrouded in fog, and we thought that this mercy would allow us some sleep. At 0330 it began to lift, and through the gloom we sighted the *Ark*. But this was only a momentary clearance. By 0420 it was thicker than before. Somerville abandoned the strike, and the entire force set course for Gibraltar.

We arrived at the Rock at 1900 on 4 July. Coincidentally the *Strasbourg* reached Toulon about the same time to what was described later as a 'wild acclamation, not only from every ship in Toulon, but most of the population'. When I finally got below at 2200 the messdecks were quiet. Everyone was dog tired, and off-duty watches were collapsed all over the ship. Many, like myself, were too exhausted to sling their hammocks. I joined a bunch of friends dozing on top of the hammock stowage. They were still fully dressed, with anti-flash gear on.

More dirty work was being shaped for us, however. All that night we refuelled and ammunitioned ship, for Somerville had been ordered to take Force H to sea at dawn and head for Dakar, where the *Richelieu* was to be given the Oran treatment. Signals were already streaming backwards and forwards from London. In Tangier the British consul general sent this 'Most Immediate' message to the War Cabinet: 'French military attaché has just told me French Air Force, based at Port Lyautey, immediate objective is *Hood*.'[2] It was relayed on to the *Hood*, and sure enough it was correct. An hour after midnight unidentified aircraft were over Gibraltar. Their efforts surprised the *Hood*, but their bombs fell in the sea.

During the hours of darkness Somerville had been communicating with the Admiralty about the state of the *Dunkerque* at Mers-el-Kebir. Reconnaissance flights over the French battle cruiser could not assess accurately her injuries. A message from the French, which had been intercepted, also stated: 'The damage to the *Dunkerque* is minimal and the ship will soon be repaired.'[3] In view of this the Admiralty cancelled the dawn sailing for Dakar and insisted that Somerville should formulate new plans for attacking again, unless he was 'certain that the *Dunkerque* could not be refloated and repaired in less than a year'.[4] The deadline given was Saturday, 6 July.

All the next morning Somerville's flag staff and the commanding officers of Force H sat down around the big blue-baize table in his cabin to work out Operation Lever. I heard through the grapevine that the *Hood* was to open the firing, and indeed this was communicated to the Admiralty in a signal made just before the meeting broke off for lunch. Whether Somerville and his advisers ate and drank themselves into a more benevolent mood, I did not know, but during the afternoon session there was a change of opinion because it was thought that renewal of the bombardment would bring further loss of French lives ashore. At 1800 that evening Somerville wirelessed the Admiralty seeking a compromise which would not embitter France to take more active measures against British warships. Oblivious to the fact that we had been under air attack already from our ex-allies, the Admiralty's alternative was that Somerville should warn the French or get them to agree to our sending a demolition party to the *Dunkerque*. The *Hood* was only two hours from sailing, and still the method of destruction had not been approved.

At 2000 we put to sea, with Captain Glennie making the ominous announcement that the force were returning to Oran; what for, we were not told. Somerville was becoming more devious now, and the fifteen ships – the *Resolution* and a destroyer were left in Gibraltar – steered a feint course into the Atlantic and then at nightfall cruised back into the Mediterranean and increased speed to twenty-three knots.

In the early hours of that night, as the off-duty watches slept in the *Hood*, Somerville was negotiating with his superiors about the form of attack. As the *Dunkerque* was aground close to the village of St André, and he feared a slaughter of civilians if the guns of the *Hood* and the *Valiant* were employed, he suggested that the *Ark Royal's* torpedo bombers should be used. At 0250, just six hours before the bombardment was due to open, the Admiralty agreed to cancel it. Instead Somerville was ordered to set up continuous attacks by aircraft until the *Dunkerque* was 'thoroughly damaged'.[5] Through the early hours of the morning the flag staff were sending out counter-orders for Operation Lever to the commanding officers of the force. In the *Ark* there were feverish preparations to ensure that the first aircraft took off just after 0500.

I awoke at six that morning – 6 July – to hear that the *Hood* was to stay on station with the *Ark* and her screen of destroyers ninety miles from Oran. We spent the next half hour or so watching the carrier's Swordfish take off in three waves. All twelve of the old 'string-bags' returned after letting loose eleven torpedoes. They left the *Dunkerque* wreathed in smoke, although it is doubtful whether the five projectiles which skewered into her exploded. I learned later that the biggest explosion was caused by the torpedoing of the patrol boat *Terre Neuve* nearby. This triggered a tremendous blast through forty-four depth charges, which breached the *Dunkerque's* hull.

After briefings had been studied, Somerville was doubtful whether the *Dunkerque* had been destroyed. Nevertheless, after three hours he ordered our return to Gibraltar. We got there at 1830 on a beerless Saturday evening (a convoy had failed to arrive). I stayed on board to write home to my mother in censor's approved style that we had seen action at Oran, but we were not allowed to name ships.

In a letter to his wife, Somerville stated: 'It doesn't seem to worry the sailors at all, as they never "had no use for the French bastards," but to all of us senior officers it's simply incredible and revolting.'[6] Somerville did not know his men. Revolting it is still to me, for the carnage of shooting into that barrel of fish which was Mers-el-Kebir was brought home to me years later when the French version of the devastation was released in Britain.

The revulsion of the French at the time was typified by a note which was sent to the *Hood* from surviving officers living in a villa at Oran. It said: 'The captain and officers of the *Dunkerque* inform you of the death for the honour of their flags on 3rd and 6th July, 1940 of nine officers and 200 men of their ship. They return to you herewith the souvenirs they had of their comrades in arms of the Royal Navy, in whom they had placed all their trust. And they express to you on this occasion all their bitter sadness and their disgust at seeing these comrades having no hesitation in soiling the glorious flag of St George with an ineffaceable stain – that of an assassin.'

With the note were mementoes – cap ribbons, the ship's crest and badges – which the *Hood*'s crew had sent to the *Dunkerque* after serving under the French flag the previous year.

Nearly 1,300 officers and men had died; four warships, totalling around 75,000 tons had been destroyed or put out of action; the remainder of the French fleet reached Toulon but was never used by Germany. Was it worth it? I believe that, even today, the bitter memories of Oran still linger on for the French and are responsible for the hostility and recrimination against Britain which exist in the European Common Market.

18

Testing the Italians

The buzz was that for the next few weeks Force H would be involved in a training programme off Gibraltar. At least this was the plan of Somerville, who during the momentous happenings of the last week considered that this 'scratch fleet' was just that. He sought time to develop a team spirit among the crews and to mould his commanding officers into a group who acted as one – and that meant anticipating his thoughts and obeying his orders implicitly.

The Admiralty had different ideas, and from the moment we returned from Operation Lever, Somerville was inundated with signals urging him to mount a raid into the central Mediterranean to test the power of the Italian fleet. It was to be a diversionary action to shield two convoys from Malta to Alexandria and was to involve a strike from the east by Admiral Cunningham's fleet, based at Alexandria.

In the eight days we had been under his command it had become obvious even to the lower deck that thankfully our new admiral was a cautious type who did not believe in wasting ships and men on hopeless causes. Somerville bore out our opinion by telling the Admiralty in forthright terms that their strategy was conceived wrongly. It meant taking crews who were 'green' to air attacks into the Tyrrhenian Sea, which was ringed by enemy bases, once the force had penetrated the narrows between Sardinia and Africa. Instead he proposed that Force H should infiltrate as far as the waters south of Sardinia, where the *Ark*'s aircraft would strike at Cagliari air base. This did not satisfy the Admiralty planners. They pressed for a bombardment by the *Hood* and the two old battleships. At the risk of being accused of having 'cold feet', Somerville again protested because the force would be hazarded by mines, coastal batteries, submarines and air attack if we were required to close to a range of around fourteen miles.

The wrangle by wireless went on inexplicably through the nights of 6 and 7 July. The stupidity of some of the Admiralty signals caused Somerville to complain that many were initiated in the small hours and this explained their lack of clear thinking in Whitehall. Finally, as time was running out, he got his way. It was to be Cagliari and no farther, with only the *Ark*'s aircraft involved.

All this was outlined to the *Hood*'s crew on the morning of 8 July, as we left Gibraltar, after only one full day there, in company with the *Valiant*, *Resolution*, *Arethusa* and *Enterprise*, the destroyers *Faulkner*, *Foresight*, *Fearless*, *Foxhound* and *Escort* of the Eighth Flotilla, *Keppel*, *Douglas*, *Vortigern*, *Wishart* and *Watchman* of the Thirteenth Flotilla, the cruiser *Delhi*, which had just joined the group – and, of course, the *Ark*. There was no 'dummying' into the Atlantic this time. We were decoys, and subterfuge was not necessary. Over the broadcasting system we were warned by Captain Glennie that air attacks could be expected. At the same time Somerville signalled all ships in what was to become a laughable under-statement: 'Object of practice is to test the quality and price of ice cream.' The ice cream? This was the admiral's way of referring to the Italians. The 'practice' meant that we went immediately to relaxed action stations, and this state did not alter all that day or through the night of high humidity, when we ploughed on towards an area south-east of Majorca, where the *Ark*'s aircraft were to fly off.

The weather was superb on Tuesday 9 July as I leaned on the flag-deck rail to watch the destroyers zigzagging on both our flanks. Was there really a war on? Only the battle bowler-hatted brigades on the upper deck prevented this from looking a typical peacetime scene, one in which the *Hood* had been involved for the last twenty years. The day passed pleasantly enough, with the searing sun tempered by a light breeze, as we more or less lazed and sunbathed away the hours. We were roused in the early afternoon by the alarm to arms – three high-pitched bugle bars, dubbed by the matelots as 'There's a bomber overhead.' From the flag deck I could see a dot in the sky, circling the fleet. It was identified as an Italian Cant flying-boat and was too high to be dealt with by our anti-aircraft guns. After a minute or so this spy disappeared. We knew that this was possibly a messenger of doom who would sound the tally-ho for the hunting packs, and the opportunity of a few minutes respite was taken to detail us off for tea. I never finished mine.

It was just before 1600 when another alarm to arms stopped me in mid-sip of my mug of tea and in a mouthful of jam. I grabbed my steel helmet and dashed up the ladders to my action station. As I made for the flag deck, our anti-aircraft guns opened up. I was just clambering to the top of the flag-deck ladder when a great roar engulfed the ship. An unseen hand seemed to pummel me in the chest, and I was hurled backwards down the iron rungs. I got up off the deck and felt a trickle of blood coming from my nose. Within seconds it had become a torrent and rushed down into my mouth. Chief Yeoman George Thomas poked his head over the top of the ladder and seeing all the blood inquired gently: 'Are you hurt, lad? What are you doing down there, anyway?' I replied plaintively: 'I don't want to play any more, Chief.' The 'plaything' which had just missed the *Hood* was a stick of bombs from six aircraft of Italy's Regia Aeronautica, now over us at high altitude. Gingerly I climbed the ladder. I wiped the blood away from my face with a handkerchief. My nose was duly inspected by the chief yeoman, who decided it was 'just a scratch'. This was no time to worry about it, anyway. The racket from our pom-poms and four-inch anti-aircraft weapons cancelled out my fear of the bombs which were tumbling down from the planes above. The azure sky was pockmarked with grey smudges of bursting shells as the fleet maintained a tremendous barrage. The multiple machine-guns were crackling away, although it seemed perfectly obvious, even to someone as young and inexperienced as myself, that the raiders were hopelessly out of range. The *Hood* maintained top speed, but even so bomb bursts alongside sent shrapnel rattling against our sides.

Approximately five miles off I could see the *Ark Royal*, which was the main target. At times she disappeared behind huge columns of erupting sea as bombs plummeted around her. More than once I thought: 'She's had it this time.' But then the 'unsinkable *Ark*' would appear again from out of the Italian-made mist, like a fiery whale, with all her ack-ack guns spuming defiance. Suddenly, it was all over; the planes had gone; the cease-fire came. Our toiling gunners, stripped to the waist, were able to relax for a smoke, but only for thirty minutes. At 1750 the Italians were back in a tight formation of eighteen planes and using altitude again.

Somerville had a healthy respect for the accuracy of the raiders by now and ordered the fleet to 'stagger the line'. Up went a general shout of 'Here they come again.' I felt helpless on the flag deck as this second attack looked more concentrated. Sticks of bombs were screaming in closer, and tons of water were cascading on our deck. The *Ark* had managed to fly off her fighters, but the Italians had height in their favour. Smoke suddenly spouted from a plane heading for home, but it flew on. Then came another lull.

But the raiders returned. The pattern continued like this with two more waves of twenty-two bombers until 1840, when we were able to discard our steel helmets for the first time in nearly three hours, as darkness began to close in. Somerville was realizing that the cost of his ice cream was going to be very high if he continued to press on towards Cagliari. All that had been achieved was the certain destruction of one Italian plane by fighters and a claim, later refused, that the *Hood* had shot down a second. While we were at supper, Somerville signalled Vice-Admiral Wells in the *Ark Royal*: 'In view of the heavy scale bombing and the nature of our objective, do you think continuance of operations justified?' Wells had no doubts. 'Definitely not,' he replied by light from the ten-inch signal projector. The next thing we knew was a sudden divergence in course to 246 degrees and the reassuring voice of Captain Glennie telling us that the force were returning to Gibraltar. Somerville was disappointed at what he described as 'an unsatisfactory outing'[1] and his frustration increased just when it seemed the fleet would enter Gibraltar without casualties. Off the Rock early on 11 July the lurking Italian submarine *Marconi* torpedoed the destroyer *Escort* and scuttled away. A tug managed to get the damaged ship in tow but had to abandon her and she sank.

Despite Somerville's dejection, the diversionary sortie had

worked. The two British convoys arrived unmolested at Alexandria, while Cunningham's fleet, unhindered by the attentions of the Regia Aeronautica, had put to flight the Italian battle fleet off Calabria on 9 July. A direct hit had been scored on the flagship of Admiral Riccardi, who coincidentally had been dined in the *Hood* by Cunningham two years earlier.

During the next nineteen days we were given a rest, but Somerville was also able to initiate his somewhat rough training period. There were daytime visits by Italian reconnaissance aircraft and one night raid. But our morale was high, as in watches we were able to visit Sandy Bay and tan ourselves on the beach. Laughable Italian claims also established a team spirit in the force. One of their official communiqués proclaimed: 'Positive information has been obtained that in the course of the action in the zone of the Balearic Islands, Italian aeroplanes inflicted heavy damage on, and set fire to, the *Hood*. The aircraft-carrier *Ark Royal* was squarely hit on its deck by two large bombs. This has been ascertained by photographs taken after the action.'[2] Neither did the claims end there. The *Corriere della Sera* reported that the *Hood* had been so badly knocked about that she was being sent to dock in Britain. And on 13 and 14 July an Italian broadcast insisted that both the *Hood* and the *Ark* had been bombed out of action. We were said to have suffered hits on a turret and the main gun control position, which would need twenty days to repair. The broadcasts continued for the next week, and the final 'hoot' for the crew was the allegation that men were 'still working on the *Hood* day and night'. They always did!

All this publicity and the fact that we were seeing action made many of the *Hood*'s boys over cocky. We were inclined to swagger about and act like old salts, not only in our walk but also in our talk. Our language was as blue as our winter number one rig – until the chaplain, the Reverend Harold Beardmore, decided to have words with us. One day when we were in Gibraltar we were surprised to hear piped: 'All boys clear lower deck. Muster in the chapel.'

The tiny church in the superstructure under the flag deck was a delightful place, an oasis of serenity in a throbbing, floating iron and steel township, and we wondered why fifty of us had been assembled there. Beardmore strode in and ripped into us with four-letter words about our arrogance, the smoking, the drinking, the cursing. He used every swear word I had heard on board the *Hood*. We shuffled uncomfortably. 'You don't like it do you?' he said. 'It seems wrong coming from a "sky bosun" in this little church, doesn't it?' To our amazement he then rattled off two diabolically dirty jokes. A few tittered self-consciously, but most of us were silent and embarrassed. Then he said: 'You would not go home and say to your mum "Pass the fucking jam" would you? So why do it here?' No other words were exchanged, and he walked out. It all seemed so obscene in the quietness of the chapel, but most of us learned from his lesson. Everyone regarded him as a first-class padre. The next time I came into close contact with him was towards the end of 1941, when I was being presented with a picture of the *Hood* at an RNVR and RND dinner. He was beyond words this time. He just grabbed my hand and shook it. He was not ashamed of the tears on his cheeks, for I was the lone survivor of the boys he had lectured.

During this spell of relaxation Gibraltar also had uneasy memories for me of the controversial multiple rocket-launcher which had been installed in our last refit. It was the brainchild of Churchill and had been developed by Professor Frederick Lindemann's secret weapons department for combating low-flying aircraft. Lindemann, the brilliant Oxford physicist and mathematician who had been a crony of the premier since the 1930s, believed that rockets would be more successful than anti-aircraft guns in shooting down raiders which were close to the sea. Each launcher, which looked like an umbrella stand, carried twenty three-inch rockets, known as unrifled projectiles. These shot out seven-inch containers, each holding two thousand feet of wire. Attached to every wire was a small parachute and a two-pound Mills bomb, which was ejected at about four thousand feet. The wires were supposed to entangle a plane and pull down the grenade, which would detonate. The Director of Naval Ordnance and his team had no faith in this device. The Training and Staff Duties Department concurred with them. 'It's plumb crazy,' they opined. But Churchill, although not plumb crazy, was certainly gadget crazy, and he was instrumental in having them installed in nearly thirty capital ships. I don't think that a single rocket claimed a single victim.

In the *Hood* there were five on B turret either side of the boat deck, under the flag deck and abaft the after funnel – and ten tons of ammunition were stowed in fragile steel lockers on the boat decks, although this unprotected storage contravened Admiralty instruction. No one fancied the idea of having ten tons of explosives so exposed, and our fears were realized when one morning in Gibraltar a launcher accidentally went off with a great whoosh and a sheet of flame. I was on the flag deck and could see twenty Mills bombs flying around the area of the mole, but most exploded in the sea and there was no damage. Three sailors were badly burned, however. This scene has always been burnished on my memory because of its relevance to the demise of the *Hood*.

Our rest at the Rock was not to last much longer. I awoke on 30 July surprised to see the old carrier *Argus* moored ahead of the *Ark Royal*. This addition to Force H presaged another operation, which this time was Somerville's idea. Twelve Hurricanes destined for Malta had been shipped to Gibraltar, and the problem was how to deliver them to the island. The admiral knew that if this valuable cargo were part of a convoy it stood little chance of surviving the hazardous run to Malta. Instead, he suggested that the fighters should be assembled and tested in Gibraltar and put on the *Ark Royal*, which would sail to within flying-off distance of Malta. The Admiralty accepted his advice but preferred to use the *Argus*. They also incorporated into the operational plan an air strike from the *Ark* on Cagliari, with a section of Cunningham's fleet setting up another diversion in the eastern Mediterranean. The name of this game was 'Operation Hurry'.

At 0630 on 31 July the *Hood* left Gibraltar with the *Valiant, Resolution, Enterprise, Argus, Ark Royal* and nine destroyers. Despite the earliness of the hour, Captain Glennie announced to the crew that we were to sail in company for nearly twenty-four hours and then would part. The *Argus* would be escorted to Cape Bon to fly off the Hurricanes to Malta, while the *Hood* with the *Enterprise*, the

Ark and four destroyers would be positioned for the raid on Cagliari.

For the next twenty-four hours we all steamed steadily eastwards in perfect conditions. Everyone was at second degree of anti-aircraft readiness, but there were no spies in the sky. Then at 1750 they arrived high – but not to spy. As the alarm to arms was shrilled, I spotted them at twenty thousand feet. 'Italian Savoia bombers', came the recognition call. Our anti-aircraft defences opened up in their now familiar startling, yet settling to my stomach, chorus of cracks, whoofs, crumps, boomp-a-boomp-a-boomps. The raiders made no attempt to home in closer but let go their loads at full distance. The scream of bombs punctuated our barrage, and a stick fell harmlessly off the *Hood*'s port quarter. Within a few minutes, and after we had fired close to a hundred rounds of HA ammunition, the raiders droned off. Everyone expected the known pattern to develop of a series of strikes before sunset. But we were wrong, and just before 1900 we were stood down.

Later that clear and starlit night the force split, and soon the comparative silence on the flag deck was broken by the warming up of the Swordfish on the *Ark*. For the rest of the night we watched the blurred fire of their engines at take-off and waited for their return from the attack on Cagliari. Next day we were told that every Hurricane had made it safely to Malta. Somerville signalled his satisfaction: 'Missions accomplished. Group One [the *Hood*'s section] is awarded a bun. Group Two is awarded two buns.' He had proved that 'flying off' was the best method to reinforce Malta's flagging air defenders, and this tactic was used many times until the end of the North African campaign.

There were no pursuers as we swept westerly towards Gibraltar, and the chance was taken to make a fifteen-inch full charge practice shoot, which revealed that the rifling of two guns was defective. Just after noon on 3 August the reassuring vista of the Sierra Nevada, those Spanish mountains which pointed to a haven ahead in Gibraltar, was sighted. We moored alongside the South Mole the next day, not realizing that this was to be the last combined operation by the heavy ships of Force H.

I was expecting letters from my mother to be in the Fleet

Mail Office, but there was not one bag of correspondence for the *Hood*. A line from home meant everything on the mess decks, and most of us were disgruntled. This was offset by the announcement of shore leave until 1700 and with it the old buzz that the *Hood* was to be withdrawn soon from the Mediterranean. It was to be sooner than later. Again we were somewhat peeved when just before 1800 that night we slipped our wires, steamed out of the harbour and headed east with the *Valiant* and the *Ark*. For four hours the *Hood* stayed on this course; then, after suddenly turning about and being detached from the rest of the force, we were convinced that the Admiralty had picked us for another 'stunt'. During darkness the ship remained on a course of 260 degrees towards the Atlantic. The next morning the mess decks were seething with rumour until Captain Glennie broadcast that the *Hood* had been ordered back to Britain. Cheers echoed around the ship, despite the fact that we were bound for inhospitable Scapa Flow.

The five-day voyage was uneventful. Just after midnight on 10 August Cape Wrath was sighted, and nearly six hours later we passed Hoxa Boom and entered Scapa, for a new phase of operations and a new boss. Within three hours Somerville had left the *Hood* for good and flown to London. His flag was not struck until six o'clock that evening, with the insignia of BC1 (Second in Command Home Fleet) being hoisted in its place. An hour later another gaggle of gold braid settled in the *Hood* – Vice-Admiral Whitworth and his staff were back with us.

19

The Admirals Cry 'Wolf'

The summer of 1940 blazed by me in a blur of bewildering figures in the headlines. The Battle of Britain was being decided in the skies of southern England, and it seemed strange and frustrating that the *Hood* with her enormous ack-ack fire power should be cloistered in the dubious cosiness of Scapa Flow. In fact we were being kept out of the firing-line of the Luftwaffe in case we were later needed to combat Hitler's surface invasion forces in Operation Sealion, which was expected during September.

Each day the headlines of the *Daily Express* and *Daily Mirror* kept up the morale of the boys' mess deck with astounding claims of the destruction of German aircraft by the RAF. On 11 August, the day we arrived at Scapa, sixty 'bandits' were shot down over the Channel; two days later the score was seventy-eight, and on 15 August it had zoomed up to 180. The next day we were at sea, hammering south, convinced that the *Hood* was going into the battle zone, until it was announced that our destination was Rosyth, where the left fifteen-inch gun of A turret was to be replaced. So we were still out of the fight as the Battle of Britain roared on with seemingly hundreds of Nazi planes being downed. The eight days the *Hood* stayed at Rosyth enabled many to return to the reality of 'civilized' runs ashore, but then we retreated to the haven of Scapa again on 25 August, the night that London had its first taste of full-scale bombing.

On 13 September, with the invasion scare at its zenith, the Admiralty decided to use the *Hood*. We left Scapa in company with the *Nelson* and *Rodney*, the cruisers *Bonaventure*, *Naiad* and *Cairo* and a screen of seven destroyers, and 'to meet any possible threat' steamed south –

but only two hundred miles, to Rosyth again. Within two days – although unknown to us – the German High Command had cancelled Operation Sealion almost at the same time as newspapers were trumpeting that in one record day the enemy had lost 185 aircraft. Churchill's chiefs of staff were not so sure that the danger had passed, and the consequence was that the *Hood* was kept in a state of constant readiness.

It seemed rather odd to us, to say the least, that the Admiralty drafted to us three Free French sailors – after all it was our guns which had killed more than a thousand of their countrymen at Oran. We 'got on' with them all right, but the subject of Oran was strictly taboo. One of them was Leading Signalman Roger Loiseaux, who signed on under the *nom-de-guerre* of Dempsey. It transpired that he had not been sent to the *Hood* against his will. In later years he told me: 'I picked the *Hood* myself and did not regret it. I have unforgettable memories of the friends I made among the officers and men.'

For the next eight months we were to be involved in a succession of false alarms and fatuous emergency sailings. The first came on 28 September, when a German cruiser was escorting a convoy more than a hundred miles off Stavanger, Norway. We were soon troughing through the North Sea. The next day the flap was over; the operation was called off, and to the disappointment of the crew we were detoured to inhospitable Scapa again.

On 15 October the *Hood* was called on again to cover the return of the cruisers *Berwick* and *Norfolk* and carrier *Furious*, whose aircraft were to attack Tromsö, Norway. Screened by the destroyers *Somali*, *Eskimo* and *Mashona*, we steamed towards the rendezvous, only to run into a fog which was so impenetrable that from the flag deck I could not see our escort. It worsened at dusk, and speed was reduced to fourteen knots. Our siren bellowed out constantly, and the destroyers' searchlights were switched on spasmodically. The fog blanket did not lift the next day, and most of us realized that with a sudden change of course to 180 degrees there would be a sudden change of plans. There was, for at 0925 on 18 October – the day the air attack was scheduled – we sighted Dunnet Head, the northernmost tip of land on the Pentland Firth, which marks the turn to starboard towards Scapa. We were to be closeted in the Flow almost until the end of October, but with the 'buzz' in the air that leave was to be given soon, our sojourn became bearable.

Most of us prayed that there would be no more flaps, but on 28 October the *Hood* was summoned out again with the *Furious* and destroyer screen for another sea-game of blind man's bluff. The objective was an 'eight-inch German cruiser' and supply ships in the area between Iceland and the Faroes. But the enemy became secondary. A Force 8 gale buffeted the *Hood*, and she was awash for long periods. Hands were not allowed in the batteries – the positions where the 5.5-inch guns had been – and all upper-deck hatches on the weather side remained closed. Yet we could see men walking round the decks of the escorts. Throughout the first night waves crested over the boat deck, flooding the wardroom and mess decks. The *Hood* had always been a wet ship, and the massive increase in her top-weight tonnage since 1939 had worsened conditions. On 30 October there was not a man on board who did not welcome the cancellation of the operation and the return to Scapa. But there was no let-up for us. The *Hood* was anti-aircraft guardship for the fleet, and our gunners complained that they were required to man the four-inch armament for two hours at dusk and for another two at dawn. For the next two days there were also exercises for the HA armament crews and torpedomen.

At the beginning of November I was one of the lucky ones given leave. To facilitate our rest, the *Hood* sailed south to Greenock. But only for three days was I allowed to relish my mother's home comforts in Derby. On the fourth day I received a telegram from the ship which beckoned baldly: 'Return forthwith.' I did as I was bid, but such were the vagaries of the telegram service and the London and North Eastern Railway that when the train pulled in to Greenock the *Hood* had gone. Two hundred of the ship's company also missed the boat, but a bonus came for all of us. We were sent to Glasgow, where we were billeted in a church hall and allowed free use of the transport systems and the cinemas.

A week later, when we rejoined the *Hood*, I learned that

the recall had been another waste of time. On 27 October the German pocket battleship *Admiral Scheer* had slipped out of Brunsbüttel and edged north passed Bokna Fjord and Bergen into the Norwegian Sea. Undetected she crossed the Arctic Circle and turned west for the Denmark Strait, which she passed on 31 October. Not until 5 November did the Admiralty realize that a lethal surface raider was abroad. On this day the *Scheer* ripped into a convoy from Halifax, whose only shield was the fourteen-thousand-ton armed merchant cruiser *Jervis Bay*. In a similar way to the sacrifice of the *Rawalpindi* twelve months earlier, Captain E.S.F. Fegen turned his ship to confront the *Scheer*, although knowing that his six-inch guns were no match. The *Jervis Bay* was sunk within twenty minutes, but Fegen's heroic action, which won a posthumous VC, enabled all but five of the thirty-seven vessel convoy to escape.

It was on receiving the *Jervis Bay*'s radioed message that Admiral Tovey, the Commander-in-Chief Home Fleet, despatched the *Hood* and *Repulse*, three ships of the Fifteenth Cruiser Squadron and six destroyers to cover the approaches to Brest and Lorient to ensure that the *Scheer* could not return. Again it was a fruitless operation, for the raider turned into the South Atlantic to bedevil a series of convoys. For five days the *Hood* and her companions chased shadows, finally returning to Scapa, where I rejoined her on 11 November in time for the Armistice Day ceremony.

As the mists of autumn set in, the crew became resigned to a winter at Scapa, alternating between exercises in the Flow and hurried despatches into the North Sea. On 23 November the *Hood* was required to screen a big minelaying force north of the Denmark Strait. At dawn the next morning we were called to action stations just as the leading vessels of the 1st Minelaying Squadron, shepherded by the cruiser *Aurora*, came into view. Visibility was perfect, and from the flag deck I could see the mountains of Iceland as we hurried north. During the afternoon of the 26th in fatherly fashion Commander W.K.R. Cross broadcast to the crew a short lecture about the great ice flow which we were nearing. The chunky, dark-coloured pack ice could be seen to the north of the Denmark Strait, and during the next few hours I spotted many icebergs. But conditions were not as idyllic as the views. Spray froze immediately as it was whipped up on to the forecastle. It was our first geography lesson of the Strait, and soon we were glad to alter course and track back to Scapa.

At about 1400 on Christmas Eve at Scapa, just as the messes were preparing for the parties of the next day, special sea duty men were piped to their stations. From the flag deck I could see that five other ships – the cruiser *Edinburgh* and the destroyers *Cossack*, *Echo*, *Electra* and *Escapade* – had already weighed anchor and were thrusting out of the Flow. The *Hood* followed, and soon came the announcement over the broadcast system that our Christmas would be spent patrolling the Iceland-Faroes passage for the purpose of trying to intercept the cruiser *Hipper*, which was being chased by the *Berwick*.

It was my second Christmas of the war at sea, but we were all in the same boat and the greyness and knifing coldness of the fringe of the Arctic Circle melted below decks as carols echoed through the messes and as 'sippers' from tots were freely exchanged before the arrival of the turkey and plum pudding. Mess decks were decorated with flags and bunting cadged from the flag deck; the captain carried out a parody of 'rounds', preceded by a boy seaman dressed in a master-at-arms uniform. As far as possible discipline was relaxed below deck, but for those on watch it was 'business as usual'.

Our real Christmas present came on Boxing Day with the news that we were to exchange the howling winds of the Faroes for the lighter zephyrs of Scapa. The *Hipper* had eluded the net, and yet again the *Hood* set course for Scapa without satisfactorily completing her mission.

The Admiralty did allow us the privilege of celebrating New Year in harbour, but the following day another escort for a minelaying operation was lined up for the *Hood*. Apart from the catalytic cold it was an uneventful four days as we patrolled north of the Faroes and then to the south. The scare came just before returning to Scapa. Off Dunnet Head Light the port paravane snarled a mine mooring. It was swiftly cut and a destroyer was diverted from the screen to blow up the drifting mine with rifle fire.

The buzz had been going around the ship for several days

now that we were to have an 'extensive refit' at Rosyth and that a long leave would be granted to everyone. It was confirmed on 10 January when the boatswain's party struck the pole-masts on both the fore and main masts. This meant that the *Hood* was about to pass under the Forth Bridge on the way to Rosyth. Sure enough we sailed from Scapa that afternoon and on 13 January secured to our buoy in the Forth.

For the last twenty years the *Hood* had been in service, and it was beginning to show. She needed repairs to machinery, and at the same time the chance was taken to install gunnery radar – type 284 – which was to be mounted on the armoured hood over the gun director on the spotting top, where the fifteen-foot rangefinder had been dismantled during the previous refit. This sounded simple enough, but there was a snag. The radar transmitting and receiving aerials were unable to revolve smoothly so the foretop mast was removed and the yard, originally mounted on this mast, had to be fitted to a special support bracket abaft the spotting top. All this increased the burden of topweight, and it was necessary to reduce it by taking down the HF/DF equipment and the enclosed section of the torpedo look-out platform from the foremast. To the relief of the coxswains, the antique steam picket boats, which had been carried since her launching, were replaced by two thirty-five-foot motor launches.

I returned from leave in the middle of these alterations to find that on promotion to rear-admiral Captain Glennie was leaving the ship on 15 February, when Captain Ralph Kerr would take over. Glennie was a typical dour Scot and a four-ringed captain who wanted everyone to know it. The scar-faced Kerr was quieter, less prepossessing, and did not want everyone to get out of his way just because he was captain of the *Hood*. Eleven days after our new 'boss' arrived, the starboard watch reported back from leave and the count-down for rejoining the fleet began with cleaning the ship, scraping off the rust and painting.

A personal milestone was reached on 1 March, my eighteenth birthday, when I had to go through the ritual of requesting that I be advanced to ordinary signalman. The process seemed an unnecessary waste of time. I had to put in a request to see my divisional officer, who heard my request. Then I was required to request to see the commander. He duly heard my request, and then I was allowed to request to see the captain. The final request 'interview' was a mere formality. The master-at-arms, A.J. Chandler, read out my request to become an ordinary rating; Captain Kerr looked at it cursorily and immediately granted it. With 'man's rating' my pay went up from 8s. 9d. to 14 shillings a week, but I still had to wait another three years before I could draw my tot of rum, although I was able to drink as much as I liked ashore!

During this first week of March the ship's company were driven into a frenzy of swift painting, which puzzled us until it was announced that the King and then Churchill were to visit the *Hood*. On the day the spit and polish were switched from the ship's metalwork to our number ones as George VI was to inspect full-scale divisions. On completion we were mustered aft on the quarterdeck to be addressed by the King. As a full-blown ordinary signalman, I was on the top line for smartness, although as I came face to face with the monarch I could not help but wonder why he appeared to be wearing make-up!

On the completion of a thorough examination of the *Hood*'s propellers, rudder and underwater hull, we were shifted to the dockyard basin to round off the refit. Our 'holiday' came to an end on 17 March when the *Hood* was towed out and anchored in the midstream above the Forth Bridge. We were back under fleet orders and at 1600 the next day sailed under the bridge, through the first boom and down channel past the West Inchkeith Gate into the North Sea.

Our destination was Scapa again, and on the way we were to put the *Hood* through a series of trials, but another 'flap' changed all this. At dawn the following day action stations was sounded by bugle. 'Another exercise,' I thought, but no. Captain Kerr was soon telling us that this could be the real thing.

Although still officially an 'inefficient ship', the *Hood* was to rendezvous with the *Queen Elizabeth*, also still working up, and join Admiral Tovey in the *Nelson*, on patrol off the south of Iceland, where in company we were to steer south at full speed. And the quarry? The battleships *Scharnhorst* and *Gneisenau*.

Admiral Gunther Lutjens was in command of this powerful German raiding force, which for the first time had broken through the British blockade into the North Atlantic during January. They had been attacking the Halifax convoy route and sunk 116,000 tons of allied shipping. Now Lutjens had been commanded to leave the North Atlantic by 17 March and break back to Brest. Not until 20 March were the *Scharnhorst* and *Gneisenau* spotted by aircraft from the *Hood's* old companion, the *Ark Royal*, still with Force H, which had been hurriedly despatched north from Gibraltar. Lutjens' position was given as six hundred miles west-north-west of Cape Finisterre, and Admiral Tovey believed he had a reasonable chance of bringing the raiders to battle.

As we tore south through the seas to the west of Ireland, the commander announced that an interception was expected at 1500. Excitement and anticipation began to build up. We thought that perhaps after all the false alarms this could be the first really big surface action of the war. Yet deep down there was the feeling of 'I'll believe it when it actually happens'. Were the admirals crying 'wolf' yet again? Zero hour came and went. On the flag deck everyone was fidgety. I could imagine how pent up the top brass must have been on the admiral's bridge.

There was no sign of the Germans. Lutjens' force had slipped through. When tracked by the *Ark's* aircraft, they had turned from a north-easterly course to one of due north. As soon as the shadowing plane had disappeared, Lutjens switched back to his original track and entered Brest unmolested on the morning of 22 March. Not until six days later did a reconnaissance foray by Coastal Command discover the *Scharnhorst* and *Gneisenau* safely tucked up in the French port. Another failure to contact the enemy for the *Hood*; another return to Scapa, where we arrived on Sunday 23 March.

There were still full power trials to be worked, despite the fact that the *Hood* had turned it all on in vain during the long surge to the south in pursuit of the German raiders. Just one night was spent at the anchorage and we were off again for a measured run, during which a speed of 28.8 knots was reached with paravanes streamed. Ahead lay three onerous weeks at sea with the occasional return to Scapa for refuelling. Admiral Whitworth, now earmarked to be Second Sea Lord, made a general signal during the forenoon of 28 March that units of the Home Fleet would maintain a patrol 350 miles to the west to ensure that the *Scharnhorst* and *Gneisenau* did not creep out from Brest into the shipping lanes again. 'Units of the Home Fleet' meant that the burden of the main responsibility would fall on the *Hood* and there was no relaxation from now on. When on patrol a three-watch system of night vigilance was scheduled for one on and two off. At dusk and dawn – the times most likely for attack – it was routine to go to action stations, so those men on the middle watch had only a few hours of unbroken sleep.

Examinations for midshipmen, who were about to be promoted to sub-lieutenant, continued at sea during this period of patrolling. They began on a Sunday and occupied four days. I remember this particular session because after it was over there was a riotous party in the midshipmen's gunroom, of which the ship's company got to hear. After the gin, beer and 'el torpedo' and 'depth charge' cocktails had flowed, bottles began to fly – and trousers, too. One lieutenant was cut by a piece of shattered glass, before all the popular officers were debagged by the 'mids'. The next morning in Scapa, before the new sub-lieutenants departed, a more decorous cocktail party was held in the wardroom by Captain Kerr, at which Admiral Whitworth forecast that the war would last for seventeen years. After those long hours of patrolling I felt I could have slept away the rest of his predicted war.

It was on 18 April, after the *Hood* had refuelled at Scapa, that I first heard of the *Bismarck*. Until then to me the name had associations with a German chancellor of the misty past. We had been briefed that our next tour of duty was to be in the Bay of Biscay, but during the middle watch these orders were cancelled and new plans were drawn which necessitated a sudden alteration of course to 060 degrees. This was brought about by a signal which stated that the new *Bismarck*, a battleship, accompanied by two *Leipzig*-class cruisers and escorted by three destroyers, had slipped out of Kiel in a north-westerly direction. The next day Whitworth revealed to the crew that the *Hood*, the cruiser

Kenya and a destroyer screen were to protect the northern waters, with a smaller force patrolling the Bay of Biscay. The searchers for the *Bismarck* were to be the *Kenya* and three destroyers. If they contacted her, the plan was for the *Hood* to close at full speed. Whitworth stressed: 'If possible we will make an end-on approach, so as to present the minimum target.' It was the first time that many officers had realized the vulnerability of the *Hood* to the vertical trajectory of a shell at extreme range, because of her weak deck armour. At closer range and a flatter trajectory the twelve-inch side armour was capable of holding out to severe punishment.

No one told the lower deck about this type of Achilles heel, as we maintained the surveillance patrol during 20 April. The next day the familiar pattern evolved; the operation was abandoned and the force put into Hvalfjord, Iceland – known to us as Shovelford – which if there had been a naval league table for runs ashore would have been in the relegation zone. For eight days the *Hood* lurked here until the arrival of the cruisers *Norfolk* and *Suffolk*, who were to be linked with our destiny. At nightfall, in company with our new 'chummies', we sailed to cover two convoys against the alleged threat of the *Bismarck*. On 1 May, after three days of bone-chilling vigilance in this arid area of frost-smoke and water-laden skies, the force returned to the doubtful benefits of Hvalfjord. Within three days the erroneous menace of the *Bismarck* had subsided. She was found holed up in Gydnia, Poland, or Gotenhafen, as the Germans had renamed it, so it was time for the *Hood* to return to Scapa, where we arrived on 5 May.

It was also time to say farewell to Admiral Whitworth, whose new job was awaiting him in Whitehall. At 13.40 on 8 May the lower deck was cleared and the ship's company waved goodbye to him from the quarterdeck as he was rowed ashore in a whaler by senior officers. Although there was to be a four-day time lag before Vice-Admiral Lancelot Holland took on the role of commander of the Battle Cruiser Squadron and second in command of the Home Fleet, there was no respite for the *Hood*. In the Pentland Firth a practice of the four-inch guns and the main armament was carried out. The four-inch crews achieved several hits on a sleeve target, towed by a Blackburn Roc, while the fifteen-inch gunners straddled a seaborne target, towed by a drifter. We were confident that our aim would be steady if our path crossed that of the *Bismarck*.

20

'Perhaps This is the Big One'

It was my job to collect messages for the flag lieutenant and take them to his cabin after members of the wardroom had dined. At 8 p.m. on 21 May I looked at a signal addressed to Admiral Holland from Admiral Sir John Tovey, the Commander-in-Chief of the Home Fleet. It seemed routine and read: 'Flying your flag in *Hood* and taking *Prince of Wales, Acates, Antelope, Anthony, Echo, Icarus* and *Electra* under your orders sail at 0001 on May 22 and proceed with moderate despatch to Hvalfjord.' I knew that it was only a confirmatory message and placed little importance on it. We had received dozens of similar signals in the last year, and generally they led to freezing watches at sea in northerly waters. 'Oh God, another cold, late night,' I thought.

The *Hood* was at Scapa Flow, and it was obvious to harbour-watchers that soon we would not be there. In the early evening there had been an abnormal amount of comings and goings between the *Hood* and the *King George V*, Tovey's flagship. Soon after, ominous, blacker streams of smoke began to emerge from the funnels of the fleet, signifying the usual controlled urgency of wartime preparation for sea. Later that evening I was hurrying to Lieutenant-Commander Wyldbore-Smith's cabin again with a confidential signal from the C-in-C. This urged: 'Raise steam with all despatch and be prepared to leave harbour 0001 on May 22.'

As special sea duty men fell in this Thursday night, light rain and a thin mist turned the flow into a lacy veil. My station on the compass platform with the admiral's staff allowed me a commentary-box view of the fleet, and a little before midnight our destroyer escort slipped their moorings in Gutter Sound, formed a line ahead and paraded through the Switha Gate to wait for us on the edge of the Pentland Firth. When the procession had ended, the *Hood* was swung around on her engines and headed southwards to the Hoxa Gate. In our wake came the newly constructed *Prince of Wales*, still with dockyard civilians on board. At the gate the massive underwater mesh of anti-submarine netting was hauled aside by the crew of the boom vessel, and we glided through with the destroyers taking station ahead.

The wind was scything into us from the north already, and although it was a May night the cold soon began to penetrate into anyone not below decks. It was a typical, boring six-hours spell at sea, one which in two days time I was to yearn for. The next day, while I was breakfasting on the mess deck, Commander Cross's calm and carefully controlled voice briefed us over the broadcasting system. He revealed that the *Bismarck* and a *Hipper*-class cruiser — at this stage no one knew she was the *Prinz Eugen* — were expected to leave Bergen, and that our squadron were proceeding to Hvalfjord to cover an area to the north and close to Iceland, while Tovey in *King George V* and the rest of the Home Fleet guarded a section further south. Aircraft and a line of cruisers were patrolling the area affected, and we were assured there would be a definite warning of the approach of the Nazi raiders. The announcement did not cause a stir. We had heard it all before and nothing had happened. We were fairly confident it would not happen this time, and if it did, the *Hood* was capable of handling any 'jumped-up German pocket battleship'. What in fact we did not know was that the *Bismarck*, far from being a mini-battle cruiser was superior in every way to the *Hood* and also to the *Prince of Wales*, which had just left the dockyard, had not completed gunnery trials and was still having trouble with her turrets, on which civilian experts were working even at this moment.

It is necessary here to fill in the vacuum of misinformation which lay between the lower deck and the wardroom. Although listed as 35,000 tons to comply with the London Naval Treaty, the *Bismarck* was in reality 42,000 tons in standard displacement and 52,700 tons when loaded with fuel, stores and crew, which meant she was 4,700 tons heavier than the *Hood*. She had been launched on St

Valentine's Day 1939 at the Blohm & Voss Yard in Hamburg and was intended by the Nazis to be as unsinkable as a ship could be. She was nearly 300 yards long and at her widest was 118 feet, seven feet more than us. Unlike the *Hood*, she was built to withstand the fiercest of bombardments. A $12\frac{3}{4}$-inch armour belt of Krupps steel girthed her, and this was backed by an ingenious double system of armoured decks of four inches and two inches. Similar to the hardest-hitting ships of the Royal Navy, her main armament was eight fifteen-inch guns. This 'unsinkable gun platform' held in Germany a similar naval prestige as the *Hood* had in 1921. She was not as comfortable for the crew, yet this gave her more protection. Because of its disadvantage in numbers of ships compared with Britain's, the German Navy operated on a wartime system of short, limited raids, and when vessels returned to their home bases, the crews lived ashore. We in the *Hood* stayed onboard, and therefore our quarters were broadside mess decks, which meant that in action the ship could not withstand as much punishment as the *Bismarck*, which was honeycombed with tiny compartments, easily shut off if holed. It had taken fifteen months to fit her out, and she was handed over to the German Navy on 24 August 1940, but not destined to be rushed into action, although Grand Admiral Eric Raeder was short of ships. To keep her away from the eyes and talons of the RAF, the *Bismarck* was sent to the Bay of Danzig and based at Gydnia, while the crew trained. Within a few days she was joined by another new ship, the heavy cruiser *Prinz Eugen*. Although she was more than thirty thousand tons lighter than the *Bismarck*, her outline was similar to her bigger fleet sister, and at a distance it was difficult to distinguish one from the other. This piece of German cunning was tortuously to change the course of my entire life.

The two ships were planned to form a squadron and also a partnership with the *Scharnhorst* and *Gneisenau*, currently being refitted at Brest. Raeder had evolved Operation Rheinubung (Rhine Exercise), which was designed to slaughter the Atlantic convoys supplying besieged Britain. The *Bismarck* and *Prinz Eugen* were intended to break out from Germany by using the northerly route through the Denmark Strait and rendezvous in mid Atlantic with the

Scharnhorst and *Gneisenau*. Five oil-tankers, two supply ships and spying U-boats were also involved. The orders for fifty-one-year-old Admiral Gunther Lutjens, who was to be in charge of the operation in the *Bismarck*, after his exploits with the *Scharnhorst* and *Gneisenau* in the Atlantic raid four months earlier, were to avoid contact with British warships during the break-out but once out into the Atlantic to concentrate firepower on lone battleships protecting convoys, while the other three ships massacred the smaller escorts and merchantmen carrying the lease-lend supplies and armaments promised to Britain by Roosevelt. Raeder also anticipated that, to ferret out the most formidable German force to be at sea since Jutland, the Royal Navy would have to withdraw units from the Mediterranean, where the Italian Navy could reasonably be expected to take the initiative.

It was a bold plan, coming on the heels of the highest monthly toll of British losses during the April, when 687,901 tons of shipping were destroyed. Fortunately for Britain, Bomber Command knocked the *Gneisenau* out of action in Brest, and the *Scharnhorst*, which had machinery defects, was contained in port by a curtain of three hundred mines 'drawn' by the minelayer HMS *Abdiel*.

Hitler was loath to gamble his 'unsinkable' super-ship *Bismarck* in this heady operation, but on 18 May it was triggered when in company with the *Prinz Eugen* she sailed from Gydnia. The first inkling that a break-out might be attempted came when the Swedish cruiser *Gotland* sighted them in the Skagerrak, and this information filtered through to the Admiralty in London. There had already been a false alarm on 19 April, when it was rumoured that the *Bismarck* was heading north, so Admiral Tovey was prepared now for the reality of the operation and set up cruiser patrols in the possible break-out channels. The eight-inch gunned cruisers *Norfolk* and *Suffolk* were assigned to the Denmark Strait, the six-inch armed cruisers *Birmingham* and *Manchester* to the Iceland-Faroes gap, and four more smaller cruisers joined him at Scapa.

On 21 May Coastal Command reconnaissance planes spotted the German ships in Korsfjord and Kalvanes Bay, near Bergen, where they were refuelling, but they were described as '*Hipper*-class cruisers'. This was discounted when film was developed and revealed that the *Bismarck* and the *Prinz Eugen* were the '*Hippers*'. It was this information which sent the *Hood* scurrying north.

While we slept that night, thirty aircraft attempted to bomb the embryonic raiders in two strikes, but failed abysmally to find the targets. By dawn the *Bismarck* and *Prinz Eugen* were racing on past Trondheim with Lutjens despatching his escort of three destroyers back to the safety of home waters.

So, unknown to us, the Germans were lost. Oblivious to the situation, we steamed on until 2230 on 22 May, when we were about to enter the approaches to Hvalfjord. Then I carried this signal from Tovey to the compass platform: '*Bismarck* and consort sailed. Proceed to cover area south-west of Iceland.' Half an hour earlier the 'lost' ships were reported no longer at their anchorage by an observer in a Maryland of Coastal Command, which sparked Tovey, still biding his time in Scapa, to sail in the *King George V*, with the carrier *Victorious*, the cruisers *Galatea*, *Hermione*, *Kenya* and *Aurora* and seven destroyers, to take up covering positions to the north-west.

As soon as the *Hood* had altered course in accordance with the 2230 signal of the C-in-C, Commander Cross updated the ship's company of the situation, and for the first time the nervous feeling of an approach to battle began to build up. 'Perhaps this is it.' I wondered. 'Perhaps this is the big one.' The feeling that I was hungry, yet did not want to eat, nagged at my stomach. Looking around me, I could see my mates yawning nervously and trying to appear unconcerned. We all knew it was an act, yet we did not discuss the possibilities of action seriously.

I slept undisturbed that night, surprised to awake in the morning to find that there had been no alarms. The nervous tension of the night before had vanished. It was, after all, another unnecessary foray, another false alarm. We were all wasting our time here on the fringes of the frozen north. Routine was back to normal until 7.30 that evening, when I was playing a quiet game of solo with Frank Tuxworth, Ron Bell and Jimmy Green on the mess deck. The broadcasting system spluttered into life and ordered: 'Flag lieutenant's messenger report to the SDO at the double!' I did as I was piped and dashed to the signals distribution office, where I was told to rush a message to Lieutenant-Commander Wyldbore-Smith in his cabin. It always seemed laughable to me that I had to rush paper missives, even though the recipient had already been told by telephone of their contents. This particular signal was at least dramatic and deserved the classification 'rush' for it stated: 'From *Suffolk* – enemy in sight.'

The *Bismarck* and *Prinz Eugen*, which had reduced from twenty-seven knots to twenty-four when entering the mush ice pack, had been blessed with mist to obscure their movements, but in the late afternoon it lifted. Able Seaman Newell, *Suffolk*'s starboard after look-out, had sighted the two at a distance of seven miles. The time was 1922, but *Suffolk*'s signal did not reach her co-searcher, the *Norfolk*, because of icing on her aerials. From that moment the shadowers of the *Bismarck* continued to send in a stream of amplifying coded reports. 'OCAS 240-25', for example, meant 'Enemy course 240 degrees and speed twenty-five knots.' 'OSTA4' indicated that the enemy were altering course to forty degrees starboard.

By now Admiral Holland had decided to abandon his normal occupancy of the admiral's bridge and to conduct the operation from the compass platform in company with Flag Captain Kerr. As the dogsbody messenger I was required to be close to Wyldbore-Smith's elbow. The 1922 report from the *Suffolk*, which was plotted in the *Hood*, put the enemy due north of us and around three hundred miles away. This prompted Holland, who was at the chart table, to order at 1945 an increase of speed to twenty-seven knots and a course alteration of 295 degrees for the interception.

With this sudden diversion the ship's company were alive again to the realization that deadly action could be just ten hours away. The back of my neck began to prickle with excitement, and I found myself stuttering slightly, a nervous habit which until then I had managed to conquer since the age of ten. Although we had still to be called to action stations, most departments were preparing for the thunder of guns. The tension was heightened by *Norfolk*'s report at 2032: 'One battleship, one cruiser in sight.' This was the first signal to reach Tovey of the position of the *Bismarck* in the Denmark Strait, because *Suffolk's* radio was still on the blink. The *Norfolk*, whose radar was inferior to the *Suffolk's*, had run straight into the enemy but had turned about at a range of six miles, had made smoke and, despite being straddled by the *Bismarck's* fifteen-inch guns, had managed to retreat into the murk to continue shadowing with the *Suffolk*.

By now the weather was roughening. We were bumping around a great deal as snow flurries began to whip into us, and I could see the destroyer escort disappearing in great troughs and then ploughing out of them like wounded porpoise. Their plight became apparent when the senior officer of the screen signalled: 'Do not consider destroyers can maintain present speed without danger.' At 2055 Holland replied: 'If you are unable to maintain this speed I will have to go on without you. You should follow at your best speed.' But the tenacity of the tiny vessels was tremendous; for the next half hour their skippers attempted to keep with us, and then gradually they were forced to accept the inevitable, reduce speed and drop astern.

The hubbub of activity between the compass platform and the bridge wireless office continued into the night, and at one stage I could not contain my nervousness and took the unprecedented step, for an ordinary signalman, of asking Wyldbore-Smith: 'What's happening, sir?' He should have admonished me; instead he took pity on my callowness and replied: 'It looks like definite action within the next few hours, Briggs.' His prediction became known to the rest of the ship's company around 2200 when Commander Cross confirmed in a broadcast that the *Bismarck* and a '*Hipper*-class cruiser' had been contacted and were being shadowed by the *Norfolk* and *Suffolk*. 'We are expected to intercept at 0200 tomorrow morning,' he confided. 'We will go to action stations at midnight. In the meantime prepare yourselves and above all change into clean underwear.' This last sentence galvanized the mess deck, where I had returned to collect a cup of 'kiy' (cocoa). The only other time we had been warned to put on clean vests, pants and socks, in case dirty garments infected a wound, was at Oran, where we had fired our guns in anger, although reluctantly. Apprehension was heavy in the air. I think that most of my mates, like myself, were fearing not instant oblivion but the horror of being fearfully wounded or mutilated and screaming out in painful insanity. I had the depressing dread of being afraid of fear and showing it. Yet I was not feeling afraid – just wound up. I wanted the action to be hurried on, and yet at the same time I did not want it to happen. Wouldn't I wake up tomorrow in my hammock and find it was all a mistake? I could sense the feeling around me of quiet confidence in the ship's ability, but a bravado about one's own capability.

Just before midnight I changed into clean underwear and socks, put on my number three suit, tied up my lifebelt, or Mae West, over it, buttoned up my Burberry on top of this bulk and then completed the ensemble by donning anti-flash gear, with my gas-mask slung in front on my chest and a 'battle bowler' on my head. It was not yet time to report, but I did not want to miss anything. I picked up signals from the SDO and was on my way up the ladder to the compass platform when Tuxworth, one of my best chums, stopped me for a quick chat and a joke, which was to become indelible on my memory. 'Do you remember, Briggo,' he said, 'that when the *Exeter* went into action with the *Graf Spee* there was only one signalman saved?' I laughed and cracked back: 'If that happens to us, it'll be me who's saved, Tux.' We were interrupted by the shrill bugle call summoning us to action stations right on midnight.

I clattered up the ladder to the glass-screened compass platform and squeezed in through the door. In the dimness of the binnacle and chart-table lights I could make out a stage-like setting. On the starboard, facing forward, stood the robust figure of Commander E.H.G. 'Tiny' Gregson, the squadron gunnery officer, and Lieutenant-Commander G.E.M. Owens, the admiral's secretary. Alongside, centre of stage, in the captain's chair was Admiral Holland, with Captain Kerr on his right. Then on the port side were Wyldbore-Smith, Commander S.J.P. Warrand, the squadron navigating officer, eighteen-year-old Bill Dundas, action midshipman of the watch, Chief Yeoman Carne, who was attending the captain, Yeoman Wright, who looked after the demands of the officer of the watch at the binnacle, and myself, who was required to attend the flag lieutenant and answer voice-pipes. All the officers, except Holland and Kerr, were huddled in duffle coats, over which was anti-flash gear, topped off by steel helmets. Some had their gas-masks slung on their chests. It seemed incongruous to me that I, the most junior of all, should be wearing shoes and they sea-boots. The short, slim admiral preferred to emphasize his rank by wearing his 'bum-freezer' type of greatcoat. He sat bolt upright, with his binoculars' strap around his neck, his fingers somewhat nervously tapping the glasses themselves.

Holland, with whom I had not come into close contact before, activated my curiosity. He was smaller and milder-tempered than Admiral Whitworth, his predecessor, and rarely raised his voice. Whitworth had filled me with awe every time he approached, but the quieter attitude of Holland made me want to discover what made him tick and to find the key to his advancement in the navy. I had ambitions, too! Although he was only fifty-four, his hair was almost white. He appeared to be extremely shy and withdrawn, but officers put this down to the fact that his only son, an eighteen-year-old, who seemed to have a brilliant future as both poet and painter, had died of polio five years earlier. The tragedy had left its mark on both the admiral and his wife. Holland was a gunnery specialist and had invented gadgets to improve anti-aircraft control in warships. He was commodore of Portsmouth Barracks in 1935 and two years later became Assistant Chief of Naval Staff. At the outbreak of war he was put in command of the Second Battle Squadron. His only battle experience had been seven months earlier, when he had led five cruisers against the Italian fleet off Cape Spartivento. The Italians had not waited to give full battle, however, and fled before the British could get at them.

Holland had already signalled his plan for action to Captain John Leach in the *Prince of Wales*. With the *Hood* leading the way, both ships were to concentrate their fire on the *Bismarck*, with the *Suffolk* and *Norfolk* taking on the *Prinz Eugen*. Because we were maintaining radio silence, however, the cruisers did not receive these orders. Radar was banned unless action was imminent, in case the *Bismarck* picked up transmissions and changed direction. At midnight the enemy were believed to be a hundred miles away, and

Holland deduced that if both squadrons continued on their courses at similar speeds the *Hood* would cross their intended track sixty miles ahead, at about 0230, or approximately forty minutes after sunrise in these days of long light.

After I had been on the compass platform about fifteen minutes, Holland stirred himself, as if he had forgotten an important factor. Then he commanded: 'Hoist battle ensigns.' The order was repeated and then passed on to the flag deck. The great flag rustled to the yardarm. At twenty-four feet long and twelve wide it was one of the largest in the Navy and whistled towards the stern to increase the anticipation of everyone who saw it. But it was anticlimax, for almost simultaneously the signal came from *Suffolk*: 'Enemy hidden in snowstorm.' Then silence. The news that contact had been lost was broadcast through the ship, and the crew were allowed to assume 'relaxed action stations'. Holland got to his feet and conferred with his flag staff around the plot. The product of this short conference was a reduction of speed to twenty-five knots and a change of direction to due north.

As I had been successful in questioning Wyldbore-Smith about the situation the previous day, I tried again, and during the next two hours my queries turned into a bombardment for information. He was extremely considerate and patiently gave me more details than it was necessary to disclose to a very junior rating. He explained that the admiral was in a quandary because of the cessation of reports from the shadowing cruisers and had to guess the movements of the enemy. Because Lutjens – of course no one knew he was the admiral in command – was aware his ships were being tracked, it was expected he would make a big divergence in course to shake off the pursuers. But a major switch towards the west was impossible because the edge of the Greenland ice pack was on the *Bismarck*'s starboard side. Holland, therefore, had concluded that Lutjens would alter to a southerly course, or just to the east of it. The consequence of this tactical guess was a reduction in the speed of the *Hood* and the *Prince of Wales* and the alteration to due north. Now Holland intended to keep to this course until 0210, when we would turn about.

The strain of this game of hide-and-seek began to show on the face of the little admiral as he turned restlessly in his swivel chair. We thundered on through snow flurries, with spray coming over the forecastle, oblivious to the knowledge that we had no definite destination. Just after two o'clock Holland ended his dilemma by first ordering a turn to the south and then another to the south-east. Again Wyldbore-Smith interpreted this manoeuvre to me. If the *Bismarck* had successfully side-tracked the *Norfolk* and *Suffolk* by altering to the south, Holland wanted to consolidate his position on the enemy's bows. If the *Hood* and *Prince of Wales* had persisted towards the north, Holland's interception course would have put us too far ahead, and a great deal of the squadron's gun-bearing advantage would have been given away on the enemy pair racing south. To ensure that there was a British force searching to the north still, Holland spread the destroyer escort to this area.

Apart from the muttered comments of officers around me, the compass platform became a strangely somnolent citadel. The cold fingers of the Arctic draughts were whistling through the platform, and I was sent down to the galley to bring off a dixie of 'kiy' for the ratings, while Midshipman Dundas was ordered on a similar mission to the wardroom kitchen for the officers.

But at 0247 came another stimulant. The *Suffolk*, veering south at thirty knots, reported she was in touch with the *Bismarck* and her consort again. On our plot this put the Germans thirty-five miles to the north-west, with the *Hood* and *Prince of Wales* a few miles ahead. Unknown to foe and friend alike, the four ships had been on slightly divergent courses. We were on 200 degrees, and Lutjens' squadron were on 220 degrees. The difference was that we knew they were there now, but they were still unaware that two British capital ships were stalking them. As the *Hood*, still ahead of the *Prince of Wales*, swung back to the north again, the news was broadcast to rouse the sagging figures below from their attempted slumber. The *Hood* began to shudder more as speed was raised to $28\frac{1}{2}$ knots, the maximum she could attain from her engines after months of over-use. From the billows of blackish, purple smoke emitted from the stacks, there was no doubt that the 'chief stoker was sitting on the safety valves'. She was at her fastest, and not another decimal of a knot could be coaxed from the ageing engines.

The next hour was to be the edgiest of my life, as the *Hood* screamed into battle. There was little for me to do in the build-up to action, and I became a somewhat frightened observer. Dawn had been at 0200, and now I could see great patches of cloud that threatened rain, if not more snow and sleet. There was a heavy swell from the north-east, which slapped the great ship and produced a haze of water that showered over the bows on to the long forecastle and beat against the side of A and B turrets. Under a grey sky on a grey sea we charged towards an enemy who threatened the lifelines to Britain. Even a technicolor film of this morning would not have brought out a brighter hue.

Momentarily I was snatched from my reverie by the message that the *Bismarck* had been picked up by our radar 'bods' and was twenty miles off to our north-east. This was no false errand now. If there were any doubts that a full-scale naval action was about to be fought, they were dispelled at once. In an hour we would be upon the enemy.

I could visualize how the mates I knew in other departments would be preparing. Ron Bell was on the flag deck at the other end of the voice-pipe I was manning. His voice did not betray any signs of funk, as I was sure mine did. Near him would be Tuxworth, helping to handle the halyards and still joking, no doubt. Alongside in charge of the flags I guessed that Yeoman Bill Nevett would be as outwardly calm as ever, despite the pallor of his face.

On the boat deck I knew another mate, Petty Officer Stan Boardman, would be readying the crew of Sally, the starboard multiple pom-pom. Would he be thinking of his adored wife and his newly born baby or would he be questioning what on earth he could do with his anti-aircraft guns against the *Bismarck*'s fifteen-inchers? And what of the sick-bay, where I had spent the first few days of my life in the ship? There the 'tiffies' under Surgeon Commander Hurst and Sick-Bay Petty Officer Stannard would be sterilizing operating instruments, laying out blankets, making sure bandages were handy – God, don't let me be wounded. I guessed a lot of blood would be flowing there today, and it made my own feel colder.

Other shipmates would be under cover and unable to see – and some unable to hear – the impending action and relying on the chaplain, the Reverend R.J.P. Stewart, who had now taken over from Commander Cross as broadcast 'commentator', to keep them briefed, and still uncertain of each movement of the ship. At least I had a grandstand view and would not die unknowingly in darkness. Death? I'm not, and never have been, a religious zealot, nor a churchman, but my last thoughts in these moments of inaction were of the peaceful little chapel under the flag deck. It reminded me of Nelson's own prayer, 'May the great God, whom I worship ...' and I offered up a pitiful silent prayer of my own for personal courage and stamina and for a British victory. I suppose it was rather like keeping your fingers crossed!

Dead on 0500 the imminence of a high-explosive fight sent a shudder of fear through me. 'Prepare for instant action,' Holland warned, although not a man in the *Hood* and the *Prince of Wales* could not have been ready by now. There was no friendly conversation on the compass platform. Everyone was staring into the steely blend of sky and sea towards the northern horizon. At 0535 the enemy were spotted from the *Hood*. The sighting was reported by voice-pipe from the spotting-top as 'Alarm starboard green 40.' I did not have any binoculars, so I could not see the top-masts, which everyone else was focusing on, but the maximum visibility from our perch was seventeen miles at this time. Almost in a whisper Captain Kerr commanded: 'Pilot, make the enemy report.' Lieutenant-Commander A.R.J. Batley called Chief Yeoman Carne to his side at the binnacle and dictated: 'Emergency to Admiralty and C-in-C., Home Fleet. From BC1 – one battleship and one heavy cruiser, bearing 330, distance 17 miles. My position 63-20 north, 31-50 west. My course 240. Speed 28 knots.' Carne copied it on to his signal pad as: 'Y-Z – Admiralty, C-in-C. H.F., V.B. Cone, IBS ICH 330-17-632°N, 315°W, 24-28.' This message was repeated by Carne through the voice-pipe to the bridge wireless office. A few minutes later came the confirmation through the voice-pipe in my hand that the message had been sent.

Then the order went from Holland to the flag deck to hoist

'Blue 4'. This meant making a turn of forty degrees together to starboard and with it the knowledge that the after batteries of the *Hood* and *Prince of Wales* would be unable to bear on the *Bismarck* or the *Prinz Eugen*. Holland was concentrating on closing the range as rapidly as possible to make the trajectory of the enemy shells flatter and to reduce the chances of the *Hood*'s being penetrated by plummeting shells where the armour was weakest.

All that could be heard now of human activity was the steering orders of the officer of the watch and the piped repetition from the quartermaster in the barbette under the foremost director. I whispered to Yeoman Wright: 'How long do you think this is going to last, Yeo?' He answered this silly question with an equally vacuous answer: 'I think it'll all be over within the next couple of hours, Ted.'

21

'Now I Lay Me Down ...'

Ting-ting, ting-ting, ting-ting – the weak chinking, yet shrilly insistent urgency of the fire gong came through the loudspeaker at the back of the bridge. Holland had already ordered the preparatory signal to the *Prince of Wales* to open fire, and flag 5 was bent on the halyards ready for hoisting. Normally flag signals are not executed until they are hauled down, but flag 5 gave captains of ships the right to fire immediately it was at the mast-head. I could see our A and B forward turrets' guns lift slightly. When the range was down to thirteen miles, Holland said in a quietly modulated and polite voice: 'Open fire.' Chief Yeoman Carne shouted more peremptorily to the flag deck: 'Flag 5, hoist.' A minute earlier the gunnery officers of both the *Hood* and *Prince of Wales* had been ordered by the admiral to concentrate their fire on the *Bismarck*, which, he told them, was the left-hand ship of the fast-approaching enemy. In the background I could hear the helmsman repeating his orders, and the closing ranges from the gunnery control position above us being sung out. Captain Kerr then ordered: 'Open fire.' From the control tower the gunnery officer bellowed: 'Shoot.' And the warning gong replied before the *Hood*'s first salvo belched out in an ear-pulsating roar, leaving behind a cloud of brown cordite smoke, which swept by the compass platform. Seconds later a duller boom came from our starboard quarter as the *Prince of Wales* unleashed her first fourteen-inch salvo.

The menacing thunder of our guns snapped the tension. All my traces of anxiety and fright left me momentarily. I was riveted with fascination as I counted off the seconds for our shells to land – 20, 21, 22, 23, 24, 25 ... then tiny spouts of water, two extremely close to the pinpoints on the

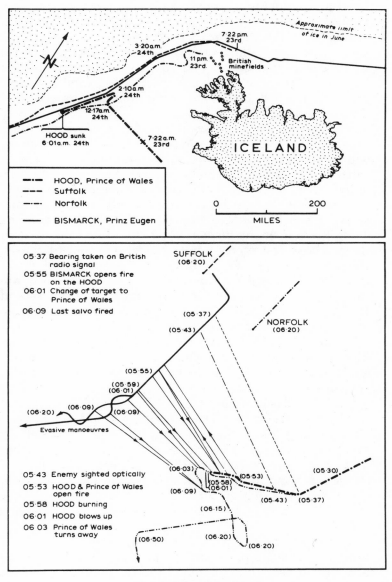

The sinking of the *Hood*

horizon. Suddenly a report from the spotting-top made Holland realize he had blundered. 'We're shooting at the wrong ship. The *Bismarck*'s on the right, not the left.' Our shells had been falling near the *Prinz Eugen*, which many hours earlier had begun to lead the German raiding force when the *Bismarck*'s forward radar failed. Holland seemed hardly perturbed and in the same monotonous voice said: 'Shift target to the right.'

Within the next two minutes the *Hood*'s foremost turrets managed to ram in six salvoes each at the *Bismarck*. I counted each time, expecting to see a hit registered. The first salvo pockmarked the sea around her, and the third appeared to spark off a dull glow. I thought we had got in the first blow, but I was wrong. Suddenly it intrigued me to see four star-like golden flashes, with red centres, spangle along the side of the *Bismarck*. But I had no time to admire them. Those first pretty pyrotechnics were four fifteen-inch shells coming our way, and deep, clammy, numbing fear returned. That express train, which I had last heard when the French fired on us at Oran, was increasing in crescendo. It passed overhead. Where it landed I was not sure. My eyes were on the two ships rapidly becoming more visible on the starboard bow. They were still winking at us threateningly. But the next salvo was not just a threat. Not far from our starboard beam there were two, no three, no four high splashes of foam, tinted with an erupting dirty brown fringe. Then I was flung off my feet. My ears were ringing as if I had been in the striking-chamber of Big Ben. I picked myself up, thinking I had made a complete fool of myself, but everyone else on the compass platform was also scrambling to his feet. 'Tiny' Gregson walked almost sedately out to the starboard wing of the platform to find out what had happened. 'We've been hit at the base of the mainmast, sir, and we're on fire,' he reported, almost as if we were on manoeuvres.

Then came a crazy cacophony of wild cries of 'Fire' through the voice-pipes and telephones. On the amidships boat deck a fierce blaze flared. This was punctuated by loud explosions. The torpedo officer reported by phone: 'The four-inch ready-use ammunition is exploding.' I could hear the UP rockets going up, just as they had roared off accidentally in Gibraltar a year earlier. Fear gripped my intestines again as agonized screams of the wounded and dying emitted from the voice-pipes. The screeching turned my blood almost to ice. Yet strangely I also began to feel anger at the enemy for the first time. 'Who the hell do they think they are, hitting our super ship?' I thought ridiculously.

As the AA shells continued to rocket around, Captain Kerr ordered the four-inch gun crews to take shelter and the fire and damage control parties to keep away from the area until all the ready-use ammunition had been expended. But the bursting projectiles were making a charnel-house of positions above the upper deck. The screams of the maimed kept up a strident chorus through the voice-pipes and from the flag deck. I was certain I heard my 'oppo' Ron Bell shouting for help. These agonizing moments did not appear to trouble Holland, Kerr or Gregson. Their binoculars were still focused on the enemy. I wondered how they could be so detached, with chaos and havoc around them. This, I supposed, was the calmness of command, and some of it transferred to me like a form of mental telepathy.

By this time the range had been cut down to approximately 8½ miles. We had been under fire for just two minutes, which already had taken on the time-scale of two hours. It was the moment for Holland to try to bring our aft turrets, X and Y, to bear, because we were being hopelessly outgunned. 'Turn twenty degrees to port together,' he commanded. Chief Yeoman Carne passed the word on to the flag deck, where surprisingly someone still seemed to be capable of obeying orders. Two blue – flag 2, a blue pendant – went up the yard-arm. I remember musing: 'Not everyone on the flag deck is dead then.' As the *Hood* turned, X turret roared in approval, but its Y twin stayed silent. And then a blinding flash swept around the outside of the compass platform. Again I found myself being lifted off my feet and dumped head first on the deck. This time, when I got up with the others, the scene was different. Everything was cold and unreal. The ship which had been a haven for me for the last two years was suddenly hostile. After the initial jarring she listed slowly, almost hesitatingly, to starboard. She stopped after about ten degrees, when I heard the helmsman's voice shouting up the voice-pipe to the officer of the watch: 'Steering's gone, sir.' The reply of 'Very good' showed no signs of animation or agitation. Immediately Kerr ordered: 'Change over to emergency steering.'

Although the *Hood* had angled to starboard, there was still no concern on the compass platform. Holland was back in his chair. He looked aft towards the *Prince of Wales* and then re-trained his binoculars on the *Bismarck*. Slowly the *Hood* righted herself. 'Thank heaven for that,' I murmured to myself, only to be terrorized by her sudden, horrifying cant to port. On and on she rolled, until she reached an angle of forty-five degrees. When everyone realized that she would not swing back to the perpendicular, we all began to make our way out in single file towards the starboard door at first. Then some turned towards the port door and attempted to break panes of reinforced glass in the foreport of the platform. But it was all done as if in drill. There was no order to abandon ship; nor was a word uttered. It just was not required. The *Hood* was finished, and no one needed to be told that.

I was surprised by my cold yet uncontrolled detachment, as I made my way to the door. 'Tiny' Gregson was in front of me with the squadron navigation officer. As I reached the steel-hinged door, Commander Warrand stood aside for me and let me go out first. I looked back over my left shoulder and saw Holland slumped on his chair in total dejection. Beside him the captain tried to keep to his feet as the *Hood*'s deck turned into a slide. I began picking my way down the ladder from the compass platform to the admiral's bridge. Then the sea swirled around my legs and I was walking on the side of the bridge, instead of the ladder. I threw away my tin hat and gas-mask and managed to slip off my anti-flash gear, but my lifebelt was under my Burberry and I could not get at it to inflate it. There was no one else in sight, although I knew that at least two officers were nearby, as the water engulfed me with a roar.

Panic had gone. This was it, I realized. But I wasn't going to give in easily. I knew that the deckhead of the compass platform was above me and that I must try to swim away from it. I managed to avoid being knocked out by the steel stanchions, but I was not making any progress. The suction was dragging me down. The pressure on my ears was increasing each second, and panic returned in its worse intensity. I was going to die. I struggled madly to try to heave myself up to the surface. I got nowhere. Although it seemed an eternity, I was under water for barely a minute. My lungs were bursting. I knew that I just had to breathe. I opened my lips and gulped in a mouthful of water. My tongue was forced to the back of my throat. I was not going to reach the surface. I was going to die. I was going to die. As I weakened, my resolve left me. What was the use of struggling? Panic subsided. I had heard it was nice to drown. I stopped trying to swim upwards. The water was a peaceful cradle. I was being rocked off to sleep. There was nothing I could do about it – goodnight, mum. Now I lay me down ... I was ready to meet God. My blissful acceptance of death ended in a sudden surge beneath me, which shot me to the surface like a decanted cork in a champagne bottle. I wasn't going to die. I wasn't going to die. I trod water as I panted in great gulps of air. I was alive. I was alive.

Although my ears were singing from the pressure under water, I could hear the hissing of a hundred serpents. I turned and fifty yards away I could see the bows of the *Hood* vertical in the sea. It was the most frightening aspect of my ordeal and a vision which was to recur terrifyingly in nightmares for the next forty years. Both gun barrels of B turret were slumped hard over to port and disappearing fast beneath the waves. My experience of suction seconds before forced me to turn in sheer terror and swim as fast and as far as I could away from the last sight of the ship that had formulated my early years.

I did not look back. There was a morass of debris around me as I pushed through the sea, which had a four-inch coating of oil on it. Fortunately before we had left Scapa the ship had been equipped with three-foot-square rafts, which replaced the older and larger Carley floats. There were dozens of these around in the sea and I managed to lug myself half on to one. I held on face downwards and then levered myself to look round to where the *Hood* had been. A small patch of oil blazed where she was cremated. Several yards away I could see the stern of the *Prince of Wales* as she pressed on with her guns firing. She was being straddled by shells from the *Bismarck* and *Prinz Eugen*, and I did not give much of a chance to her survival. As I watched her veer away, I began to wonder about my chances of survival, too. I knew, of course, that a ship in action could not stop to pick up survivors, but this did not prevent a feeling of deep and helpless frustration.

The oil fire, which was still burning, instilled a spirit of self-preservation in me. I feared that larger patches of fuel, in which my raft was swilling, might be ignited, and with both hands I paddled out of the brown, sickening coating. Although I still had on my Burberry, number three suit, lifebelt, shoes and socks and had been in the water only some three minutes, the cold was beginning to numb my arms, fingers, legs and toes. My frantic efforts to propel the raft away from the fire helped to circulate my blood, but soon I was out of breath. I looked back and saw that the fire was out. On the horizon I could just make out the smoke from the *Norfolk* and *Suffolk*. About fifty yards away I suddenly saw life from another raft. A figure on it began to wave at me. Parallel to this was another raft with a man flapping his arms. I tried to find other signs of life. There was none – just us. We all began to paddle towards each other. The two linked up first, and then I puffed towards them. On one raft was Able Seaman Bob Tilburn and on the other was Midshipman Dundas, who had been on the compass platform with me.

Dundas had managed to sit up on his raft. For some odd reason it infuriated me that he was perched comfortably and perfectly balanced. As I neared the other two, I was crazily determined that I would 'enter their water' sitting up on my raft, too. I hauled myself into a central position, knelt up and then toppled back into the sea. I tried again and the raft capsized. I clambered back and was bucked off for a third time. I was crying with frustration when six-foot Tilburn, who was now alongside, helped me back on and said: 'Come on now; you're all right, son.' I realized I was making a fool of myself and finally gave up. I stayed sprawled out after this as we clutched the ratlings of each other's raft to bind us together.

Dundas took command not because he was an officer – the most junior one at that – but through his cheerfulness. He kept us singing 'Roll Out the Barrel' to ensure that we stayed awake. After an hour my mind was as numb as my body. I was overcome with a great drowsiness and the feeling again of 'What will be, will be.' All I wanted to do was to sleep my way to death, but I was roused by Tilburn shouting: 'There's a plane.' I looked up and saw a Sunderland flying-boat in the distance. The three of us yelled 'Help, help, help' and splashed the sea with our hands, although it was obviously a futile attempt to attract attention. The Sunderland flew on. Later I learned it was piloted by Flying Officer Vaughan, who, although having a grandstand view of the battle, understandably missed us in the debris. At least his plane had awakened me from my sleep of exposure, and now I was aware of the perishing cold that set my teeth chattering again. Dundas was determined that we should not drop into a coma, and to prevent this he suggested we tell our stories of how we got out of the *Hood*. The escape of twenty-year-old Tilburn, who had been in the Navy for four years to this very day, was the most dramatic, and he related it something like this:

'I was manning one of the four-inch AA guns on the port side, but when the shooting began, we were ordered to take cover on the boat deck. Some of the men took cover in the aircraft hangar. The first hit was a small one, right near the anti-aircraft rockets. It must have been a small one, because a bigger shell would have gone through the deck. There was a tremendous fire, all pinkish with not much smoke. It seemed as if the UP ammo had exploded, but it might have been the four-inch ammo lockers. Petty Officer Bishop, who was in charge of the four-inch guns, told us to put out the fire, but then the bridge ordered us to take shelter again until all the ammo had gone off. So we all lay face down flat on the deck as everything began going off like Chinese crackers. Just after we had turned to port, the whole ship shook like mad. Bits of steel showered down on us, and bodies started falling from above all over the deck. A part of a man fell from aloft and hit me on the legs. Bodies without arms and legs were falling all around. One of my "oppos" was killed; another was blown away, and a third had a splinter in his side and his guts ripped out. I felt violently sick and rushed to the side to spew up. Then the ship began to vibrate even worse, and she seemed to stop. I first noticed that she was going down by the stern after listing to port. She began to tilt at such an alarming angle that I got up and jumped on to the forecastle, which was nearly under water. I ripped off my gas-mask, coat and helmet, and the sea washed me over the side. Just before I went in, there was a flash of flame between the control tower and B turret. As I was swimming, I looked back and saw her coming over on top of me. Some part of the mast hit me on the legs, and I was partly pulled down by a tangle of wires around one of my sea-boots. Luckily I still had my knife on a lanyard, and I slashed at my boot until it was loose and I could kick it off. When I came to the top, the *Hood*'s bows were stuck out of the water, practically upright – and then she slid underneath.'

Dundas, who was only a few feet away from me on the compass platform, was a keener observer than I, for this is what he told us:

'I reckon that the *Bismarck*'s first salvo fell off the starboard side and the second off the port bow. It was after the third that the cordite fire began on the starboard side of the boat deck. The fourth salvo seemed to go through the spotting-top without exploding, although bodies began to fall from it. It was the fifth salvo that really did for us. Wreckage began raining down again, and I saw a mass of brown smoke drifting to leeward on the port side. As we began listing heavily to port, I found I could not get to the door, where you and the others got out, Briggs. I scrambled uphill and kept kicking at the window on the starboard side until I made a big enough hole to squeeze through. When I was halfway through, the water came underneath me, and I was dragged down quite a bit. The next thing I knew was that I shot to the top, and I was swimming on the surface.'

We were all still dazed by the sudden demise of the *Hood*, especially as none of us could recall hearing any loud or catastrophic explosion before she sank. I was the only one who had escaped without a scratch. Tilburn had wounded himself on the knee, where he had cut away his sea-boot, while Dundas had sprained an ankle when he kicked in the armoured glass window in desperation. What intrigued me was that Dundas and I had gone into the sea from the starboard side, yet I was the one who had emerged on the port side. I must have gone right under the ship.

All this talking had tired us, and our stiffened fingers involuntarily lost their grasp on the ratlings and we drifted apart, to four hundred and eight hundred yards. Through the sleepy mist that was snarling my eyes and brain I could hear the distant voice of Dundas, who had started up another chorus of 'Roll Out the Barrel'. My mind urged me to listen, but then I thought: 'Oh why don't you shut up, man, so I can get some sleep.' Later Tilburn revealed that he believed he was about to die and remembered that the best way to go in extreme cold was to close your eyes and sleep the deepest sleep of all. Fortunately for him he stayed awake. Suddenly Dundas stopped his raucous singing and began to cry: 'There's a destroyer coming along. She's seen us.' I looked up wearily in disbelief, but Dundas was right. She was heading towards the rafts. I recognized the pendant number – H27. 'It's the *Electra*,' I screamed. Then I began to bawl crazily. '*Electra*! *Electra*! *Electra*!' The other two joined in, and we waved our arms desperately. She had certainly seen us. She cut her engines and began to steer in towards us. Men with hand-lines were stationed around her sides. Scrambling-nets were already rigged, so we had obviously been spotted before we had noticed her. In jubilation Dundas sang: 'Roll out the barrel, let's have a barrel of fun ...' and began conducting an imaginary orchestra. As low in spirit as I was, I could not but admire his bravado.

Slowly the *Electra* approached my raft, on which I was prostrate. Then a rope sailed into the air in my direction. Although I could not feel my fingers, somehow I managed to cling on to it. A man yelled unnecessarily at me from the scrambling net: 'Don't let go of it.' I even had the heart to retort: 'You bet your bloody life I won't.' Yet I was too exhausted to haul myself in and climb the net. After nearly four hours in the sea my emotions were a mess. Tears of frustration rolled down my oil-caked cheeks again, for rescue was so close and I could not help myself. I need not have worried. Several seamen dropped into the water, and with one hand on the nets they got me alongside and manhandled me up to the bent guard-rail, which had been battered by the storm, and into the waist of the *Electra*.

The sheer thankfulness of being saved acted as a

tranquillizer on me. I was laid out on deck, and gentle hands cut and eased away the frozen clothes from my body. I remember thinking: 'There goes my Burberry and number three suit.' Then someone forced a cup between my lips and said: 'Here, drink this.' I did, and although I had been in the Navy for three years, this was my first taste of rum. I vomited it up immediately. My idiotic attempts to sit up on the raft, which had led to my swallowing a mixture of brine and oil, made it impossible for me to keep anything down for the next few hours. Swathed in blankets and with the ship's doctor, Lieutenant W.R.D. Seymour, massaging my hands and then my feet, I was soon joined by Tilburn and Dundas, whom I heard say to the No. 1 after he was hauled up to the main deck: 'Sorry I can't salute, sir. I'm afraid I've lost my cap.' It was his last show of cheeky cheerfulness. He immediately collapsed into a heap. He, too, was massaged and then bundled off protestingly to the wardroom. Tilburn and I were carried bodily to the sick-bay. I was helped into a bunk, and then a sick-berth attendant gave me a blanket bath. But sleep did not come easily after this, because as my circulation returned I was seized with a series of cramps, which made my body rigid again. The SBA tried to massage me back to suppleness, but even this did not ease my pain. Finally I fell asleep.

22

Just the Three of Us Left

When I woke up, about four hours later, the cramps had
subsided, although I was still stiff. The first lieutenant,
whom I later discovered to be Lieutenant Richard
Jenner-Fust, was called and he told us that we were being
landed at Reykjavik in Iceland. This officer also related that,
when the simple signal 'Hood sunk' was received at around 6
a.m. from the *Prince of Wales*, no one on the *Electra*'s bridge
believed it. The yeoman who brought the news was in tears,
however. The destroyer and the rest of the escort had been
spread at fifteen-mile intervals to search towards the north,
as ordered by Holland. Wake-Walker in the *Norfolk*, who
had taken over as senior officer, signalled them to turn south
and hunt for survivors around the *Hood*'s last reported
position, which was sixty miles away. Commander S.A.
Buss, skipper of the *Electra*, obeyed instantly. He knew that
survivors could not last for more than a couple of hours in
the refrigerator that was the sea and asked the engine-room
to 'give him everything they had got'. During the previous
night the heavy weather had stoved in the ship's motor-boat
and whaler. Only one other whaler was serviceable, and on
the way to the rescue Jenner-Fust and the chief buffer had to
work out ways of picking up the hundreds of survivors who
were expected. The doctor recruited a work party to turn the
tiny mess decks into hospitals, and stewards were instructed
to have the officers' bunks ready for the overflow. The cooks
prepared hot soup and tea, while a special supply of rum was
indented for from stores. The *Electra* managed to race to the
scene of the disaster fifteen minutes ahead of her estimated
arrival time, mainly because of a plot given by Flying Officer
Pinhorn, the pilot of a Hudson of Coastal Command, who
had also watched the battle. A sliver of smoke was seen by a

look-out, which raised hopes of finding the *Hood* still afloat, but this turned out to be a solitary merchantman who had straggled away from a convoy and was scurrying home.

With the sea seemingly empty, Lieutenant-Commander Buss had begun to think that the *Electra* was off course, but large patches of oil and tangled unrecognizable masses of wreckage were sighted. Then they spotted us. The seaboat was launched, and what they believed was to be a big rescue operation got into full swing. Soon the *Icarus* and *Anthony* joined in the search. No one could believe it; there was not another sign of a man, dead or alive. Only then, when Jenner-Fust told us the story, did we realize that the three of us were the luckiest men to be alive. But this did not buoy me up.

Depression held me in its grip for the next few days. Poor old 'Dingle' Bell; poor old 'Tux'; poor old Stan. Old? Far from it. Bell and Tuxworth were my own age, and Stan Boardman, at twenty-one, had just received his first good-conduct badge. But I was not the only one who was hard hit by the realization of the death of more than fourteen hundred shipmates. The crew of the *Electra* were also in low spirits as the search was abandoned because her fuel was running low and the ship headed for Iceland.

On the passage to Reykjavik the ship's company did their best to cheer up Tilburn and me. We were invited to the seamen's mess, and there we had sipper after sipper of rum to make us forget. If we had drunk everything which was offered, it would have been more lethal than the sea that nearly claimed us. Both of us were also kitted out with odds and ends of clothing donated by the crew. I ended up with a blue jersey, the bottom half of someone's old number one suit, a watch-coat, thick sea-boot socks and a pair of battered boots.

Not until the *Electra* berthed alongside at Reykjavik during the dogwatch of 24 May did we begin to realize that suddenly we were VIPs. There was an ambulance waiting on the quay, and as soon as the gangway was in place, we were helped ashore. In the last few hours I had been in a dreamland of uncertainty and incredulity that this was really happening to me. Once ashore the enormity of what we had gone through dawned on me, mainly because of the hustle that was generated around us. We were hurried into the ambulance and driven at speed to the nearby military hospital. There we were met by a padre, who took our names and addresses and those of our next of kin so that telegrams saying we were safe could be sent. It was a kindness that was to save hours of anguish, for I later learned that my mother in Derby received the telegram just sixty minutes after the delayed official announcement on the radio that the *Hood* had been sunk with very little hope of survivors being picked up.

The three of us were told next that we were to bath and get to bed. As I lazed in the balm of just Lifebuoy soap and hot water, a young nursing sister entered the bathroom to help me. Still young and innocent, I insisted that she turn her back before I got out. She did as I asked, but as I stood up I slipped dizzily back into the bath and blacked out. I came round sitting on the side, with my head on the sister's shoulder. As I opened my eyes, she assured me: 'Don't worry, laddie, I'll look after you.' Indeed she did. She helped me to dry and then was my crutch as I staggered back to bed to sleep the sleep of the vanquished.

Next morning we were informed by an army doctor that we were being sent back to the UK in the *Royal Ulsterman*, a trooper operating between Iceland and Greenock. After a lazy day confined to the hospital we duly joined the ship and were placed immediately in a benevolent kind of 'solitary'. Unlike the hundreds of other ordinary bods on board, Tilburn and I were given a cabin to ourselves. Dundas, being a midshipman, had one to himself. We were warned by the first mate that we must not reveal our identities while we were on board and must not discuss with anyone the battle with the *Bismarck*, our rescue or, indeed, any part of the operation. But we did discuss it among ourselves during the four-day passage to Greenock.

It was still difficult to believe that we were the three men 'chosen' to escape from the *Hood*. Why did no more of our shipmates survive? My own theory was – and still is – that the fire and exploding ammunition accounted for many lives and that the final blast killed a large number in the open on and above the upper deck. And of the hundreds below decks, the concussion would have knocked most senseless, while the sudden capsize would not have allowed those who had survived to clamber up crazily elevated ladders and out of oddly contorted hatches. I had to chase from my mind grim thoughts of how they died. Anyone else who managed to get into the sea in the three minutes it took the *Hood* to sink would have been encumbered, as I was, by heavy clothing and the difficulty in inflating lifejackets, which were worn ridiculously under Burberries or oilskins.

The *Royal Ulsterman*'s officers and stewards treated us like conquering heroes, instead of abject, deflated survivors. Our depression became almost suicidal when it was announced on the radio that the *Bismarck* and *Prinz Eugen* had managed to elude Tovey's massive hunting force. Had our comrades in the *Hood* been sacrificed in vain? Were the enemy raiders even now committing mayhem among the convoys from the United States? But revenge came on Tuesday 27 May when we heard that the *Bismarck* had been found again – strangely by a namesake, Flying Officer Briggs – and destroyed by the most fearsome massing of units of the Royal Navy in search of a lone prey. Wounded by a torpedo dropped by one of the *Ark Royal*'s Swordfish aircraft, brought to action by the *King George V* and *Rodney*, battered to a helpless hulk and finally put out of her misery by torpedoes from the *Dorsetshire*, the defiance of her admiral, captain and crew filled us with grudging admiration for a truly great fighting ship. She had taken on the full weight of the British Home Fleet, plus emergency help from the Mediterranean Fleet, and had nearly got away with it.

When the *Royal Ulsterman* arrived at Greenock on 29 May, we were still unaware of the dramatic stir that the sinking of the *Hood* and our survival had caused. A Royal Navy car was waiting on the dock to pick us up. We landed first, like admirals, and were whisked off to the headquarters of the Naval Officer in Charge, where we were all kitted out in correct uniform again. Railway warrants were handed to us, and Dundas was briefed that we were to travel by overnight train to London and report to the Admiralty on arrival.

The VIP treatment continued. That night an officer escorted us to the train, where a special compartment had been reserved for us. Before distributing cigarettes, sweets, soft drinks, newspapers and magazines, he insisted: 'Keep your mouths shut.' Could careless talk cost any more lives? I wondered. On the long journey south I took the time to catch up on the news and found the papers still full of the *Hood* disaster and the triumph of the pulverizing of the *Bismarck*. The loss of our old battle cruiser was a morale-shattering blow, not only to the Navy but to most Britons. She symbolized the sheer supremacy of British naval power, even though she had outlived her day. Civilians could be excused for thinking that she was unsinkable, but naval officers who should have known better were horrified when the unthinkable news was announced. This is how the Admiralty communiqué phrased it on the 9 p.m. news on 24 May.

'British naval forces intercepted early this morning off the coast of Greenland German naval forces including the battleship *Bismarck*. The enemy were attacked and during the ensuing action HMS *Hood* (Captain R. Kerr, CBE., R.N.) wearing the flag of Vice-Admiral L.E. Holland, CB, received an unlucky hit in the magazine and blew up. The *Bismarck* has received damage and the pursuit of the enemy continues. It is feared there will be few survivors from HMS *Hood*.'

The loss of not only a great ship but 94 officers and 1,324 ratings caused many a sailor to break down and cry that day.

In Britain the seeds of controversy were being sown already – and by none other than Admiral of the Fleet Lord Chatfield, who, although living in retirement at Winchester, Hampshire, wrote this letter to *The Times* on the day that we arrived back in Britain:

In your leading article of today on the destruction of the *Hood* you write that she was the largest and most powerful warship afloat; that she was blown up by a lucky hit, although she had been specially designed to be invulnerable to that kind of danger. You conclude that this raises the technical question whether a miscalculation was made in her design. As great concern has resulted from this misfortune it is important that the nation should realise the reason of it.

1. The *Hood* was not the most powerful warship afloat. True she was the largest, but she was constructed 22 years before the *Bismarck*. In those 22 years engineering science and the power weight ratio have changed beyond imagination.

2. It cannot be quite truly said 'she was destroyed by a lucky hit'. There are numerous magazines in a capital ship, in addition to the four largest ones, which lie beneath the main turrets. If, therefore, a heavy shell penetrates the armour at the angle of descent given by long ranges, the chance of one of the magazines being ignited is quite considerable.

3. The *Hood* was the most powerful ship of her speed that could be constructed in those days. But after the war the sailor made up his mind, after much experiment, that a very fast ship cannot afford to sacrifice armour to get that speed.

4. So in the *Nelson* class speed was sacrificed to ensure protection against sudden annihilation by shell, torpedo or bomb.

5. Since the *Nelson* was built, modern engineering has closed the gap between the two factors.

The *Hood* was destroyed because she had to fight a ship 22 years more modern than herself. This was not the fault of the British seamen. It was the direct responsibility of those who opposed the rebuilding of the British Battle Fleet until 1937, two years before the Second Great War started. It is fair to her gallant crew that this should be written.[1]

Thousands of words have been set in type, and millions more have flowed in verbal argument about the demise of the *Hood*, but in the last thirty years I have never seen nor heard a more crystallized or sensible theory than this surprisingly uncensored criticism by Admiral Chatfield, who had visited the ship on many occasions in peacetime.

23

A Naval Curio in Demand

The three of us were unlikely companions – Tilburn, tall, muscular, confident and able to assert himself; Dundas, approximately the same age as I, did not seem to want to communicate, which was surprising after his extrovert behaviour in the sea – and myself, still a shrinking lad but liable to blurt out an impertinence. Nevertheless, the fact we had survived was enough to bind us, albeit loosely, for the next twenty years.

When the train drew into King's Cross at 6 a.m. on a drizzling, chilly May morning, Dundas told us: 'We've been ordered to stay in this compartment until we are met by some top brass from the Admiralty.'

We waited until an officer peered through the window, realized we were his contacts and entered the carriage to introduce himself. 'I've orders to take you to the old Admiralty building,' he said. I for one did not expect this, but we were soon on the move again in another special RN car, which was alongside the platform. We were deposited at the office of the duty captain, who was the most affable four-ringer I have met. He shook hands and said: 'The Second Sea Lord, Vice-Admiral Whitworth, wishes to see you.' I gulped back my anguish. Whitworth was the admiral I had sent sprawling on the *Hood*'s bridge a year earlier. 'Not to worry,' I reassured myself. 'He won't recognize a mere OD like you.'

The agreeable captain asked us whether we had breakfasted. When he heard we had not eaten since the previous night, he sent away his secretary to organize eggs, bacon, sausages, toast, marmalade and coffee. As we waited, he set a kettle on a gas-ring, waited for it to boil and made us a pot of tea. When he poured out three cups, Dundas,

Tilburn and I sniggered at each other and then burst out laughing. The captain looked surprised, until Dundas explained: 'It seems very funny to us three very junior bods to have tea poured for us in the navy's holy of holies by no less a person than you, sir, a four-striped captain.'

'And why not, after what you lads have been through?' was the jovial reply.

After we had gobbled down breakfast we were ushered into the inner sanctum of the Second Sea Lord's office and presented to Admiral Whitworth. We were introduced in order of seniority, which meant I was last to be grasped by the hand. Whitworth stared at me with a forbidding frown on his furrowed, straggling eyebrows. His eyes held mine and then he growled: 'I know you, don't I?'

I stammered: 'Yes, sir. I was the flag lieutenant's messenger when you were in the *Hood*.'

His memory did not need jogging; a smile eased the straightness of his lips, and a softness came into his eyes. 'Oh yes, I remember. Nice to see you, son,' he nodded. 'You'll be all right – after a haircut!'

He sat down and began to probe us about the battle, the *Hood*'s destruction and our survival. For an hour he rifled in questions and listened attentively. At the end he said: 'I must impress on you not to say anything to any outsiders until we have held a court of inquiry.'

Before dismissing us, he wanted to know what orders we had been given. Dundas said we had been instructed to report to our respective depots. Whitworth turned to his secretary. 'Oh no, you're not. Send these boys on leave.'

I had enough temerity to ask: 'For how long, sir?' Again that softness of eye melted his stern face and he replied: 'Indefinitely. We'll send for you when the court of inquiry comes up.'

The secretary bustled us into the outer office, where railway warrants, ration cards and cash were given us. We practically gambolled down the steps of the building and shared a taxi to King's Cross Station, where we parted. It was when I was alone on the train from St Pancras home to Derby that the nerve-shattering experiences of the last week began to affect me. Until then I had been a staunch brother in arms, a rollicking musketeer of the sea, who had cut a certain dash. Now by myself and left to my thoughts I became a jangling mass of nerve-ends and confused emotions. Why me? Why should I have survived when 1,418 died? Was I really here? Perhaps it was all an illusion.

I had managed to send a telegram of my arrival time to my mother, and she was at the station with a taxi to meet me. Without a word, she hugged me tightly. On the way home very little was said, apart from banalities like: 'It's not a very nice day;' 'How long are you home for?' 'Were you hurt?' 'Are you hungry?' As she opened the front door of our house at 108 Nuns' Street, the last barricade of self-control disintegrated. I became a gibbering, quivering young lad from the war returning.

For the next ten days this nervous wreck from the wreck of the *Hood* was cosseted back to a reasonable frame of mind by his mother. The normal survivor's leave – although I still felt abnormal – was at least fourteen days, and on Whitworth's word I expected more, but on the tenth day I received a letter from the commanding officer of the RN Signal School, at Portsmouth Barracks, ordering me to report there when a fortnight's leave had expired. I might have been a war veteran at eighteen, but I was still green, for I duly reported to barracks at the correct time. Not until I met Tilburn again nearly three months later did I learn that he and Dundas had received similar orders but replied that they had been given indefinite leave until the inquiry. Their leave continued; mine was at an end.

It was when I went to the joining office at the signal school that I realized I was a naval curio. The usual officious master-at-arms looked at me imperiously through the glass hatch, booked me in and took down my details. 'Name? Briggs, Albert Edward. Official number? PJX 157404. Rating? Ordinary Signalman. Last ship? The *Hood*.' He threw down his pen, glared and barked: 'What's that? You'd better not be pulling my pisser, lad.'

I assured him I was not joking. His whole attitude changed. 'Come round here and let me shake your hand.' I went into the office; he grabbed me by the hand, clapped me on the back and bawled to the rest of the regulating staff: 'This lad got out of the *Hood*.'

My fame spread. I was marched into the first lieutenant's

office, who got me to tell my story. From there I was taken to the signal school's captain to repeat it. The ritual did not end there. My final call was on the commodore, who wanted to hear it all first hand. By the time my serializations were finished, they had decided what to do with me. The first lieutenant said that the school – to be known as HMS *Mercury* – was on the threshold of moving to East Meon, near Petersfield, Hampshire. I was to go there until the inquiry. It was expected any day, but the weeks rolled on until I finally was ordered to be at Dorland House, Regent Street, London, on 27 August.

I arrived at the appointed 10 a.m. and was shown into a small ante-room with three chairs in it. Soon after, Tilburn entered. We expected Dundas to join us, but he did not turn up. Tilburn was called first, and then at 11.30 it was my turn to face a galaxy of gold braid, including Rear-Admiral H.T. 'Hooky' Walker, the *Hood*'s last pre-war captain, who was the board's president, Captain R.J. Duke and Captain L.D. Mackintosh. They were assisted by Mr D.E.J. Offord, chief constructor of the Naval Construction Department and Captain J.F.B. Carslake, of the Torpedoes and Mining Department. I was apprehensive, and my nervous stammer seemed about to explode, but Walker put me at ease by saying: 'Just sit down quietly and answer our questions to the best of your ability. Don't be nervous; try to be natural.'

I told my story yet again, but behind the inquiry itself was another story. Years later I discovered that this was the second board of inquiry. The first was nearly three months earlier, when a different board had reported on 2 June, while I was on leave. Dundas gave evidence, but neither Tilburn nor I was wanted: neither were many others who saw the *Hood* blow up. Apparently the first board, headed by Vice-Admiral Sir Geoffrey Blake, who had been carried off the *Hood* with a heart attack and then invalided out of the Navy for a spell in 1938, had bungled. Whoever had convened the inquiry into Britain's most devastating naval loss of face so far in the war forgot to make sure a shorthand writer was present. Blake let the inquiry go on, so there was no formal reporting, apart from a summary composed of the rough notes of the members. Admiral Sir Dudley Pound, the First Sea Lord, primed by his Vice-Chief of Naval Staff,

Admiral Sir Tom Phillips, was outraged by this slip-up. Two other factors forced him to reconvene a second inquiry. The first was the failure to call every possible witness – such as Tilburn and me – and the second was a theory that the *Hood* had been destroyed by her own torpedoes.

Sir Stanley Goodall, the Director of Naval Construction, pleaded with the Sea Lords not to accept the findings until evidence was heard from more eye-witnesses, including survivors from the *Bismarck*. The subject was rightly too big an issue to discuss lightly, and that was how I came to be called to Dorland House.

The board seemed interested in my evidence about the exploding ammunition, the loss of steering, the absence of a loud explosion and the fact that I, like Dundas and Tilburn, was dragged down into the sea and then shot to the top. Although they seemed puzzled that only three of us had reached the surface, it was explained to me that we probably owed our lives to the underwater explosion of a boiler, from which we were capsulated in air bubbles and propelled to the top. I could only wonder why others had not survived this way.

As every witness gave evidence *in camera*, I did not know, of course, what else was said, but when the official documents of the inquiry were released thirty years afterwards, they made interesting reading. I did not realize until then that the average sailor could be a purple-patched poet. Stories had changed from those roughly documented at the first board, and this forced the second inquiry to note the difference in evidence. But against Tilburn's deposition was the comment: 'A very clear-headed and intelligent man, though inexperienced and still obviously shaken by his ordeal.' I was tagged: 'Another quite intelligent witness ... in a position to overhear the talk of some officers.' There were derisory descriptions of other witnesses, however, because they had either over-elaborated or romanticized.

When they reported on 12 September, the board left the argument virtually open for generations to come. The passage headed 'Cause of the ship's destruction' warned that, because a great deal of the evidence was 'contradictory and inconclusive, many points in connection with the loss of the *Hood* can never be proved definitely.'[1]

They scuttled the theory that the explosion was caused by the *Hood*'s torpedoes by stating that they were not convinced the warheads would have caused her to sink so fast and that damage to the after part was considerably greater than would have been possible if two torpedoes had detonated. Nevertheless, they left the controversy half open by stressing: 'We have therefore come to the conclusion that although the explosion or detonation of two warheads cannot be entirely excluded, this was not the direct cause of the sinking of the ship.'[2]

Unfortunately, the second board of inquiry accepted the findings of the first board that the third salvo from the *Bismarck* had turned the boat deck into a charnel-house. In fact, they denied the full credit of brilliant marksmanship to the gunnery officer of the *Prinz Eugen*, which was loosing off accurate rounds every twenty seconds. Instead, the board took heed of Kapitän Leutnant Burkard von Mullenheim Rechberg, who was interrogated on the *Dorsetshire* after he had been picked up from the sunken *Bismarck*. If they had examined him more closely, they would have not placed such credence on his evidence. He said that the *Hood* 'made smoke', which helped the *Bismarck*'s gunners find the range. He could have meant that there was a great volume pouring from the funnels – which it always did when the *Hood* was at full speed – but if he intended to indicate that a smokescreen was put down, he deposed wrongly, for at no part of the action did either Holland or Kerr order this. He claimed that his ship's second and third salvoes crumped into the *Hood* and that a 'very vivid bright, white flame was seen, but no smoke'. This absence of smoke and whiteness forced the *Bismarck*'s officers to believe that petrol storage tanks for the aircraft were hit. But there were only two gallons of petrol nearby, and this would have been unlikely to have started a big fire. He also told the inquiry that the fourth and fifth salvoes landed on the *Hood*. If this were the case, it meant that the *Bismarck* was off target only with the first salvo. Most of this so-called evidence should have been struck out.

Rechberg was later to write:

Having been ordered to keep our old fellow travellers, the

Norfolk and *Suffolk* under continuous observation, in case they launched torpedoes at us, I could no longer watch what was going on off our port beam. I had to depend on what I could hear over the fire control telephone ... I heard Schneider order the first salvo and heard his observation on the fall of shot, 'short.' He corrected the range and deflection, then ordered a 400-metre bracket. The long salvo he described as 'over', the base salvo as 'straddling' and immediately ordered, 'Full salvos good rapid.' He had thus laid his battery squarely on target at the very outset of the engagement. I had to concentrate on watching the *Suffolk* and *Norfolk*, but I must say I found it very difficult to deny myself glimpses of the morning's main event ... I continued to hear Schneider's calm voice making gunnery corrections and observations. 'The enemy is burning,' he said once, and then 'Full salvoes good rapid.' The forward gunnery computer room was telling him at regular intervals, 'Attention, fall.' ... Convinced that the *Suffolk* and *Norfolk* would leave us in peace for at least a few minutes, I entrusted the temporary surveillance of the horizon astern through the starboard director to my petty officers and went to the port director. While I was turning it toward the *Hood*, I heard a shout, 'She's blowing up.' 'She' – that could only be the *Hood*! The sight I then saw is a thing I shall never forget. At first the *Hood* was nowhere to be seen; in her place was a colossal pillar of black smoke reaching into the sky. Gradually, at the foot of the pillar, I made out the bow of the battle cruiser projecting upwards at an angle, a sure sign that she had broken in two. Then I saw something I could hardly believe: a spurt of orange coming from her forward guns! Although her fighting had ended, the *Hood* was firing a last salvo. I felt great respect for those men over there.[3]

Rechberg did attempt to straighten the record forty years later when he wrote: 'At 0557 one of our observers had spotted a quick-spreading fire forward of the *Hood*'s after mast: the second salvo from the *Prinz Eugen* had set fire to ready ammunition.' This vindicated Tilburn, the only on-the-spot witness alive, who always insisted that the first hit was an eight-inch (20.3 centimetres German size) and that a 15-inch shell from the *Bismarck* at a range of 26,500 yards would have penetrated the deck and probably have killed him. Another German prisoner confirmed that all the *Bismarck*'s secondary armament shells fell short of the

Hood. It was surprising, therefore, that most experts had forgotten the role the *Prinz Eugen* had played in this German victory, bearing in mind that because she was the leading ship she had been mistaken for the *Bismarck* originally. But the board did admit: 'There is no very definite evidence of the fall of shot from *Prinz Eugen*, though one salvo was described as falling astern of the Hood.'[4]

The fierceness of the fire which the *Prinz Eugen* caused also made no impression on the board, who intended to concentrate on the final blast. Actor Esmond Knight, a lieutenant in the *Prince of Wales* who lost his sight in the action, said:

> The fire was on the forward part of the boat deck and spread immediately afterwards. It was a most enormous fire; it seemed to burst into flames so rapidly. High, licking red flames and dense, pitch black smoke. I remember thinking that they would have a very hard job to put it out. It was so complete that it seemed to involve the after part of the ship almost. It appeared to me as if some ready-use cordite had probably caught fire and was burning. At the same time I think the *Prinz Eugen* was firing some HE, which was bursting into the air, bits of which were spraying into the water all around. I did not understand that at all as I could not understand how they could be using their LA guns to explode these shells on a time fuse at such great range. They were going off with a crash just astern of the Hood.[5]

It is likely that the shell bursts in the air which Knight saw were either the UP missiles, which most of us in the *Hood* hated, or four-inch ammunition. The 'rockets-on-a-string' have constantly fuelled arguments that they were responsible for the last dramatic explosion. Captain J. Leach and Commander H.F. Lawson, of the *Prince of Wales*, were not asked by the board to give an opinion whether this was possible, neither did they venture one, yet they are alleged to have given their views to Captain G.H. Oswald immediately after the battle, when interviewed at Scapa. Both claimed: 'The rocket weapons and the unsafely stowed ammunition were the direct cause of the loss of the ship, probably through the explosion of the ready-use cordite penetrating the flash proofing of X turret.'[6] Captain Leach was unlikely to have given this opinion lightly. He had been Director of

Naval Ordnance from 1939 until taking command of the *Prince of Wales* and obviously knew what he was talking about. I saw the damage the rockets could do when they were detonated accidentally at Gibraltar a year earlier. With ready-use ammunition exposed nearby – as it was when the *Hood* went into action in the Denmark Strait – the detonation would have been shattering. The actual stowage of the $9\frac{1}{2}$ tons of refill rockets was a dangerous one because it was immediately below the launchers in splinter-proof lockers and above the armour. Most of the Navy's top brass thought the weapons were useless. Rear-Admiral A.D. Nicholl has revealed that everyone – apart from Professor Lindemann and Churchill – thought the rockets ludicrous, but the chiefs of staff in the War Cabinet were not prepared to invoke the anger of the Prime Minister by speaking out against them. This controversy over one apparently useless weapon might have blurred the judgement of Leach after the loss of the *Hood*, but it seems certain that the board of inquiry were not prepared to cross words with Churchill over one of his pet contraptions, and consequently not one of the explosive experts was asked whether the UPs could have been the primary cause of the final blast.

The mis-directed inquiry – I call it this because to me its findings are very much open to question – ended with this conclusion: 'The sinking of the *Hood* was due to a hit from *Bismarck*'s 15-inch shell in, or adjacent to, the four-inch or 15-inch magazines, causing them all to explode and wreck the after part of the ship. The probability is that the four-inch magazines exploded first.'[7] In fact, the findings of this second board, although longer, were virtually a carbon copy of the first inquiry.

There were immediate repercussions after the report had been circulated. Although no blame had been attached to the UP apparatus, it was removed from every ship which had the misfortune to be fitted with it. In the *Renown* a section of the upper deck foward torpedo armament, similar to that in the *Hood*, was dismantled. The lesson of sending battleships – which the *Hood* was not, of course – into action with insufficient armour was also learned. Protection was increased in the *Nelson*, *Rodney*, *Queen Elizabeth*, *Warspite*, *Duke of York*, *Anson*, *Howe* and *King George V*.

The Outdated Heavyweight

In what to many seemed deference to the dead, the strategy of Admiral Holland was not questioned by either board of inquiry. The 'lucky hit' announcement when the *Hood* was sunk was the line that the Admiralty expected the public to swallow. Admiral Pound, the First Sea Lord, certainly did not want to bring Holland's name, or that of any officer, into disrepute. In a memorandum which virtually concluded the affair he signified: 'No blame attaches to the vice admiral commanding the squadron, the captain or anyone else.'[1]

But as the years healed the wounds and eased the sorrow of the mourners, Holland's whole approach to the battle has been re-examined time and again, and some critics have made the admiral, and not the ship, the scapegoat for one of the most debasing days in British naval history. I must admit that on hindsight it does seem to me that in his last breathing minutes Holland must have realized that his tactics had failed abysmally. As I left the compass platform, he did not seem paralysed with fear as he sat in his chair. He had more the look of a man who preferred to die with his ship, instead of fighting for a chance of survival and possible ignominy. Why did no one issue an order? Why did no one shout or cry out? Why was there no rush for the exit? All these questions are unanswerable, as also are those which have been posed in several books written by both experts and the unknowledgeable. To analyse them it is preferable to take the incidents in chronological order.

Holland's decision to turn north just after midnight has been interpreted in two ways. In his first volume of *War at Sea*, Captain S.W. Roskill accepts the normal theory that Holland made this deviation after the *Suffolk* and *Norfolk* had lost contact with the *Bismarck* in the snowstorm. But

Ludovic Kennedy in *Pursuit* argues that the *Suffolk*'s signal nine minutes after midnight reported 'Enemy hidden in snowstorm' and that the admiral had no more reason to suppose that the *Suffolk* had lost radar contact than when earlier that night for nearly an hour she was reporting that the enemy was hidden in fog. Kennedy gives the time of despatch of the signal at 0020, although the *Norfolk* is supposed to have received it four minutes earlier. Because Holland decided to turn from 285 degrees to 340 degrees at twelve minutes after midnight, Kennedy aligned himself with the opinion of another expert, Commander Pitcairn Jones, that Holland altered to the north, not to search for the *Bismarck* but to bring on the action. It is suggested that five minutes later – probably on decoding the *Suffolk*'s signal that the *Bismarck* was hidden in a snowstorm – Holland ordered another fifteen-degree turn to due north to allow for the chance of the *Bismarck*'s having altered to the south. This is possible, but as I remember it, although the *Suffolk* had not said it in so many words, it was broadcast around the *Hood* that the shadowing cruisers had lost contact and the men were allowed to go to relaxed action stations. If it was Holland's intention to 'bring on the action', we certainly would not have been allowed to relax.

The most contentious debate has centred around the approach to the enemy which Holland embarked on. The sharp-angled run-in of the *Hood* and *Prince of Wales* meant that the A arcs – the after turrets of both ships – could not be brought into action until Holland ordered a turn. The alterations during the night led to a loss of bearing, and the switch to forty degrees to starboard at 0538 brought the squadron to a true course of 280 degrees, and when the 'open fire' was ordered they were steering 300 degrees. Consequently, instead of bearing the *Hood*'s full destructive power of eight fifteen-inch guns and the *Prince of Wales*'s ten fourteen-inch armament against the *Bismarck*'s eight fifteen-inch guns and the *Prinz Eugen*'s eight eight-inchers, the British advantage was eroded. It became sixteen to nine to Lutjens, although in big guns it was still nine to eight in Holland's favour.

The admiral was forced to take this risk because he knew of the thinness of the *Hood*'s upper deck armour, and by steering as close to head-on as he could get, he was presenting a target of only a hundred feet – the *Hood*'s beam – as against a target of nearly 860 feet, her length broadside on. The end-on approach was not just a phobia of Holland's; in fact it was the favourite tactic of Admiral Tovey, the commander-in-chief, who habitually recommended it to every flag officer and commanding officer in the Home Fleet. This was based on the idea that, if A arcs had to be sacrificed in an effort to close the range rapidly, the least dangerous method was to steer straight for the enemy and disregard the loss of bearing. It was claimed that the end-on run-in shortened the time when A arcs were closed and also reduced the target for the enemy. But it was essential that the approach be as straight as possible, and Tovey suggested only a ten-degree deviation. The *Hood*'s course was thirty degrees off a straight line. So Holland had put his ships in the worst possible position, and Captain Russell Grenfell in *The Bismarck Episode* – which I regard as a trifling title – wondered whether the admiral had Tovey's end-on theory in mind at all. Certainly Tovey must have been doubtful, because when he discussed the tactic with the First Sea Lord, who criticized the approach, the commander-in-chief replied that he wished Holland 'had been steering in more still'. Pound called it 'going into battle with one hand, when you have two'.[2] Tovey was on the point of signalling the tactics to be employed to Holland but decided that the admiral on the spot should be allowed to devise these.

Lieutenant R.G. Robertson, who was taken off the *Hood* because of a perforated duodenal ulcer just before she sailed to her death, recalls: 'On 20th April the admiral [Tovey] again made known his intentions if an "enemy in sight" report was received we would close the enemy at speed and, so far as possible, our approach would be "bow on". The fact that in the initial stages of any action our after 15-inch guns would not be able to bear was outweighed by the necessity of presenting the minimum target to the enemy. It was imperative that any action be fought at as close a range as possible when the trajectory of the enemy shells would be flatter and so less likely to penetrate our weak deck armour.'[3]

Grenfell posed the other possibility that Holland based his tactics on the Admiralty's printed fighting instructions, which had been handed down from the seventeenth and eighteenth centuries, revised in 1918, but were still in use from the outbreak of the Second World War. This was later to bring the comment from Roskill: 'Grenfell was never a man to pull his punches when he considered criticism to be justifiable and he is highly critical of the manner in which Holland took his battle cruiser into action. I will only say that had Grenfell seen a copy of the Fighting Instructions then in force in the Royal Navy, he might, I think, have strengthened his criticisms of the rigidity of such instructions, but modified his strictures on the vice-admiral. For Holland actually took the ships into battle in the manner recommended in the current Fighting Instructions.'[4]

Be that as it may, this still does not absolve Holland from the blame of the formation of his two-ship squadron. It would have been reasonable to suppose that he should have led the attack in the *Hood*, and yet Tovey had been on the threshold of signalling him to put the infinitely heavier armoured *Prince of Wales* in the van. Captain Leach also considered this the best plan, but he too did not inform Holland. The vice-admiral probably preferred to place the *Hood* first because the *Prince of Wales* had still to be worked up properly; her guns were suspect – indeed one fired just a single round before jamming – and while the gunnery of the *Hood* was known to him, that of his consort was not. Nevertheless, there was no reason why he should have insisted on the *Prince of Wales* keeping close order – a distance of a thousand yards, the standard between two capital ships – during a fast approach. If Leach had been allowed to play a solo part, his ship could have stood off, employing all her guns in broadsides, while the *Hood* raced in to minimize the danger of a plunging shell on her thin armour and then to open A arcs. Instead the *Prince of Wales* was required to work in unison with the result that when the *Hood* was destroyed it was relatively simple for the *Bismarck* to switch to the new target – and hit her immediately, seven or eight times.

Grenfell questioned this order of approach thus:

Why was it necessary for the range to be shortened so quickly that A arcs had to be closed? It would surely seem that if the

Bismarck was capable of decisive gunfire at 25,000 yards, the British big ships should have been equally able to fight at that range. Indeed, they almost certainly were. The *Bismarck* was well within their gun range and since they were firing at her with half their guns they could obviously have fired at her with all. The use of their full broadsides was not incompatible with a closing range; the only condition was that closing with A arcs open meant closing a little more slowly. But it was early morning and the British ships had plenty of time. Why then the hurry to get in? The answer is not very obvious.[5]

Indeed, the answer is far from obvious, but Grenfell also missed another point, which had been to Holland's advantage. Surprise was in his favour. Not until the *Hood* opened fire was Lutjens aware that British capital ships were in the vicinity. At first it was believed that the approaching vessels were light cruisers. If the German admiral had known earlier that he was about to confront the *Hood* and the *Prince of Wales*, it is doubtful whether there would have been a battle, for his orders were to avoid conflict with any force superior to his own.

Holland's major mistake has also obscured partially two other regrettable omissions, which might have saved the *Hood*. It was his intention for the *Suffolk* and *Norfolk* to attack the *Prinz Eugen* from the rear and so reduce the enemy's fire power. Although this battle plan was signalled by light to Leach in the *Prince of Wales*, because of the insistence on radio silence from the *Hood* it was not communicated to those who mattered – Admiral Wake-Walker and the captains of the *Suffolk* and *Norfolk*. In the event, only the *Suffolk* loosed off a few desultory rounds, which were hopelessly short of the *Prinz Eugen*.

Holland either forgot to recall the destroyer screen, still searching to the north, or considered it best to have them hunting there in case he did not intercept the enemy – and that showed a remarkable lack of confidence in himself and his staff. The destroyers' torpedoes could have caused the *Bismarck* and *Prinz Eugen* to have taken avoiding action and so upset the accuracy of their gunnery. Instead, the escort took no part in the battle and were only recalled by Wake-Walker to pick up survivors after the *Hood* had been obliterated. If the smaller of the enemy had been properly engaged, it would have been unlikely for her to have hit the *Hood* and caused the distracting, to say the least, fire on the boat deck.

It is possible that Holland feared that the *Bismarck* would make a dramatic and drastic turn to port as the British were sighted, and that might have meant business for the destroyers. It was an unlucky ploy and indicated that, despite his somewhat reckless race towards the Germans, he was cautious enough to try to cover all eventualities.

Throughout the search, the chase and the subsequent confrontation with the enemy, Holland had clamped down on the use of radar, still in its infancy and not trusted by the Royal Navy. This at least did obtain a degree of surprise in the early stages and, together with his signal that radar should not be used until action was imminent, was a wise enough precaution. But several of his critics contended that when the squadron were steaming 'blindly' without the eyes of the cruisers, he should have relied on radar. Most missed the point that radar at this stage of the war was not fully effective beyond twenty miles. However, as the distance narrowed between the two squadrons, there was no valid reason why the guns of the *Hood* at least – the *Prince of Wales'* set, like most of her gadgetry, was not functioning correctly – should not have been ranged by radar. The result was that fire was opened relying on optical rangefinders, a difficult operation when spray was cascading on to both ships and misting the lens. Radar sets should have been tuned ready for the meeting, especially when the plot put the enemy at around twenty miles distant. Lutjens already knew just after 5 a.m., twenty minutes before the battle commenced, that two fast-moving vessels – he had no idea they were capital ships – were approaching on the port bow. The sound of the screws of the British squadron had been picked up by the Germans' long-range underwater sensitive listening device, which they called GHG. Sixty of these were fitted in the *Prinz Eugen*. Although a check was made on radar, there were no blips on the screens, and not until the third gunnery officer, from a rangefinder in the foretop position, spotted smoke far away to the south-east was the GHG report definitely confirmed. So the *Hood*'s radar could have been used to range and allied to the element of surprise would have improved the efficiency of the gunnery. Nevertheless, the fore turrets were aimed by mistake at the *Prinz Eugen*, and Holland's detractors wondered whether his subsequent order to shift the target to the *Bismarck* ever became known to our main armament control. I can confirm that it was and that fire was opened eventually on the 'correct' ship.

As a 'naval curio' I have been asked scores of times to give an opinion on Holland's handling of the squadron. In the years immediately following my survival I had no definite views, apart from the 'lucky hit' theory. But this was because I was still a young and novice sailor, of course. In my more mature years after the war and into the 1970s, when more 'secret' facts became available to the public and I became an officer, I formed the opinion that, although Holland was at fault in many of his decisions, the blame for his being placed in a position where he would falter was primarily that of Admiral Tovey. To send a suspect battle cruiser and a battleship which was a long way short of being an efficient fighting unit and still had dockyard men on board, to take on the world's most up-to-date battleship was not the best of decisions. Even allowing that Tovey had no other capital ship available, apart from his flagship *King George V*, I question whether it would not have been beyond the realms of his command to have put to sea himself in the *King George V* in company with the *Hood*. This would have given the *Prince of Wales* a vital twenty hours to have rectified the gunnery faults at Scapa. Whether it was feasible to expect Tovey to conduct the search for the *Bismarck* from afar at sea and without a flag admiral in command of the bulk of the Home Fleet left behind at Scapa is debatable, but bold moves were necessary, and a more positive approach might have saved the *Hood*.

Perhaps it is loyalty which repels me from inculpating Holland entirely. Instead I still point to the lack of foresight of the Governments in the 1920s and 1930s, who clung to the false image of their show-ship being the world's greatest example of naval power. Our heavyweight champion had a knock-out punch but a glass chin and a paunch which was too heavy for her. She was carrying more than four thousand tons of extra weight with all her wartime trappings, and yet the additional armour prescribed for her was missing. Even in her design days there was the problem of stopping the 'bending' movement expected in her hull because of her great length and tonnage. As we have seen, she was always wet aft, but with supplementary equipment the quarterdeck became virtually an island in heavy seas, with waves constantly pounding it. I believe that this seriously weakened her frame, and when the ultimate explosion came she split in half. When I saw her raddled bows vertical in the sea, they seemed – and must have been – completely separated from the rest of her. No explosion alone could have achieved this.

The irony of it was that, if she had been put out of commission in 1939, more depth could have been given to her wafer-thin $1\frac{1}{2}$ inches of armour on the forecastle deck, her tawdry two inches on the lower deck and, above all, those grossly inadequate three inches on the upper deck. It was planned to offset this additional weight by dispensing with those always unnecessary above-water torpedo tubes and the massive conning tower. Our heavyweight would have been slimmed by shedding nearly four thousand tons. Instead the *Hood* slogged on through the war, lending her apparent power and prestige to operations which could have proceeded without her. Would she have been missed on those long, forlorn searches towards the Arctic Circle? Would she have been missed at Oran? Would she have been missed in the Mediterranean sorties? I doubt it. In a similar way to pre-war crises, she was used as a frightener, and if someone had realized at the Admiralty that the frightener needed protecting immediately, the *Hood* disaster would have been averted.

No one in the top echelon of the Royal Navy was prepared to admit that she was no longer a super ship, and her epitaph was written by Admiral Lord Chatfield soon after her name became synonymous with the extinction of the battle cruiser: 'The *Hood* was destroyed because she had to fight a ship 22 years more modern than herself.'

References

Chapter 1
1 Arthur J. Marder (ed.), *Fear God and Dreadnought*, Volume III (Cape, 1959), p.163
2 Maurice Northcott, *Hood Design and Construction* (Bivouac, undated), pp 7-13

Chapter 3
1 Geoffrey Bennett, *Cowan's War* (Collins, 1964), p.54
2 Cowan memorandum, 6 June 1921 (Cowan Papers, 13/2)
3 Ibid., 17 January 1922 (Cowan Papers, 13/2)
4 Ibid.
5 Elkins Papers
6 Ibid.
7 Cowan Papers
8 Ibid.

Chapter 4
1 V.C. Scott O'Connor, *The Empire Cruise* (private, 1925), p.30
2 *Cape Argus*, 23-30 December 1923
3 Ibid.
4 Ernle Bradford, *The Mighty Hood* (Hodder & Stoughton, 1959) p.69
5 C.R. Benstead, *Around the World with the Battle Cruisers* (Hurst & Blackett, 1925), p.105
6 O'Connor, p.125
7 Benstead, pp.135-6
8 *Vancouver Sun*, 26 June-5 July 1924
9 Bradford, pp.87-8

Chapter 5
1 Admiral Sir Frederic Dreyer, *The Sea Heritage* (Museum Press, 1955), p.287
2 Commander N.K. Cambell letter to authors

Chapter 6
1 Admiral E. Longley-Cook, speech to Hood Association, 24 May 1980
2 David Divine, *Mutiny at Invergordon* (Macdonald, 1970) pp.88-9
3 Stephen Roskill, *Naval Policy between the Wars* (Collins, 1976), p.98
4 Divine, p.131
5 Ibid.
6 Captain Patterson's Report of Proceedings, ADM 178/110
7 Roskill, p.102
8 Len Wincott, *Invergordon Mutineer* (Weidenfeld & Nicholson, 1974), p.110
9 Roskill, p.103
10 Tomkinson Papers
11 Patterson's RoP
12 Ibid.
13 Divine, pp.156-7
14 *Norfolk's* RoP, ADM 178/110
15 Divine, p.165
16 Ibid.
17 Ibid., p.167
18 Ibid., p.166
19 Ibid., p.170
20 Ibid.
21 Patterson's RoP
22 Roskill, p.108
23 Divine, p.171
24 Patterson's RoP
25 Roskill, p.109
26 Divine, p.176

Chapter 7
1 Divine, p.176
2 Ibid.

3 ADM 178/66
4 Divine, p.193
5 Kelly Papers
6 ADM 178/114
7 Ibid.
8 ADM 178/114 and ADM 1/19160
9 Admiralty letter NL M.02855/31

Chapter 8
1 Admiral Sir William James, *The Sky Was Always Blue* (Methuen, 1951), pp.13-14
2 Admiral Longley-Cook's speech to Hood Association, 24 May 1980
3 Roskill, *Naval Policy between the Wars*, p.129
4 James, p.163
5 Ibid., pp.172-4
6 ADM 1/8770/1319
7 Ibid.
8 James, p.176

Chapter 9
1 Chatfield papers
2 *The Times*, 27 February, 1935
3 *The Times*, 28 February, 1935
4 Ibid.
5 Ibid.
6 Peter C. Smith, *Great Ships Pass* (William Kimber, 1977), p.64
7 Kelly Papers
8 *The Times*, 8 March 1935
9 Pridham Papers
10 Chatfield Papers

Chapter 10
1 Chatfield Papers – and for the ensuing correspondence concerning Tower
2 Pridham Papers
3 Ibid.
4 James, p.184
5 Arthur J. Marder, *From the Dardanelles to Oran* (Oxford University Press, 1974), pp.99-100

6 Pridham Papers
7 Ibid.
8 Ibid.
9 Chatfield Papers
10 Dreyer to Chatfield, 19 October 1942, Chatfield Papers

Chapter 11
1 Pridham Papers
2 Ibid.
3 Chatfield Papers
4 FO 371/21352
5 ADM 116/3514
6 *The Times*, 15 April 1937
7 ADM 116/3514
8 *The Times*, 21 April 1937
9 FO 371/21353
10 ADM 116/3514
11 James Cable, *The Royal Navy and the Siege of Bilbao* (Cambridge University Press, 1979) pp.87-90; ADM 116/3516, 3514
12 Pridham Papers

Chapter 12
1 Admiral Sir Andrew Cunningham, *A Sailor's Odyssey* (Hutchinson, 1951), pp.181-2
2 Ibid., p.186
3 Ibid., p.187
4 Ibid.
5 Admiralty letter NL 1201/32, 12 August 1932
6 Cunningham, p.189
7 Pridham Papers

Chapter 13
1 Smith, *Great Ships Pass*, p.22

Chapter 16
1 Warren Tute, *The Deadly Stroke* (Collins, 1973) pp.21-8
2 Ibid.
3 Marder, *From the Dardanelles to Oran*, p.233
4 Unattributed quotations come from Lt. Briggs' own knowledge as a boy signalman during this period.

5 Tute, pp. 89-92
6 Ibid. p.135
7 Ibid. p.148

Chapter 17
1 Marder, *From the Dardanelles to Oran*, p.241
2 Tute, pp.171-2
3 Ibid. p.187
4 Ibid.
5 Ibid. p.191
6 Marder, p.268

Chapter 18
1 Captain Donald McIntyre, *Fighting Admiral* (Evan Bros, 1961), p.75
2 Unattributed quotations from Lt. Briggs

Chapter 22
1. *The Times*, 28 May 1941

Chapter 23
1 ADM 116/4351, p.103
2 Ibid.
3 Baron Burkard von Mullenheim Rechberg, *Battleship Bismarck* (Bodley Head, 1980), pp.107-10
4 ADM 116/4351, p.19
5 Ibid.
6 Marder, *From the Dardanelles to Oran*, pp. 116-17
7 ADM 116/4351, p.108

Chapter 24
1 ADM 116/4351, p.76
2 Captain Russell Grenfell, *The Bismarck Episode* (Faber & Faber, 1957), p.63
3 *Ships Monthly*, June 1975, Lieutenant R.G. Robertson
4 Roskill Papers
5 Grenfell, pp. 64-5

Bibliography

Bassett, Colonel Samuel, *Royal Marine* (Peter Davies, 1962)

Beesly, Patrick, *Very Special Admiral* (Hamish Hamilton, 1980)

Bekker, Cajus, *Swastika at Sea* (William Kimber, 1953)

Bekker, Cajus, *Hitler's Naval War* (MacDonald, 1974)

Bennett, Geoffrey, *Cowan's War* (Collins, 1964)

Benstead, Lieutenant C.R., *Around the World with the Battle Cruisers* (Hurst & Blackett, 1924)

Bradford, Ernle, *The Mighty Hood* (Hodder & Stoughton, 1959)

Cable, James, *The Royal Navy and the Siege of Bilbao* (Cambridge University Press, 1979)

Cain, Lieutenant Commander T.J. and A.V. Sellwood, *HMS Electra* (Hutchinson, 1959)

Carew, Anthony, *Lower Deck of the Royal Navy* (Manchester University Press, 1981)

Chalmers, Rear Admiral W.S., *The Life and Letters of David Earl Beatty* (Hodder & Stoughton, 1951)

Colven, Ian, *Vansittart in Office* (Gollancz, 1965)

Cunningham, Admiral Sir Andrew, *A Sailor's Odyssey* (Hutchinson, 1951)

Dawson, Captain Lionel, *Sound of the Guns*, (Pen in Hand Publishing, 1949)

Divine, David, *Mutiny at Invergordon* (MacDonald, 1970)

Dreyer, Admiral Sir Frederic, *The Sea Heritage* (Museum Press, 1955)

Edwards, Kenneth, *The Mutiny at Invergordon* (Putnam, 1937)

Farman, Christopher, *The General Strike* (Rupert Hart Davis, 1972)

Grenfell, Captain Russell, *The Bismarck Episode* (Faber & Faber, 1957)

Hoyt, Edwin, *The Life and Death of HMS Hood* (Arthur Barker, 1977)

James, Admiral Sir William, *The Sky was Always Blue* (Methuen, 1951)

Kemp, Lieutenant Commander P.K., *Victory at Sea, 1939-1945*, (Frederick Muller, 1957)

Kennedy, Ludovic, *Pursuit* (Collins, 1974)

King-Hall, Commander Stephen, *My Naval Life* (Faber & Faber, 1930)

MacIntyre, Captain Donald, *The Thunder of the Guns* (Muller, 1959)

MacIntyre, Captain Donald, *Fighting Admiral* (Evans Brothers, 1961)

Marder, Arthur J., *From the Dardanelles to Oran* (Oxford University Press, 1974)

Marder, Arthur J., *Portrait of an Admiral* (Cape, 1952)

Marder, Arthur J. (ed.), *Fear God and Dreadnought*, Volume III (Cape, 1959)

Northcott, Maurice, *Hood Design and Construction* (Bivouac, undated)

Pack, Captain S.W.C., *Sea Power in the Mediterranean* (Arthur Barker, 1971)

Pack, Captain S.W.C., *Cunningham the Commander* (Batsford, 1974)

Padfield, Peter, *The Battleship Era* (Hart Davis, 1972)

Poolman, Kenneth, *Ark Royal* (William Kimber, 1956)

Roskill, Stephen, *The War at Sea* Volume I (HMSO, 1954)

Roskill, Stephen, *The Navy at War, 1939-45* (Collins, 1960)

Roskill, Stephen, *Naval Policy between the Wars* (Collins, 1976)

Roskill, Stephen, *Churchill and the Admirals* (Collins, 1977)

Smith, Peter C., *Great Ships Pass* (William Kimber, 1977)

Smith, Peter C., *Hit First, Hit Hard* (William Kimber, 1979)

Steer, G.L., *Tree of Guernica* (Hodder & Stoughton, 1938)

Thomas, Hugh, *The Spanish Civil War* (Hamilton, 1965)

Tute, Warren, *The Deadly Stroke* (Collins, 1973)

Varillon, Pierre, *Mers-el-Kebir* (Amiot Dumont, undated)

von Mullenheim Rechberg, Baron Burkard, *Battleship Bismarck* (Bodley Head, 1980)

Warner, Oliver, *Cunningham of Hyndhope* (John Murray, 1967)

Wincott, Len, *Invergordon Mutineer* (Weidenfeld & Nicolson, 1974)

OFFICIAL RECORDS AND PAPERS

Chatfield Papers (Greenwich Maritime Museum Library); Cowan Papers (Greenwich Maritime Museum Library), Cunningham Papers (British Museum); Pridham Papers (Greenwich Maritime Museum Library); Elkins Papers (Greenwich Maritime Museum Library); Kelly Papers (Greenwich Maritime Museum Library); Roskill Papers and Somerville Papers (Churchill College Archives Centre, Cambridge); Tomkinson Papers (privately held)

Public Record Office, Kew:
Hood's ships logs – ADM 53/78910 to 78966 conclusive; ADM 53/104194 to 104217; ADM 53/109191 to 109202
World cruise – ADM 1/8662; ADM 199/131; ADM 116/2219; ADM 116/2254, 2255, 2257
Invergordon Mutiny – ADM 167/83 and 89; ADM 178/50, 64, 66, 79, 110, 114, 129
Mutiny rumours – ADM 1/8770/1319
Abyssinian Crisis – ADM 116/3487
Bilbao blockade – ADM 116/3514, 3516, 3534, 3679; F.O. 371/21352, 21353; CAB 27/639; CAB 24/269
Oran – ADM 1/10321; ADM 205/4
Hood boards of inquiry – ADM 116/4351, 4352

INTERVIEWS, OR CORRESPONDENCE, WITH:

Captain Kenneth Aylwin RN (retd.), Captain G. Blundell CBE RN (retd.), A.E. 'Windy' Breeze, J.J. Brown, Lieutenant L.E. Brown RN (retd.), John Bush, Commander N.K. Cambell MBE, DSC, RN (retd.), William Cass, Commander Gerald Cobb OBE, RN (retd.), William Collier, Lieutenant S. Donovan MBE, RN (retd.), the late Commander J.G. Gould, RN and Mrs J.G. Gould, R. Hall, Lieutenant-Commander Frederick Hard RN (retd.), Lieutenant-Commander William R. Harding RN (retd.), Reginald Harper-Smith, W. Hawkins, Commander C.T. Haynes, Stanley Hazell, Robert Hector, Harry Holderness, L. Hudson, E. Hughes, Gunther Janzen, Latham Jensen, Ned Johns, Rear-Admiral C.F. Kemp CB

Vice-Admiral E. Longley-Cook CB, CBE, DSO, Mrs R. O'Sullivan, Commander A.F. Paterson RN (retd.), Harry Purdue, Lieutenant F.J. Revell RN (retd.), Vice-Admiral Sir Guy Sayer KBE, CB, DSC, Harry Smith, Commander Vernon Smyth RN (retd.), E.J. Taylor, A. Thomas, Robert Tilburn, Captain H. Watch RN (retd.), Surgeon Commander William Wolton RN (retd.)

Index